New Zealand Graves at Brockenhurst

Clare Church

93 New Zealand soldiers remembered from World War One

Front cover: New Zealand graves and cenotaph in the cemetery at St. Nicholas Church, Brockenhurst

Published by Clare Elizabeth Church,
Lymington, Hampshire, SO41 8DN

© Copyright Clare Elizabeth Church
2002

ISBN 0 9543341 0 8

No part of this publication may be reproduced, stored in a retrieval system, or transmitted, in any form or by any means, electronic, mechanical, photocopying, recording or otherwise, without the written permission of the publisher

All photographs except where otherwise ascribed are the property of the author

CONTENTS

Preface	vi
Acknowledgements	viii
List of maps	x
Abbreviations	x

Part I - Chapters

Immigration	3
Military Training	7
Theatres of War	18
Medical Care	32
Remembrance	37

Part II – Biographies

Enlisted 1914:

Frank Clark	42
George William Haxton	43
Cedric Gilbert Adams	46
Norman Douglas Fraser	47
James McAnulty	50
Frederick Selwyn Fendall	53
Albert Kennedy	56

Enlisted 1915:

Kiri Rapona	61
William Edward Johnstone	62
Samuel Allington	66
Sydney Allan Davies	68
Darcy Roycroft Newell	70
Andrew Gilbert	74
William Munro Duncan	76
Alfred Benjamin Booker, MM	78
William Leslie Morice	80
Wilfred Blythe Kirk	83
Thomas Cyril Broadbridge	86
Herbert Lionel Edman	88
Alexander Miles Stirrat	89
James Hayter Barter	90
John James Monahan	91
Rakapa Akena	92
Tuheke Tui Matenga	93
Herbert Joseph Baird	95
Potene Tuhoro	97
William Charles Page	98
William David Dunbar	101
Charles Frederick Game	102

Enlisted 1915 (continued)

Christopher Roy Tait	103
William Ainslie	104
John Blackham	106
Richard William Lynch	108
Alfred Leonard Harris	109
William Collett Cooper	112
Samuel Bennett	113
Anthony Arrowsmith	114
Harry Rhoades	115
Charles James Lankey	118
William Henry Steele	119
Andrew Woodley	120
Raukawa Hura	125
Ewen Donald Campbell	126

Enlisted 1916:

Edward Percy (Perce) Meek	131
Ernest **Guy** Giblin	137
Thomas Charles Adams	140
George Hurrell	142
John Geoffrey	143
William Holt	145
William Healey	147
James Ernest Cliff	149
Hugh O'Connor	150
Fred Hallett Brown	151
Percy Lawrence Williams	152
William James Mogg	155
Wilfred Cecil Bedford	159
Ernest Nicholson Player	160
George Eckford Law	163
William Milne Morrison	166
William John Smail	167
Claude Raymond Read	168
Walter Whyte	170
Farquhar McDonald	172
Jerry Rata	174
Christian Diedrich Marcussen	175
Henry Wi Waka Wi	177
Joseph Briggs	178
Harry Phillips	181
George William Heslop	183
Andrew Hamilton Stobo	185
Harold Levi Eion Hambling	188
Arthur Cole	191
Henry Charles Sidford	193
Edward William Henry Lawrence	195

Enlisted 1917:

Thomas Campbell	198
William Douglas Mayall	200
Cyril Ernest Rogers	202
Joseph William Bower	206
William James Rainey	208
Horace David Matuschka	209
John Tana Warena	210
John Thompson Connelly	211
James Lilley	212
Percy Emanuel Holst	213
Cletus Patrick O'Brien	214
Robert William Marshall	216
James Williams	218
William John Shotter	220
Matthew James Watson	222
David Ivon Porteous	223
Temete Smith	225
Meihana Huta	226
Llewellyn Gilbert Grooby	227

Appendix A1	New Zealand Immigrants 1840-1849	230
Appendix A2	New Zealand Immigrants 1850-1859	231
Appendix A3	New Zealand immigrants 1860-1870	232
Appendix A4	New Zealand Immigrants 1871-1880	233
Appendix B	NZEF Departure from New Zealand	234
Appendix C1:	Evacuation from the Somme September/October 1916	238
Appendix C2:	Evacuation from France October 1916-December 1917	239
Appendix C3:	Evacuation from France 1918	241
	Bibliography	244
	Index	247

Preface

This book is about the 93 New Zealand Expeditionary Force (NZEF) Soldiers from World War One (WW1) who lie buried in the Commonwealth War Graves Commission (CWGC) cemetery attached to St. Nicholas' Church in Brockenhurst, Hampshire, England.

I am commemorating the descendants of two groups of pioneers - those who left their original country and settled in New Zealand. The first pioneers are Maoris who arrived in New Zealand from Polynesia and were well settled by the 14th century, and possibly even earlier. Of the 93 men who are buried at Brockenhurst, 12 were Maoris. The second group are the Europeans (Pakeha; as the Maoris called them) who emigrated to New Zealand from 1840 onwards.

You may question, "Why is an English person delving into the histories of families who lived on the other side of the world and are not personally known to the author?" I had better explain the situation. A short while after my husband and I had returned from a holiday in New Zealand I was approached by John Cockram of Brockenhurst – who has recently published *Brockenhurst and the Two World Wars*. John asked if I would like to research the backgrounds of the 93 New Zealanders, as this required a separate study, which had not been appropriate for his work. In view of my interest in genealogy I took up the challenge.

My investigation has been the opposite of John Cockram's. Whereas he has written about the men from Brockenhurst who died in both World Wars and are buried throughout the world (in fact many have no known graves) the men I have researched are all buried in the same cemetery, but came from all corners of New Zealand, four of them even having parents living in England.

I am not an expert in WW1 history; this project has been a learning experience as I have progressed in my research. This book is written from the family and social history perspective, and includes (where known) stories of these soldiers' forebears and their roots. Nevertheless, brief mention must be made of the major battles in which the men were involved – full details can be obtained from the Regimental Histories listed in the bibliography.

I already knew the names of the next of kin and addresses of the NZEF men which had been obtained from the CWGC website, so I set forth emailing genealogy contacts in New Zealand whom I had found on relevant websites. Progress was slow during the first few months and I was on the verge of giving up when someone in New Zealand suggested that I put an advertisement in the bi-monthly *New Zealand Genealogist* journal. Thanks also to an email being converted into a letter and placed on page one, a tremendous response ensued.

I am delighted that it has been possible to trace living relatives who have provided invaluable information. In one or two cases cousins have discovered each other as a result of my enquiries into their family histories. But, of course, with so many New Zealanders interested in their forebears' roots, Brockenhurst is well known to them. Often members of their family were patients at No. 1 New Zealand General Hospital during WW1, the majority thankfully returning to their home country.

The next stage in my research was a visit to New Zealand during February/March 2001 when I had the privilege of meeting many New Zealanders who have associations with those buried at Brockenhurst. All were so kind even to have me to stay in their homes, though I had never met them beforehand. Whilst I was touring around both islands I visited the home townships of the NZEF soldiers and took photographs of their parents' graves on which their own names were often mentioned. The experience of seeing the word "Brokenhurst" or "Brockenhurst" on several headstones made my visit to the other side of the world most memorable.

The chapters in Part I include details on Immigration to New Zealand in the 19th century, Military Training organisation, Theatres of War in which the men were involved and the Medical Care they received upon injury or sickness. Part I concludes by describing how Brockenhurst remembers these brave men.

Part II comprises the individual biographies, which will be of particular interest to family members and anyone who has any connections with New Zealand. I apologise for not being able to contact all relatives of the NZEF men, but in view of the distance involved, and the desire to publish this book within a reasonable timeframe, I have made an appropriate effort by making enquiries via email and letter. I must also consider the assistance I have received from individuals who have contacted the media in New Zealand without my prompting. Indeed, I feel it is only right that those people who have provided me with information and photographs should see the results of their efforts without too much delay.

I have found this research to be extremely rewarding and have learnt a great deal along the way. Hopefully, what I have written will stimulate further interest and bring forth information that I have failed to include. I should also be grateful to receive corrections for any errors. I have sometimes been dependent upon secondary sources that I could not corroborate. Family history research is never ending; the multi-faceted jigsaw is never complete!

Clare Church   2002

ACKNOWLEDGEMENTS

and SOURCES

This book would not have been written without the help of many contributors. Those who have provided specific information about a particular soldier, I have listed at the end of the individual biography. Others to whom I am most grateful are:

Manuscripts and Archives and Oral History Sections of Alexander Turnbull Library, National Library of New Zealand, Te Puna Matauranga o Aotearoa (ATL), Wellington for helpful service during my visit in March 2001, plus permission to use photographs

Auckland City Libraries for permission to use photographs on pages 46 and 142

Arthur Banks for the use of map on page 29, from his book *A World Atlas of Military History 1860-1945*

Elizabeth Beer for help with research

Kevin Bourke for advice re Alexander Turnbull Library resources

John Cockram for help and guidance on military matters

Commonwealth War Graves Commission (CWGC) website: www.cwgc.org

Friends of Brockenhurst Association for financial assistance

The Francis Frith Collection, Salisbury, Wiltshire SP3 5QP, www.francisfrith.co.uk

Adele Graham for contacting the media on my behalf

Richard Green for embarkation details, plus family burial records

International Genealogical Index (IGI)

John Hall for information from "Chronicles of the N.Z.E.F"

Betty Image, Secretary of Canterbury Branch of New Zealand Society of Genealogists

Library staff of the Imperial War Museum, London

The Reverend Te Rangi Matanuka Kaa, Tikitiki, East Coast

Naval & Military Press, Uckfield for the use of map on page 26

Peter Marks for the use of photographs on pages 12, 14, 16, 17, 20, 74, 104, 170

Otago Daily Times for publishing my request for information in Prester John's Talk of the Times column

Penguin Books New Zealand for the use of maps on pages 11, 23, 24, 25, 27, 28, 30, 31 and 179 - from *The New Zealand Division 1916-1919 – A Popular History Based on Official Records* by Col. H. Stewart, published by Whitcombe & Tombs Ltd. 1921

Allan Pope for material from a paper on military training

Neil Richardson for the use of map on page 22, from his book *Fallen in the Fight*

Alison Ryan, New Zealand Society of Genealogists

Joan Snow for the use of photographs on page 36

Ruth and Dal Walker of Dannevirke and many other New Zealanders who were so hospitable during my time in New Zealand

Olwyn Whitehouse, South Canterbury Branch of New Zealand Society of Genealogists

Lynly Yates (Personnel Archives Officer) and colleagues at New Zealand Defence Force, Trentham Camp, Upper Hutt re Army Service Records

Finally, my task would have been so much more demanding but for the patient support of my husband, Tony, whose aptitude for detail has been so valuable for the proofreading and literary correctness.

If I have forgotten to acknowledge anyone who has assisted me in my research I offer my apologies.

LIST OF MAPS

Egypt	9
Training area in France	11
Gallipoli Peninsula	22
Northwest France	23
Armentières and Vicinity	24
Area of the Somme Battlefield (1916)	25
Battle of Flers-Courcelette: 15th-22nd September 1916	26
Messines and Ypres	27
Basseville	28
Passchendaele	29
The Upper Ancre	30
Le Quesnoy	31
Bapaume	179

ABBREVIATIONS

AIF	Australian Imperial Force
ATL	Alexander Turnbull Library
Bn	Battalion
Bty	Battery
CCS	Casualty Clearing Station
Coy	Company
CWGC	Commonwealth War Graves Commission
GH	General Hospital
HMNZT	His Majesty's New Zealand Troopship
HS	Hospital Ship
IGI	International Genealogical Index
MDS	Main Dressing Station
NZASC	New Zealand Army Service Corps
NZEF	New Zealand Expeditionary Force
NZFA	New Zealand Field Artillery
NZGH	New Zealand General Hospital
NZMC	New Zealand Medical Corps
NZRB	New Zealand Rifle Brigade
NZSG	New Zealand Society of Genealogists
RAP	Regimental Aid Post
Rft	Reinforcement
RMO	Regimental Medical Officer
WW1	World War 1
WW2	World War 2
YMCA	Young Men's Christian Association

Part I

Chapter 1

IMMIGRATION

Early Days

Prior to 1840 there were only about 2000 non-Maori living in New Zealand. From 1792 onwards sealers had settled in Dusky Sound, Southland. Other pioneers were whalers, traders, missionaries, and immigrants who had come via Australia, not to forget escaped convicts seeking a new life.

In 1826 the British ship *Rosanna* arrived at Port Nicholson (Wellington) with 25 immigrants on board. A fledgling unformed organisation called the "New Zealand Association" in London had ordered the skipper, Captain James Herd, to find a suitable site for settlement in New Zealand. This first attempt was a disaster. Wellington's surrounding countryside was totally unsuitable for settlement owing to the steep hillside rising from the harbour, so the ship sailed northwards to Hokianga, where the immigrants went ashore. However, they soon returned to the ship because they had heard stories that ferocious Maori natives lived nearby, and they persuaded Captain Herd to take them on to Sydney, Australia.

In 1837 the New Zealand Association was properly established for the purpose of colonising New Zealand. The driving force was Edward Gibbon Wakefield who enticed settlers to leave England and Scotland and begin a new life on the other side of the world. The British government insisted that a company should be formed to subscribe capital for the venture, and a further proviso was that the Maoris must give consent before any area in New Zealand was earmarked for settlement. The New Zealand Association was thus dissolved and the New Zealand Company was founded with £400,000 capital. Captain William Hobson was chosen as Governor of New Zealand.

In 1839 advertisements were placed in newspapers for settlers and trades people to migrate to New Zealand on ships provided by the New Zealand Company. The first ship to leave England was the *Tory*, which left Gravesend on 5th May 1839 with 35 passengers on board, amongst whom was Edward Wakefield who would negotiate with the Maori chiefs regarding the sale of land. The ship landed at Port Nicholson on 20th September, and fortunately ten days later a deal had been struck. Unbeknown to Edward Wakefield and the surveyors on board, and before the successful news had filtered back to England, three further vessels had set sail with immigrants, the *Oriental, Aurora* and *Adelaide* with over 800 people on board. The ships' captains had no idea where their passengers were to land; they had merely been instructed to sail for Port Hardy, D'Urville Island (Cook Strait).

Several of the pioneer families, whose descendants eighty years later lie buried in the land they had left, became prominent members of their community after they had settled in New Zealand.

1840-1852

Between 1840 and 1852 there were three main groups of British migrants to New Zealand. The largest group were assisted passengers to the five New Zealand Company settlements. During the first two years settlers landed at Wellington, Nelson and New Plymouth. Then between 1848 and 1852 renewed assisted migration was offered for settlers to Otago and Canterbury.

The second group of settlers were free migrants, i.e. paying passengers. The Prebble family were on board the *Aurora*, the first ship to arrive in Port Nicholson, on 22nd January 1840, which had left Gravesend, Kent on 18th September 1839. The Prebbles ultimately settled near Christchurch and the township Prebbleton was named after them. Their daughter Maria Jane married into the Harris family.

Another prominent character was Walpole Cheshire Fendall, son of the Vicar of Crambe, Yorkshire, who departed from Gravesend on 8th September 1850 on board *Sir George Seymour* and arrived in Lyttelton on 17th December. The area of Christchurch where he settled became known as Fendalton.

The Canterbury colonists, September 1850. Scene at Gravesend with the *Charlotte Jane, Sir George Seymour, Randoph* and *Cressy* visible in the background.
PUBL-0033-1850-199. ATL

Lastly, there was the military group of settlers, over 700 men from British regiments who were on half pay in the reserve. They emigrated as Royal New Zealand Fencibles, to provide military protection south of Auckland. The British government was short of money so the suggestion was made for these soldiers to settle in New Zealand with the bonus of a cottage and one acre of land, which would become freehold after seven years.

One such soldier was John McAnulty from Drumally, Ireland. The McAnulty family set sail from Belfast on board the *Ann* late October 1847. On the way down the Irish channel the ship grounded on the Arklow Bank, and land was not cleared until January 7th 1848. After a five-day stop at Cape of Good Hope the ship finally arrived at Auckland on 16th May 1848. An epidemic of influenza caused twelve deaths during the voyage, including a young son of John and Mary McAnulty.

The Plymouth Company was an offshoot of the New Zealand Company, which was established for settlers from Devon and Cornwall. The George family from Cornwall sailed on the *Oriental* in 1841, followed by the Rusdens on the *Blenheim* the following year. Both families settled in New Plymouth and had daughters marrying into the Newell family.

1853-70 Gold boom

During the period of the Gold boom the non-Maori population increased from about 20,000 to over 250,000. Assistance with fares was provided, and anyone prepared to settle in Auckland was given a land grant of 40 acres. Also, the lure of gold, which had been discovered in Otago in 1861 and in Westland in 1865, encouraged many people to uproot and settle in New Zealand. In 1863 the gross migration to New Zealand was 45,730 people, the maximum number settling in the country in any year to date. Many people also transferred from the Australian gold fields.

George Heslop was a miner in the Aorere Goldfield, near Collingwood, Nelson and his son, George William was born on site and spent his childhood and schooling in the midst of the workings.

1871-80: Government-assisted immigration

From 1871 the New Zealand Government offered assisted passages to selected migrants and those people nominated by relatives. The total number of assisted migrants during the ten years was over 100,000, half of the total gross migration.

1874 saw over 32,000 assisted migrants, including the Allington and Woodley families, who sailed on the *Crusader*.

The ship *Crusader* at the wharf, probably in the Port Chalmers area.
David Alexander De Maus Collection G-2016-1/1. (PAColl-3035). ATL

Other families who arrived in New Zealand during this period included the Pooles (married into Johnstone family), Christiana Foulstone (married into Holt family), and the Hamblings. There may be more, but details of their sailings are not known.

1881 onwards

The economic difficulties of the 1880s and early 1890s made New Zealand put a halt to massive migration, and assisted passages were stopped between 1891 and 1904. The Briggs and Mayall families settled in New Zealand during these years, the latter family transferring from Victoria, Australia.

Chapter 2

MILITARY TRAINING

New Zealand

The Defence Act of 1909 founded the New Zealand Army, and established a Territorial Force, which was raised by compulsory military training. At the outbreak of WW1 on 4th August 1914 New Zealand was able to offer an Expeditionary Force to support Britain. Of particular advantage was the fact that the War had broken out during the army camping season in New Zealand. 30,000 troops were in a state of readiness, and the first volunteers had to be selected by ballot.

Military training took place in semi-permanent reinforcement training camps at Trentham, Tauherenikau and Featherston, and other camps scattered round New Zealand. Trentham was the principal camp and by 1918 it could accommodate 4500 men in huts and up to 2000 in tents. Featherston Camp was established in January 1916 with a capacity of 7500, 4500 in huts and 3000 in tents.

View overlooking the military camp at Trentham. F-020728-1/2. ATL

The National Registration Act of 1st October 1915 required that men between the ages of 19 and 45 had to declare whether they had volunteered as a member of an expeditionary force for the war, and whether they had been accepted or rejected. On 1st August 1916 the Military Services Act introduced conscription.

The system of recruitment entailed passing a medical examination and completing an Attestation Form. The volunteer then waited for a notice calling him into camp. Until September 1915, reinforcements were called up every two months, and after this date every month. Infantry reinforcements spent their first five weeks at Trentham where they were equipped and carried out basic drill and musketry training.

The recruits then transferred to Featherston for eight weeks for more advanced infantry training. At the end of this period they marched back over the Rimutakas to Trentham for a final musketry course and were issued with uniforms and equipment for overseas service. They were then sent on embarkation leave.

There were variations to this routine. Engineers stayed at Trentham during the whole period of training. Artillery, mounted rifles and specialists were trained at Featherston. The Tunnelling Company and the Maoris trained at Narrow Neck Camp on high land behind Devonport, near Auckland. The New Zealand Maori (Pioneer) Battalion was formed as a Maori unit on 1st September 1917. Its forerunners were the Maori contingents that first sailed from New Zealand in February 1915. The Pioneers provided the labour force of the New Zealand Division, laying railways and building bridges and trenches.

Camp discipline was strict; minor infringements were punished with confinement to barracks, and major offences suffered detention.

The average time between entering the Army and joining a Battalion was ten months. A soldier spent four months training in New Zealand. He then faced a long sea-voyage. Until April 1916 the troops went initially to Egypt, the journey sometimes taking up to six weeks.

Egypt

The main body of 8417 men sailed from Wellington on October 16th 1914, the largest single body of men ever to leave New Zealand. The troops reached Alexandria on November 3rd and after a period of acclimatising to their new surroundings, they settled down at the various camps situated at Zeitoun near Cairo, at Moascar near Ismailia and at Tel el Kebir (between the two).

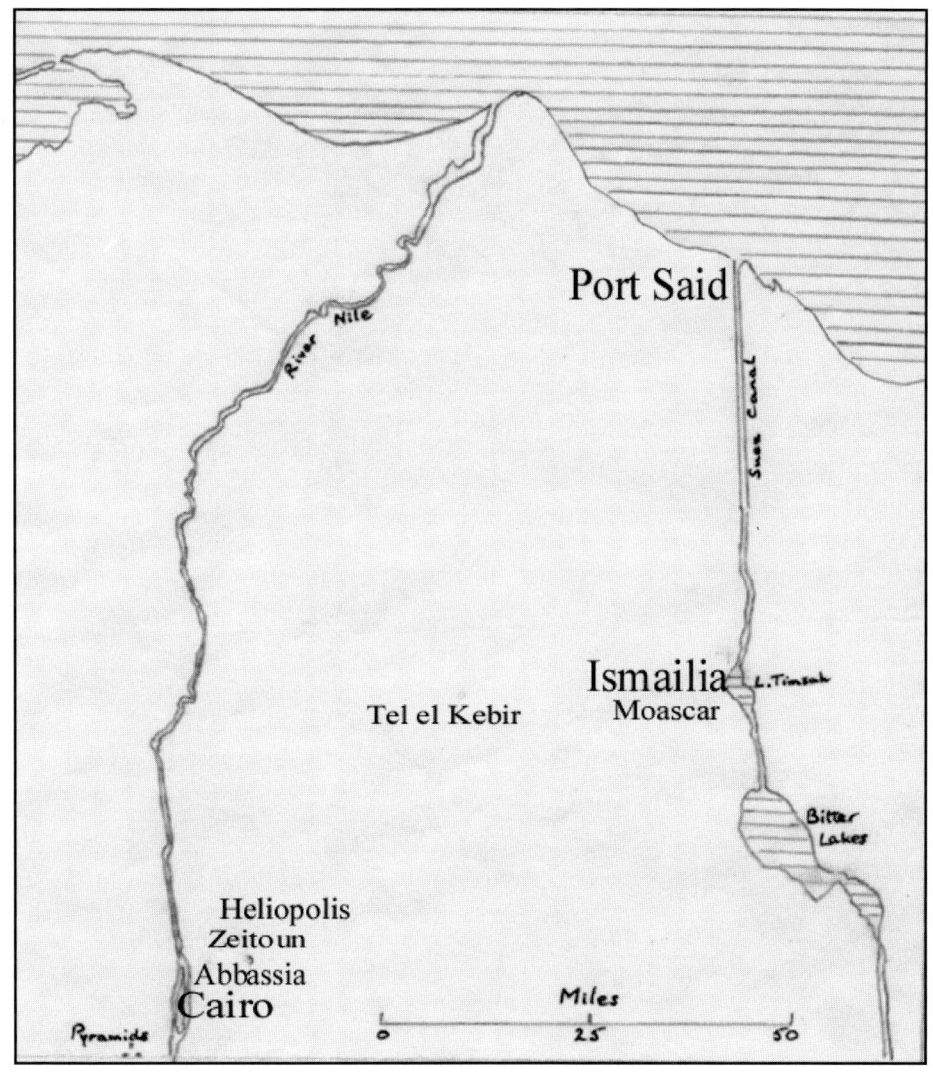

Egypt

The troops trained in the desert in preparation for fighting in Gallipoli. Reinforcements sailed from Wellington to Egypt at two-monthly intervals.

Life in camp took the form of drill, musketry, trench digging, night bivouacs and route marching. Training in the desert for the New Zealand Field Artillery (NZFA) was hard going for the horses and they found it difficult coping in the sand. A rifle range was established at Abbassia, near Zeitoun and much practice took place there.

Heliopolis was a new tourist resort near Zeitoun, and from there the electric train could be boarded for transport into Cairo where sightseeing and pleasure seeking took place in abundance!

The majority of men would at some stage visit the famous pyramids of Giza as illustrated below.

Three unidentified New Zealand servicemen on camels
during World War I in front of the Sphinx and a pyramid.
James McAllister Collection. G-012536-1/1 (PAColl-3054). ATL

In April 1916 the NZEF transferred from Egypt to the Western Front in northern France and Belgium. They sailed to Marseilles and then journeyed by train to the Divisional Area where training camps were established.

Hazebrouck was the centre of Divisional Headquarters, and the NZEF men were based at Morbeque, Steenbecque and Roquetoire. Troops were sent to army schools to learn the use of grenades, Lewis guns and defence against gas attack.

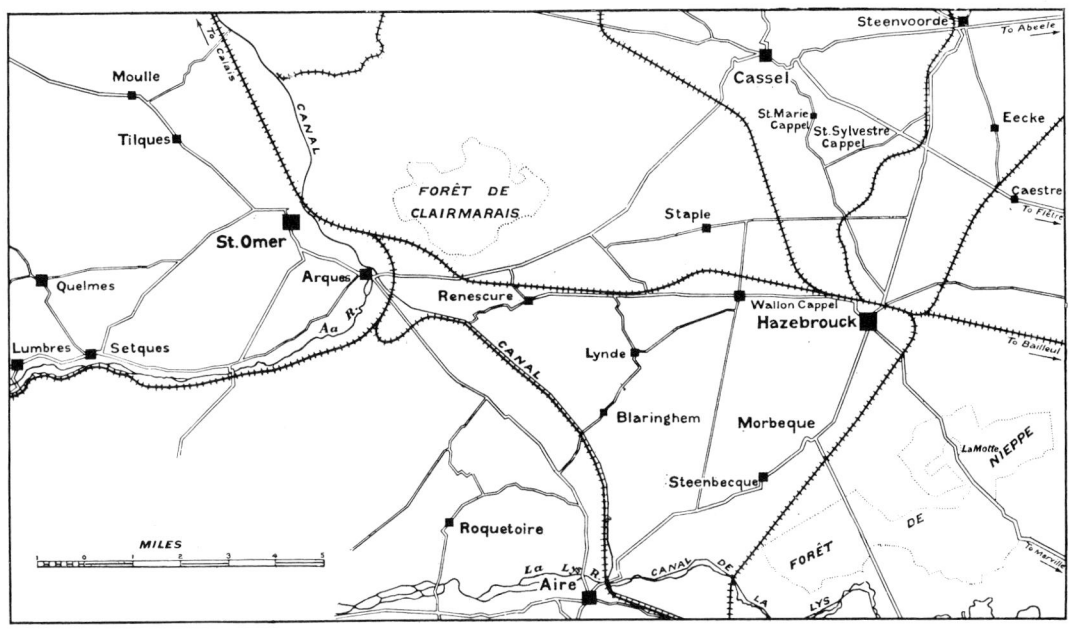

Training area in France

The 13th Reinforcements left New Zealand on 27th May 1916 and disembarked at Devonport, near Plymouth, England. From there they entrained for Sling Camp on Salisbury Plain. After arrival at the railhead at Bulford the men marched the last two miles into camp. All Reinforcements thereafter sailed direct to Britain.

Sling Camp

Sling at Larkhill on Salisbury Plain was a hutted camp, situated on rising ground close to the permanent military camp above Bulford village. Reinforcements arrived from New Zealand at the rate of about 1,000 per month and after a brief period of recovery from their sea voyage they undertook rigorous training. The New Zealanders resented having to remove their Reinforcement badges, which were regarded as the privilege of those who had already seen active service. Non-commissioned officers straight from New Zealand lost a stripe and had to pass an examination at the end of their training to retain their reduced rank. They had to put up with the fact that there were many Privates with more experience serving in France and still awaiting promotion.

The training was severe, lasting from 6.30 a.m. to 9.00 p.m., often seven days per week, but this soon improved the health of the trainees. The reinforcements were put through an intensive three weeks' training under pressure: squad and section drill, musketry, physical training, bayonet fighting, wiring, bombing, anti-gas measures and the Lewis gun. Here the men had to suffer the shouting and harshness of the New Zealand and British instructors. The parade ground at Sling was nicknamed "The Piccadilly Trot" with the marching taking place on "Piccadilly Circus", a name no doubt adopted after some Kiwis had returned from a leave period in London!

Despite the harsh circumstances in which the New Zealanders found themselves, there was time for rest and recreation with a YMCA Hut (above) provided on site.

Private William James Mogg, 26129, New Zealand Machine Gun Battalion (p. 155) was based at Sling during the Christmas of 1916/17 and one wonders whether he sent this card to his family at Wolverton, Warwickshire, or whether he was allowed home on leave for a few days?

Greetings from Sling Camp, 1916-1917. Kia-Ora.
Eph-A-WAR-WI-1916-01. ATL

France

After Sling, the men sailed for France and passed through a tented camp outside Boulogne. The story goes that the bell tents in which they were billeted were rotten and leaked like a sieve. The men were issued with just one blanket for bedding, hence the nickname "One Blanket Hill" camp.

Then there was a 20-mile march to Etaples, which was the Reinforcement Training Centre for the British Armies in France, where each Division had its reinforcement depot. At Etaples soldiers passed through another rigorous training course, covering all aspects of trench warfare before being sent forward to the Division. Here the parade ground was nicknamed "The Bullring".

Inspection of troops at the New Zealand Infantry Base Depot in Etaples.
RSA Collection. G-13716-1/2. ATL

At the end of this process the soldiers would be marched to the local station, and entrained for the Front in "Hommes 40-Chevaux 8" wagons. In the Divisional Area, reinforcements were allotted to battalions, and then they were allocated to companies.

SPECIALIST TRAINING CAMPS IN ENGLAND

Brocton

By May 1917 Sling Camp was overcrowded, so in August that year the New Zealand Rifle Brigade (NZRB) of nearly 2000 reserves moved into a temporary canvas camp at Tidworth Pennings, four miles north of Larkhill. This latter camp was only suitable for use in summer so the decision was made for the NZRB to transfer to a permanent camp at Brocton, Staffordshire on 27th September.

Brocton was a section of the Rugeley Camp, officially termed "The Cannock Chase Reserve Centre". The camp was set in 100 acres with a German prisoner of war camp nearby. The area was classified as "bleak and dreary upland, surrounded by a charming countryside dotted with quaint old-time villages".

General training included formal drill protection against gas, construction of trenches, bayonet fighting, physical training, musketry, and all-night occupation of trenches. The administration of the camp was considered to be very good.

The Quartermaster set high standards and unlike at other camps, waste was unknown. Crumbs and stale bread were baked in the large ovens for sale to Birmingham manufacturers of calves' food.

Like No. 1 New Zealand General Hospital at Brockenhurst, the camp was called "Tin-Town" because of the tin huts in which the men were accommodated.

Christchurch, near Bournemouth, Hampshire

The New Zealand Engineers were based at Christchurch, the Royal Engineers Training Centre for Southern Command. In June 1916, 150 Engineers, Signallers and Tunnellers arrived in Sling Camp from Egypt and were immediately transferred to Christchurch where they met up with the Australian Engineers Depot at Jumper's Camp outside the town. The Depot consisted of a few tents in a bare paddock. In July the 12th and 13th Reinforcements arrived from Egypt and New Zealand and undertook nine weeks training, with parades taking place at King's Park at Boscombe, Bournemouth.

In August the Signallers transferred to Hitchin to a Depot of their own.

Training at Christchurch included trench works and mining on St. Catherine's Hill, a large knoll overlooking the River Avon. Practice in construction of bridges took place on the River Stour nearby. The weather broke in October and the troops were moved to billets in Boscombe, nearby. For a temporary period the Depot moved to Brightlingsea in Essex, with the Drivers remaining in Christchurch. However in January 1917 the planning was reversed much to the satisfaction of the troops who liked the circumstances in Hampshire better than Essex. During the spring the troops returned to living in tents on the banks of the River Stour.

Early in 1918 the depot was extended to include the New Zealand Maori (Pioneer) Battalion who transferred from Salisbury Plain. The troops thoroughly enjoyed boating and bathing in the River Stour, but unfortunately the water proved fatal for one member of the Maori (Pioneer) Battalion, Private Tuheke Matenga, 16/810 (p. 93), who drowned on 14th May 1918.

In 1918 the Christchurch Engineers' Depot undertook construction and repair work at No. 1 New Zealand General Hospital at Brockenhurst and also grave-digging at the adjacent cemetery.

Ewshott

From August 1917 the New Zealand Field Artillery undertook training at a 30-acre site at Ewshott (36 miles from London), in the Aldershot command. This camp accommodated 1500 of all ranks and about 1000 horses. The Headquarters overlooked a large barrack square; on one side were the 18-pounder gun sheds with the stables opposite. The course for new men lasted for six weeks and riding lessons were available in the vicinity. The camp had all services such as a veterinary surgeon, shoeing smiths and saddlers.

The New Zealand Medical Corps (NZMC) also had its chief depot in the camp. Members of this Corps went direct to Ewshott on arrival in England. Here training courses in gas, water duties, testing of water carts and advanced dressing station work were undertaken and personnel were allocated to the New Zealand hospitals in England and the hospital ships.

Grantham, Lincolnshire

The Machine Gunners were based at Grantham. Three camps were located in the area - Harrowby, Belton Park and Chepstone. The New Zealanders were at Belton Park, the private property of Earl Brownlow. The Machine Gunners were ranked as "specialists" in New Zealand, but this was not the case in Britain. They did, however have the advantage in that the training was longer than for the infantry, which prolonged the period before being sent to the dangers of the Western Front.

BELTON CAMP.

Hornchurch

Hornchurch, in Essex was selected as the first depot in England of the New Zealand contingent. It became the Command Depot for the gathering of all men before they returned to their respective fighting units. The camp consisted of many huts clustered round a manor house called Grey Towers, set in 93 acres.

GREY TOWERS, N.Z. DEPOT, HORNCHURCH.

The first group of wounded arrived in January 1916 but by the beginning of May, Hornchurch was considered to be too small for the Command Depot base so it was converted into a convalescent hospital and the Command Depot was established at Codford in Wiltshire.

Codford

Codford was established as the New Zealand Command Depot in July 1916 and men who were convalescing from wounds or sickness were sent there. The camp hospital became No. 3 NZGH and could accommodate 10 officers and 980 other ranks.

The camp also accommodated men who had transferred from Hornchurch and were on the road to recovery. In he first instance they were generally graded B3 and given light work. The next stage in recovery was B2 when they would undertake route marches of 4 to 6 miles to build up strength. B1 grade meant that the march was extended to a maximum of 10 miles a day. "A" grade soldiers were capable of marching 14 miles a day and fit enough to return to Sling Camp and join a reserve unit.

Codford Camp, Wiltshire

Chapter 3

THEATRES OF WAR

This Chapter briefly describes the campaigns in which the New Zealand Expeditionary Force was involved.

1914   5th August   War declared

    Samoa   29th August   – unopposed landing by 1413 troops

    Egypt   16th October – Main Body sailed from Wellington
8417 troops comprising:
4 infantry battalions
4 mounted rifles regiments,
Ammunition column
reached Egypt on 3rd November

1915

    Egypt   3 February   First New Zealand combat when Turkish attack across Suez Canal was repulsed

        25 December   Senussi affair

    Gallipoli 25 April   Landing at Anzac Cove by NZEF

        5-8 May   2nd Battle of Krithia

        24 May   Armistice to bury dead

        7-21 August   Battle of Suvla

        8-20 December Evacuation of peninsula

The NZEF returned to Egypt and was reorganised and reinforced, under the command of Major-General Sir Andrew H. Russell, K.C.M.G.

Western Front

1916	April	New Zealand Division arrives in France
	13 May	Troops man trenches for the first time over a 4 mile stretch on the Armentières front
	15 September	New Zealand Division attack Flers as part of the Battle of the Somme

The winter of 1916/17 is spent on the River Lys, near Armentières

1917	7 June	Battle of Messines
	27 & 31 July	Basseville
	4 and 12 October	Attack on Gravenstafel - Passchendaele (part of 3rd Battle of Ypres)
	3 December	Attack on Polderhoek Chateau

The winter of 1917-18 is spent in the Ypres area

1918	21 March	German attack on 50-mile front
	25 March	New Zealand Division in the Upper Ancre valley
	5 April	German counter attack. Road to Amiens held
	July	Allied advance through Rossignol Wood, Puisieux, Achiet, Grevillers, Bapaume
	21 August - 1 September	Battle of Bapaume
	September	Battles of Havrincourt and Cambrai
	October	Battles of Le Cateau and Selle River
	November	Battle of the Sambre
	4 November	Battle of Le Quesnoy
	11 November	11.00 a.m. Armistice

SAMOA

The first action in which New Zealand troops were involved was the occupation of Western Samoa in the south central Pacific Ocean northeast of New Zealand. Samoa was in German possession and on 29th August 1914 a force of 1413 New Zealand troops landed and took over control. A law system was formed, defining the rights of Germans, aliens and natives, and the local police were put through a training programme. The Germans did not show any great animosity towards the troops.

During their time in Samoa many of the New Zealand troops became ill due to the climate and living conditions. They were living in low-lying land near the beach, which was an area rife for disease. They could take very little exercise owing to the extreme heat and they were fed a diet more appropriate to a cold climate. After two months the physical condition of the men declined, with ailments such as blood disorders, cuts that did not heal, dysentery and fever, and the local hospitals were full.

Apia-Samoa Hospital

EGYPT

British military bases had long been established in Egypt and were principally to be concerned with the campaigns in Palestine and the Middle East. The NZEF became involved, as, for instance assisting in the repulse of a Turkish incursion across the Suez Canal on 3rd February 1915.

Later that year, attention was diverted to Egypt's western border with Libya, where Senussi Moslems were being encouraged by Turkey to rebel against the Allies and seek to expel Italian rule from Libya. This led to the formation on 20th November of a Western Frontier Force under the command of Major-General A. Wallace, C.B. On 7th December, Headquarters was established at Mersa Matruh, 200 miles west of Alexandria and the first encounter with the Senussi took place four days later. The Western Frontier Force sailed from Alexandria on an assortment of boats between 19th and 21st December – gunboats, tiny traders and trawlers. On Christmas Day an "affair" took place near Mersa Matruh, in which men of the No. 3 New Zealand Machine Gun Company were involved.

Once the plan to open up the Dardanelle Straits had been agreed, the NZEF found itself training for fighting on he Gallipoli peninsula.

GALLIPOLI

It is unlikely that many of the New Zealanders who volunteered for the War in Europe had even heard of Gallipoli, yet it was here that so many made the ultimate sacrifice. There were a number of reasons why a campaign in this corner of the Mediterranean received support, particularly from Winston Churchill, then First Lord of the Admiralty. A successful campaign would probably have severed Turkey's allegiance to Germany, dissuaded Bulgaria from joining the Central Powers, and freed a vital sea route to Russia through the Dardanelle Straits. In the event, it led to a costly and humiliating defeat for the Allies.

The NZEF established an advanced base on the island of Lemnos, about sixty miles west of Gallipoli, the narrow peninsula overlooking the Dardanelle Straits.

On 25th April 1915, the Australian and New Zealand Army Corps (ANZAC) landed at Anzac Cove, having sailed from their base on Lemnos.

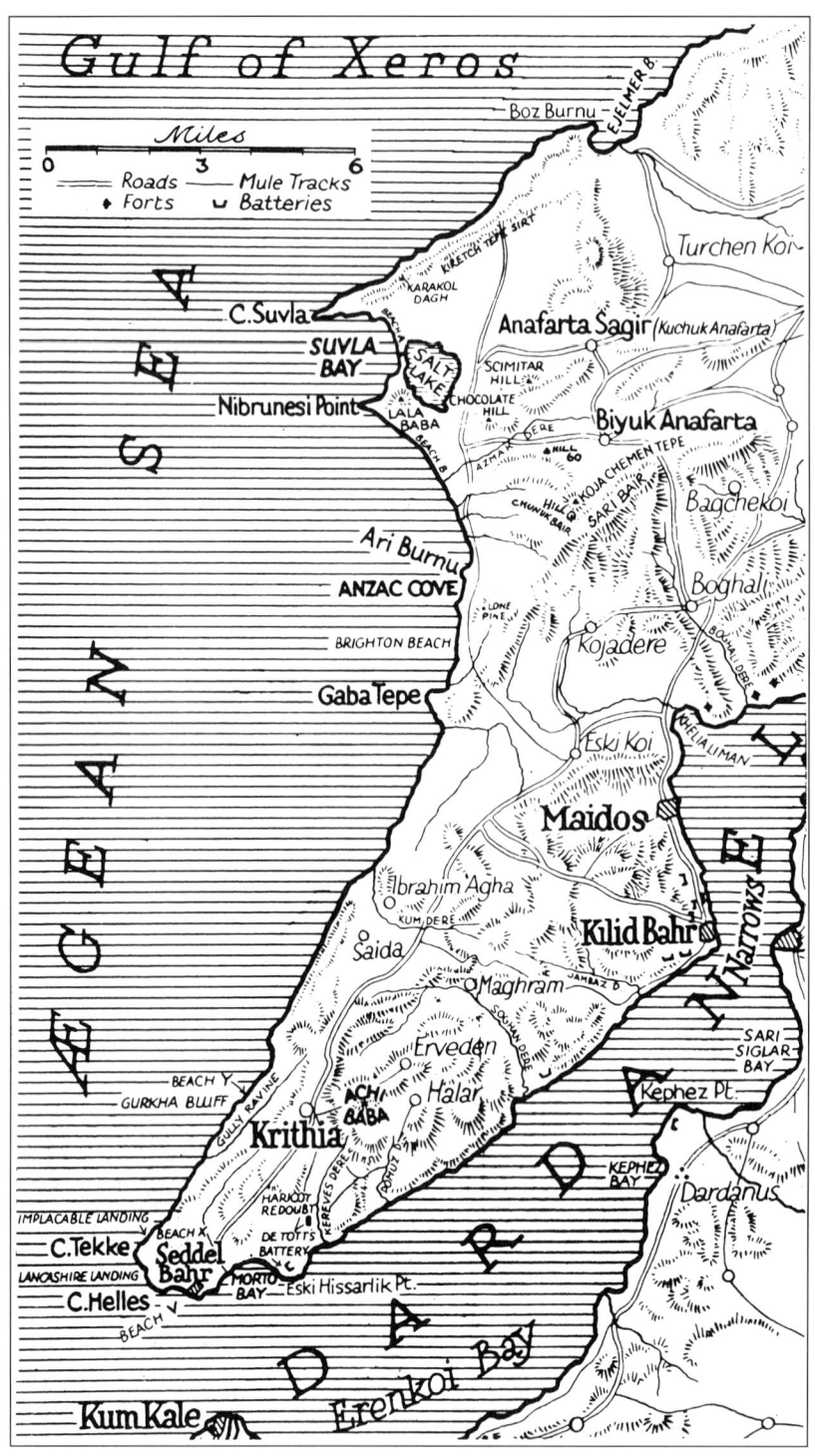

Gallipoli Peninsula

The major campaigns on Gallipoli were the Second battle of Krithia (May 6-8) and the Battle of Suvla (August 6-21). After the disastrous attempt to take control of Gallipoli by the British Army and the death, injury and sickness of over 200,000 men, the peninsula was evacuated and all New Zealand troops had left the area by 20th December. Altogether 8,556 New Zealand troops served on Gallipoli. 2,721 died and 4,752 were wounded.

THE WESTERN FRONT

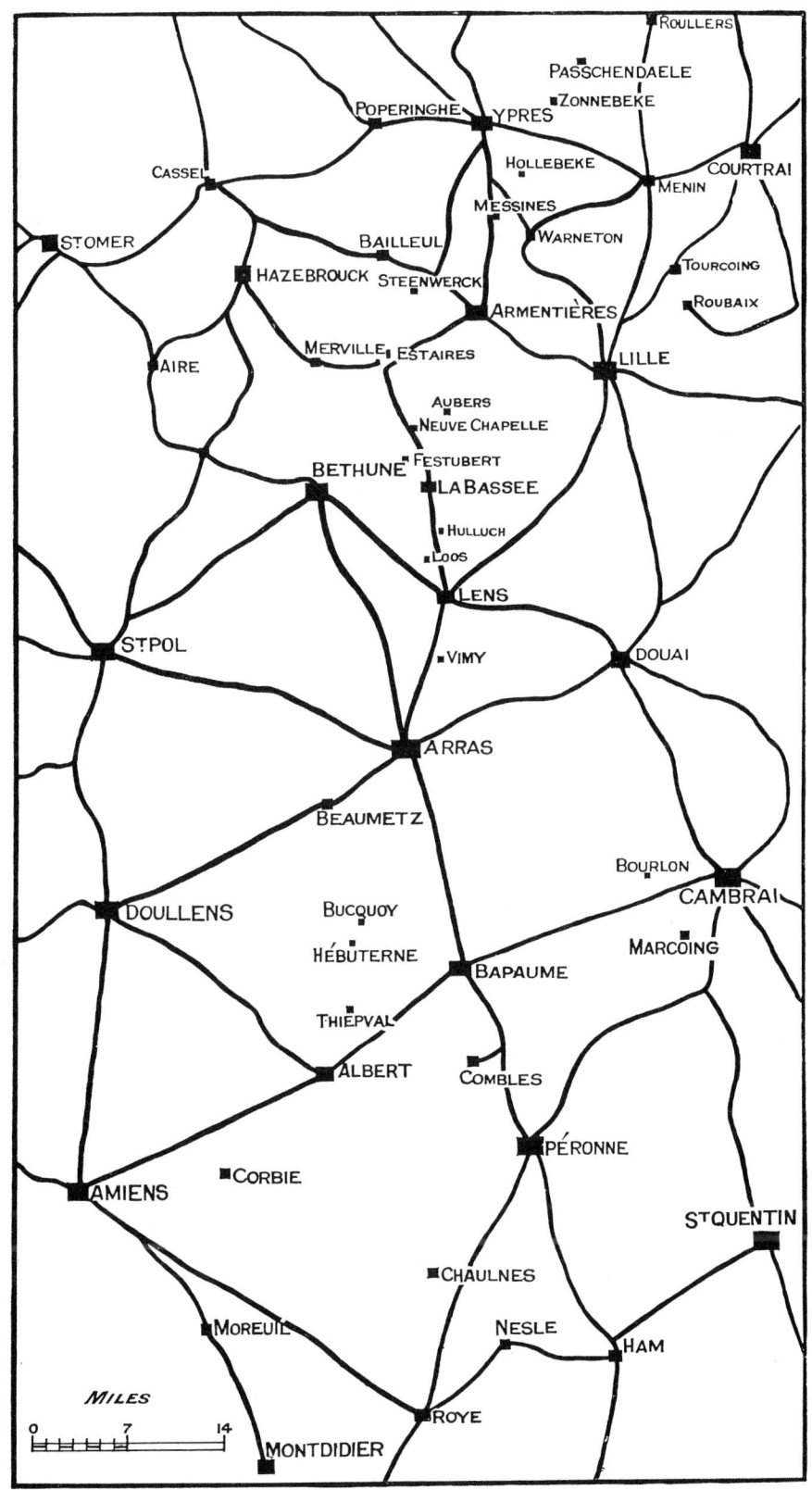

Northwest France

ARMENTIÈRES

After arrival in France in April 1916, the New Zealand Division moved into Front line trenches on May 13th, a four-mile stretch of the line in the "quiet" sector near Armentières. The whole of this area was composed of low-lying flats, criss-crossed by canals and railways, in the basin of the Lys River.

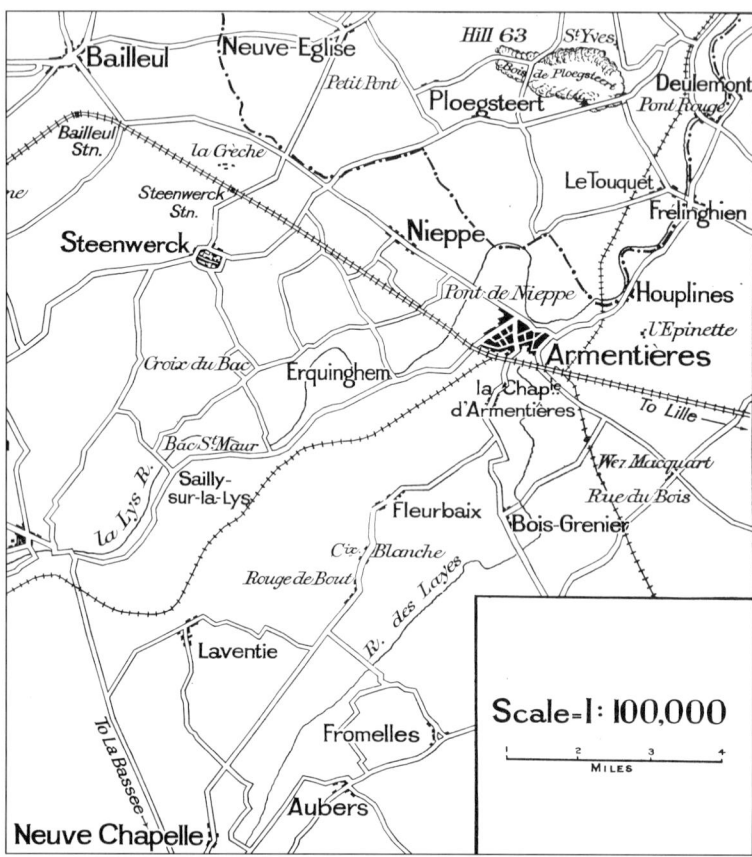

This sign is now displayed in the Queen Elizabeth II Army Memorial Museum at Waiouru, New Zealand, a long way from its original location!

SOMME

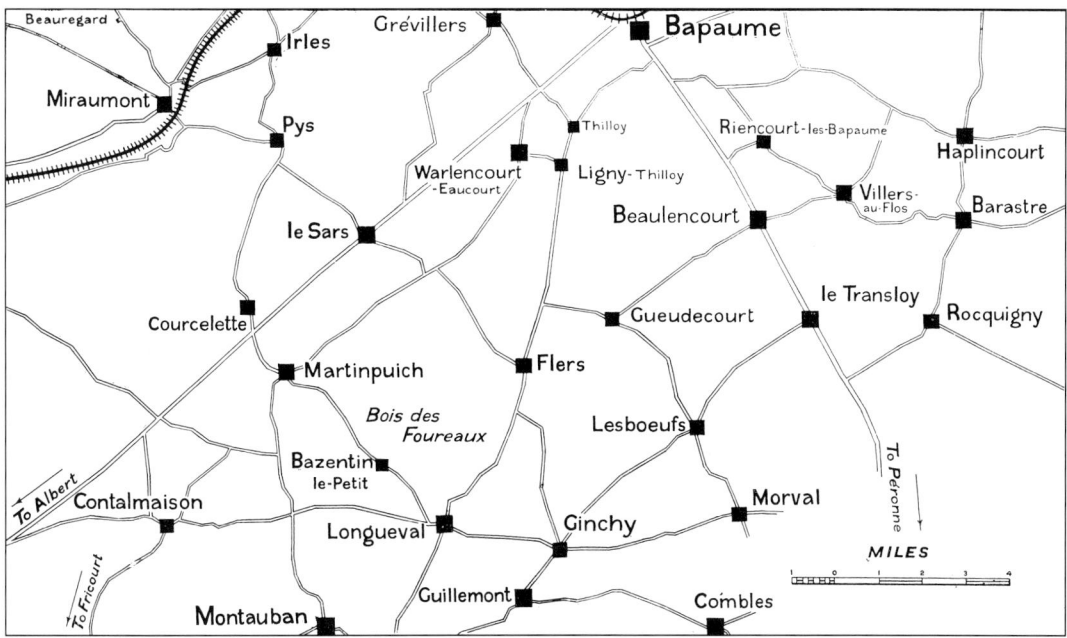

Area of the Somme Battlefield (1916)

The Somme Campaign began on 1st July 1916 near Albert, but the New Zealand Division was not involved until 15th September when they attacked the village of Flers, the first day on which tanks were used in battle. However, 31 of the 49 tanks used during the attack succumbed to mechanical difficulties.

On a second assault on September 25th the Division captured Factory Corner (due north of Flers and west of Gueudecourt). During this period the New Zealanders fought for 23 days without a break and advanced approximately two miles. They left the area on October 10th, but their artillery remained behind on the Somme.

This period saw the end of the fighting career of many 'Brockenhurst' men, several being injured on the same day. The details of their evacuation to England are laid out in Appendix C1.

(Naval and Military Press – *Imperial War Museum Trench Map Archive*)

MESSINES (7th June 1917)

The New Zealand Division's task was to capture the village of Messines and the battle began with the detonation of 19 large mines under the German lines.

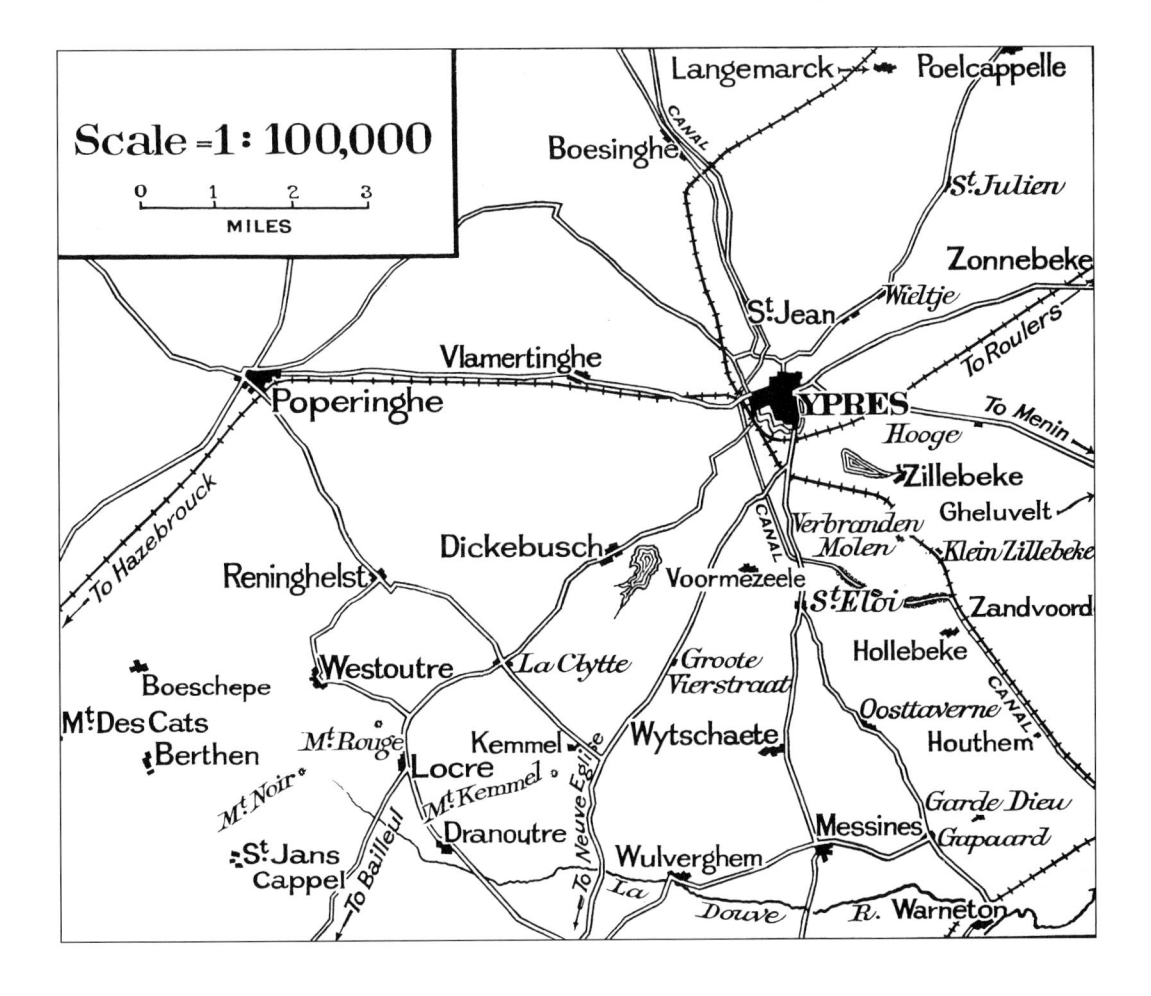

Messines and Ypres

The initial objectives were met within two days, at the cost of many dead and wounded.

BASSEVILLE

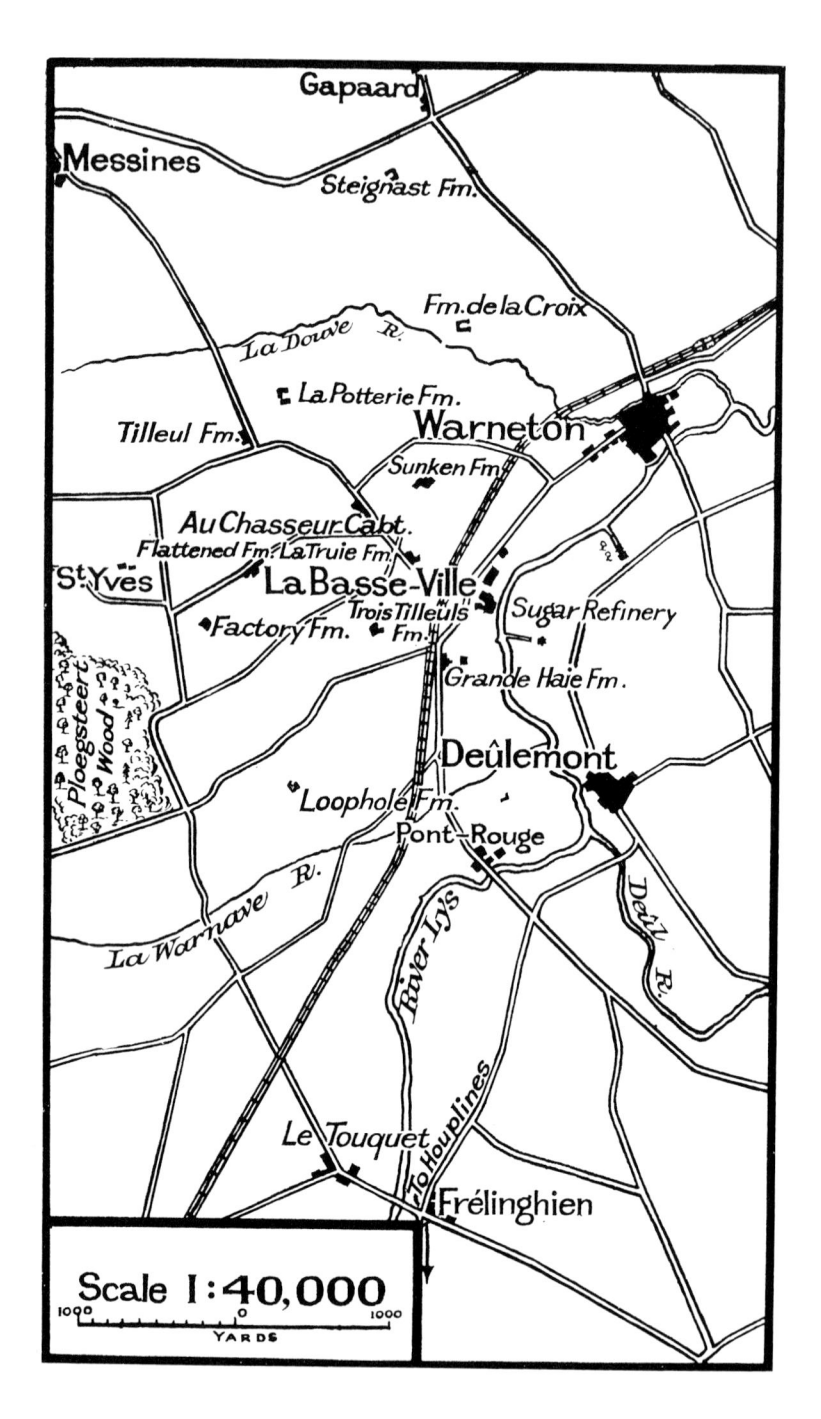

Basseville

The Wellington Battalion stormed and captured Basseville on two occasions. The village was taken on 27th July but a few hours later the Germans counter-attacked, with success. On 31st July the New Zealanders again seized the village and stood firm, and the Division stayed in the line until 31st August.

PASSCHENDAELE (3rd Battle of Ypres)

The New Zealand Division returned to battle on 4th October as part of the 3rd Battle of Ypres (Passchendaele). The battlefield occupied a low-lying, gently undulating area of reclaimed pastureland. The water table was near the surface, even during the summer months, and liable to flooding.

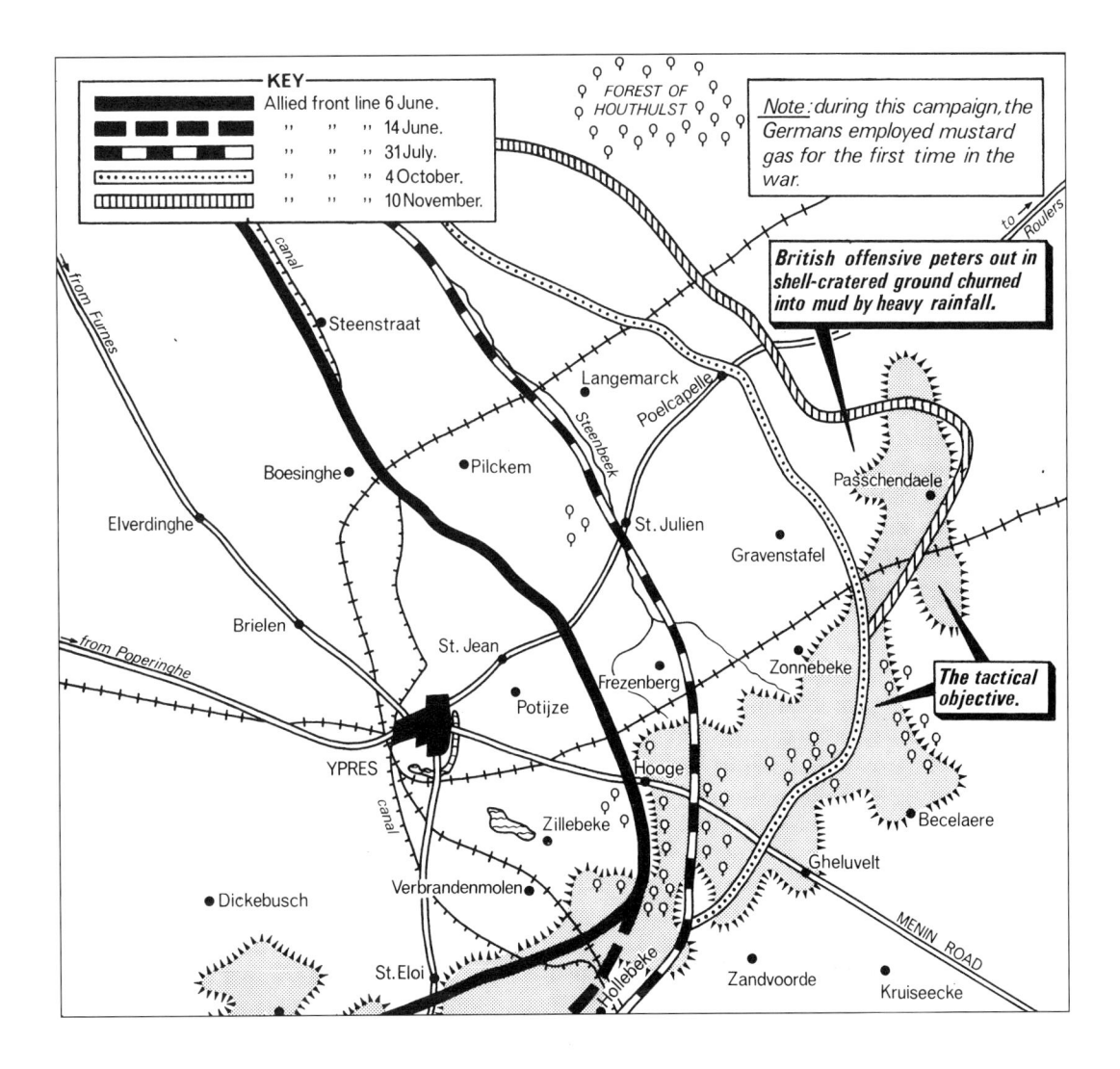

The Division attacked at Gravenstafel and after two days there were 1653 casualties (330 dead, and 1323 wounded). The troops were withdrawn and returned to the Front line on 12th October, which was the worst day on the Western Front for the New Zealanders. The weather was atrocious and the men had to struggle through thick mud without the protection of adequate artillery cover. In just four hours there were 2,700 casualties, which "broke the spirit of the Divison". Eventually, on 6th November, three weeks after the New Zealanders had aimed at their target, the Canadians took Passchendaele, which had cost in total over half a million lives over three months.

1918

The German Army began its final offensive of the War on 21st March 1918 and the New Zealand Division contributed towards preventing the Germans from obtaining the strategic centre of Amiens.

Between March and July the New Zealand Division was based in the Upper Ancre valley between Hébuterne/Puisieux-au-Mont and Englebelmer.

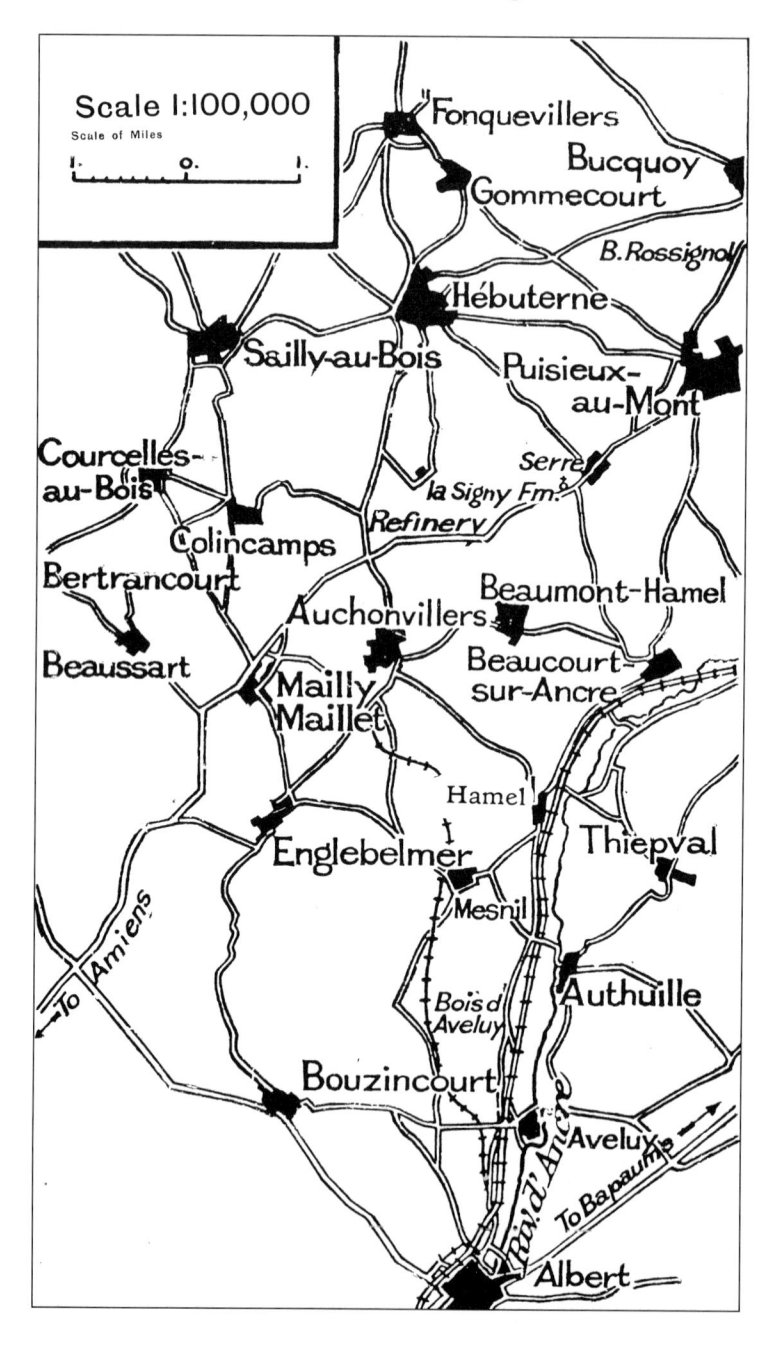

The Upper Ancre

The final battle in which the New Zealanders were involved was the Battle of Sambre (1st-11th November). On 4th November the New Zealand Rifle Brigade scaled the town ramparts at Le Quesnoy (east of Cambrai).

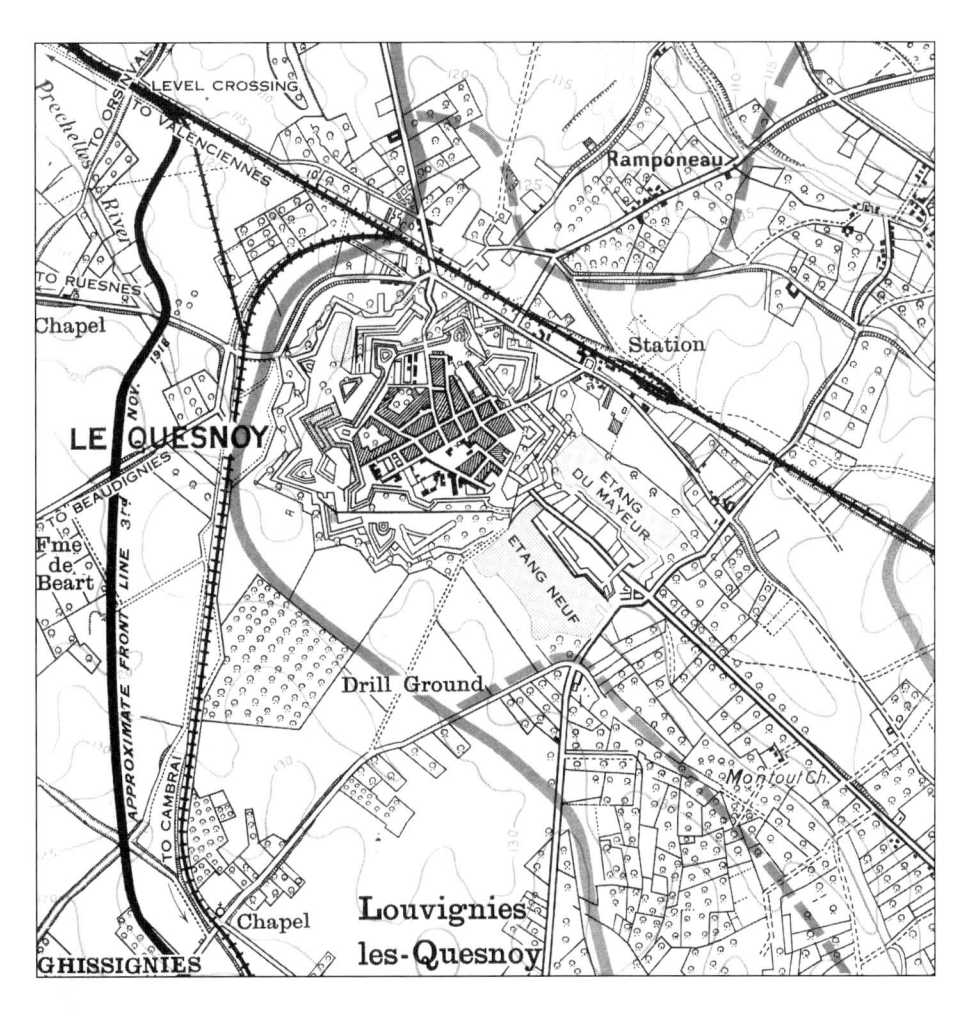

Le Quesnoy

On Armistice Day, 11th November 1918, the New Zealand Division had 58,129 troops in the field and another 10,000 in training.

Chapter 4

MEDICAL CARE

In order to understand how the 93 men arrived at Brockenhurst, it is essential to know the system of medical care once they were wounded in action or fell ill.

The typical evacuation from the Western Front is described. Appendix C gives details of an individual's journey from France to England. Most of the New Zealanders went straight to No. 1 NZGH, Brockenhurst, but a few found themselves transferred to other hospitals in England, particularly in London. Full information can be found in the individual biographies.

Regimental Aid Post (RAP)

Regimental medical personnel took care of the men when they were first wounded or fell ill. Stretcher-bearers carried the wounded from the battlefield to the Regimental Aid Post (RAP). Here the Regimental Medical Officer (RMO) was responsible for receiving and treating the patients and transferring them on the Field Ambulance.

The RAP was situated in as safe a place as could be found close behind the firing line. The RMO would check that the wound was clean, and if necessary, carry out any emergency operations. He would oversee the splinting of fractures and try to ensure that shock did not set in.

RAP near Ypres

The main objective was to prepare the person for evacuation to a safer place as quickly as possible. The quality of the treatment received at the RAP was essential for the patient's recovery. Before transfer to the Field Ambulance the patient would have a ticket pinned to his clothing giving details of his name, unit, wound, and the treatment already given.

Field Ambulance

Behind the RAP lay the Field Ambulance. It relieved the RAP of sick and wounded, gave treatment at its Main Dressing Station (MDS) and assessed future requirements. Immediate evacuation was not always possible and the men might have to stay at the MDS for longer than ideal. Therefore it was essential that the MDSs were located sufficiently far behind the lines for safety. If possible the wounded should be accommodated in as comfortable circumstances as practicable, provided with warmth and food, and given an anti-tetanus injection to combat against lockjaw.

New Zealand dressing station on the Somme, Mailly-Mallet, France.
RSA Collection. G-13108. ATL

Sometimes the MDS was by-passed and the seriously wounded men went straight from the RAP to the Casualty Clearing Station (CCS). But this only took place when the number of casualties was manageable.

Casualty Clearing Station

The Casualty Clearing Station (CCS) was the next stage in the process of a soldier's medical care. The CCSs were initially intended as sorting centres to provide rest and food for the patients and where the injured had their wounds inspected and redressed before they continued on their journey. However, as the war progressed this system of working was totally inadequate for handling large numbers of casualties on the Western Front. With the additional problem of gas gangrene the need for urgent operations was essential. Hence it was decided that facilities for surgery to take place nearer the Front line were urgently needed particularly as the Field Ambulances were not suitable for their provision. CCCs thus became hospitals near the Front line. Sir Anthony Bowlby, who had been the consultant surgeon responsible for surgery in the forward areas, devised their expansion. He recognised that they could be used for immediate surgery in order to save lives and advised Field Ambulances to send these cases onward as quickly as possible.

The CCSs were set up on open ground, using tents to accommodate the wounded. Operating theatres and wards for serious cases were housed in huts with operations being carried out under electric light provided by portable generators. A typical CCS would have an establishment of six medical officers, which included one surgical specialist, and approximately seven nursing sisters. Numbers varied according to need, and increased in times of heavy fighting. It was essential that CCSs were located in an area of good communications, near to railway stations, and suitably placed between Field Ambulances and stationary hospitals. Motor ambulance convoys of up to fifty vehicles, each accommodating eight sitting patients or four stretcher cases conveyed the patients to the stationary hospitals, which were mostly based at Etaples or Rouen.

Stationary and General Hospitals

The men were then transferred to hospitals at the army bases. Stationary hospitals had originally been established as light hospitals, accommodating 200 cases and intended as temporary accommodation between the medical units near the Front line and those at the base. But owing to the change in status of CCSs and the more speedy evacuation arrangements provided by motor ambulance convoys and ambulance trains, the role of the stationary hospital changed, and the same type of medical care was undertaken as at General Hospitals.

The General Hospitals catered for the full range of wounds and sickness and divided into two sections, a medical division and a surgical division. No. 26 General Hospital opened at Etaples in June 1915 and could accommodate 1040 cases. The sick and wounded were accommodated in wooden huts, and later in the war tents were erected to cater for the increasing number of casualties. Accommodation included two operating theatres and an x-ray room. The casualties were segregated according to their circumstances. There were separate wards for amputees, chest cases, head wounds, abdominal wounds, and compound fractures. The system was so arranged in order that the doctors could treat the patients according to their medical expertise.

Prior to 1918 some doctors at the base hospitals regarded their job as lacking excitement compared with the medical work nearer the Front line, but when the Germans launched their offensive in March 1918, surgical operations at CCSs came to a halt. From then onwards the base hospitals at Etaples were stretched to the limit and undertook many more operations than previously, thereby altering the doctors' opinion of their workload. The majority of the NZEF soldiers who ended their days at Brockenhurst spent just a brief period at a base hospital before evacuation to England.

The final journey from France to Brockenhurst

Appendix C indicates the many ships that were used to convey sick and injured patients from France to England. A ship would leave Rouen, 78 miles inland on the River Seine in France and arrive at Southampton, Hampshire in less than twenty-four hours. Several of the New Zealanders travelled on the same ship and arrived at No. 1 NZGH, Brockenhurst together. A few men died on board ship and their bodies were taken to Brockenhurst to be buried amongst comrades.

Hospital Ship *Maheno*.
J H Kinnear Collection.G-14988-1/2 (PAColl-3053). ATL

On arrival at Southampton Docks, ambulance trains conveyed the patients the twelve miles through the New Forest to Brockenhurst Station, where ambulances would be waiting to take them the few hundred yards to No. 1 NZGH.

Transfer of stretcher case into Ambulance at Brockenhurst Station

In June 1916, No. 1 New Zealand General Hospital transferred from Cairo to Brockenhurst. The main site was at Tile Barn, in the field opposite the approach to St. Nicholas' church. The New Zealanders were also nursed at Balmer Lawn Hotel and Forest Park Hotel (officers only!) in the village. I do not intend to write further about the hospital because this has already been described in the booklet *New Zealanders in Brockenhurst – The No. 1 New Zealand General Hospital 1916-1919*.

New Zealand General Hospital No. 1, Brockenhurst

Chapter 5

REMEMBRANCE

The graves of the New Zealanders were originally marked by simple wooden crosses, which were replaced by the Imperial War Graves Commission in 1924 with the familiar headstones that can be seen in war cemeteries all over the world.

Original grave markers (from Tony Johnson, Brockenhurst)

The cenotaph with its incorporated cross was erected in 1927. The soldiers are remembered each year at the Anzac Service, which is organised by the Brockenhurst Branch of the Royal British Legion and held on the Sunday nearest to Anzac Day (25th April), the day on which the ANZACs landed at Gallipoli in 1915.

Anzac Day Service at Brockenhurst, 2001

Representatives of the New Zealand High Commission and the Armed Forces attend the service, and during the ceremony the New Zealand flag is paraded and local children lay posies at each grave.

Posies being laid at the war graves by Brockenhurst children
Anzac Day Service 2001

During the service the No. 4 bell in St. Nicholas' Church is rung. This bell was presented to the church in 1924 by relatives of those New Zealanders who died in the War, and is tolled 94 times, once for each person, including the one Australian buried in the cemetery:

Private Ernest William BOLLOM, 4373
22nd Battalion, Australian Infantry
Died of sickness on 30th October 1916, aged 23
Son of George William and Margaret Bollom
Native of Victoria, Australia
Grave Ref. Plot A, Row 5, Grave 9

The graves are situated on a gently rising slope, overlooking the village of Brockenhurst and the New Forest. This area of the cemetery is maintained to perfection by a local gardener who is employed by the Commonwealth War Graves Commission. It is a sad but, nevertheless, rewarding experience to visit the Anzac graves and contemplate upon the terrible conditions the men experienced before reaching their final resting place.

Part II

Biographies

It has been difficult to decide the order of the biographies. There are several alternatives - alphabetical, age or death date order. After much deliberation I have decided to place them in order of enlistment so that links between individual soldiers can be noticed. Men who signed on within a few weeks of each other often left New Zealand on the same ship and trained together. A total of 100,444 men and women from New Zealand served overseas in World War One. 18,166 died, a greater percentage loss than was the case for any other country involved. After injury or sickness on the Western Front, some men were evacuated from France on the same hospital ship. When one considers that I am only researching the movements of 93 men out of so many thousands, these are interesting features.

One might expect that by far the majority of the soldiers died as a result of wounds. This is not the case. Of the 93 NZEF men who lie at Brockenhurst, 51 died of wounds (55%), 41 died of sickness (44%) and one man drowned in England. Details, where known, of a person's sickness or injury are indicated in an individual's biography.

In order to avoid repetition within the biographies, and because the majority of the men who are buried at Brockenhurst followed the same pattern during the last few weeks/months of their lives, details of evacuation upon sickness or injury on the Western Front are given in Appendix C.

FRANK CLARK

Private, 12/2183
1st Battalion, Auckland Regiment, 3rd Company
Died of wounds on 12th October 1916, aged 23

Frank Clark was born on 6th February 1893 at Auckland, the son of Johnson (a Customs Officer for the New Zealand Government) and Jemima (née Ferguson). The family home was opposite Butler's Store, New North Road, Kingsland. A brother, Fred, later lived at Mount Pleasant Road, Mount Eden. Frank worked as a Boilermaker for Charles Bailey (Junior), Boat builder, Beaumont Street, Auckland. Another soldier who is buried at Brockenhurst, Gunner George Hurrell, 10603, New Zealand Field Artillery (p. 142) was also employed at the same boatyard.

Frank joined the army soon after the Great War was declared, and marched into camp on 9th August 1914 in the 3rd Battalion, Auckland Regiment. Two days later he departed with the Samoan Advance Party, which took over the control of Samoa on August 29th. He returned to New Zealand on 15th April 1915 but barely had time to see his family, because two days later he was on board ship again, bound for Suez. The ship docked on 25th May and Frank was soon on his way again, this time to the Dardanelles, where he joined 1st Battalion, Auckland Regiment on 8th June.

Frank was wounded three times before his luck finally ran out. He was wounded in the shoulder on 8th August 1915, and admitted to H.S. *Dongola* for passage back to Egypt and hospital in Cairo. The injury was not too serious because he was transferred to Special Camp at Zeitoun on 20th August. Nevertheless, it is apparent that he suffered from his experience in the Dardanelles, because he spent three weeks in hospital with debility. He was still in Egypt in December at the base depot at Ghezireh and eventually rejoined his unit at Ismailia on 18th January 1916.

Frank left Egypt on the *Franconia* on 6th April 1916, bound for France. He was wounded in action (second occasion) at Armentières on 24th June, with slight gunshot wounds to his head, but was fit enough to rejoin his unit on 8th July. The first twelve days of August were spent in re-equipping, re-organising and battle training for fighting on the Somme.

Frank's final days serving his country took the following course. On 9th September he was bivouacked in fields on the edge of the battlefield at Fricourt Wood. On the morning of the 15th, 1st Auckland moved to Mametz Wood and the next day the men marched to the battlefield and took over on the line. Orders were given for an attack on Goose Alley, which were subsequently cancelled, so the Battalion dug the left defensive flank for the New Zealand Division. As some stage during that day Frank was seriously wounded (third occasion) with gunshot wounds to his left thigh, which were serious enough for evacuation to England. He was admitted to No. 1 NZGH, Brockenhurst on 24th September. He died of his wounds on 12th October 1916, and was buried two days later. Plot A, Row 2, Grave 11.

Acknowledgement: Chris Clark, Brisbane

GEORGE WILLIAM HAXTON

Sapper, 10/3592
New Zealand Engineers, No. 3 Field Company
Died of sickness on 14th November 1918, aged 26

The Haxton family originated in Fifeshire, Scotland, and forebears of George William moved to Deal, Kent in the late 18th century. His great grandfather, Andrew, was born at Deal circa 1801 and married Elizabeth Ratcliffe. They had a family of three boys, John (b.1822), James (1827-1894) and William Andrew (b.1828), and a girl Emma (b.1830). Their second son, James, emigrated to New Zealand in about 1855. He met and married his wife Jane, née Anderson (1842-1867) in 1859 at Wellington. Jane was born at the Shoreditch workhouse, London and arrived in New Zealand aboard the *Montmorency* in 1858. The couple had five children:

William Andrew	(1862-1920)
Emma Elizabeth (Mrs. Wenden)	(1863-1949)
James Haxton	(1864-1931)
Jane (Mrs. Hayes)	(1866-1955)
Armond	(1867-1935)

The marriage only lasted for eight years, because Jane died at the age of 25, just two days after the birth of Armond, George's father.

Armond and Emma, née Kemp were married in 1892, and brought up their family in Richmond Road, Carterton, near Masterton. George William, their eldest child of eight, was born on 8th October of that year.

St. Mark's Anglican Church, Carterton

Their house was in the same road as St. Mark's Church, at which George would have attended services with his parents during his childhood. The church was built in 1875 by Thomas Bennett for £210, and enlarged in 1882 by the addition of the transept and sanctuary. It is the oldest church in the Wellington Diocese and a fine example of Victorian wooden church architecture.

George is one of two men buried at Brockenhurst who served in Samoa, the other soldier being Private Frank Clark, 12/2183, 1st Battalion Auckland Regiment (p. 42). Prior to enlisting George was working as a Clerk for the New Zealand Railways Department at Marton. He signed on as a Sapper 4/96, with the Railway Regiment of the New Zealand Engineers on 10th August 1914 and departed from New Zealand with the main body on 16th October. He served in Samoa until 10th March 1915, arriving back at Wellington on 12th April. George was then discharged from the NZEF "in consequence of being medically unfit for active service, although fit for employment in civil life" and returned to work as a Clerk for the Railways at Greatford Station. He enlisted for the second time on 19th October 1915 at Trentham.

In February 1916 he arrived in Egypt on the *Maunganui*, and on 8th March transferred to No. 3 Company. He was then posted to France, and on 7th April sailed on the *Alaunia* from Alexandria.

His army sheet next records that on 2nd August 1917 he was with his unit in the field in the Basseville area. On 18th March 1918 whilst in the Ypres area, he suffered from the effects of mustard gas and slight burns, and spent time in hospital and at a convalescent depot.

He rejoined his unit at the beginning of June, when he spent a month working as a cook.

George William Haxton (from Ian Haxton, Paekariki, Wellington)

On 1st November George was wounded for the second time, receiving gunshot wounds to his right leg on the first day of the Battle of the Sambre. He immediately transferred to England, arriving at No. 1 NZGH, Brockenhurst on 6th November. He died on 14th November 1918 of lobar pneumonia. George was buried on 16th November, with the officiating clergyman the Reverend W. Bullock (New Zealand Chaplains Department). Plot A, Row 4, Grave 21.

George is commemorated on his parents' grave at Clareville Cemetery, near Carterton, on the War Memorial at Carterton and on the ANZAC Memorial at Bulls.

Armond and Emma encountered other family tragedies. A son, Wishart, died in 1902, just a few months old. Later, two daughters were killed in the 1931 Napier earthquake. Doris Emma, aged 25, and Sabina May, aged 26, were working as pastry cooks when they died at a baker's shop at Heretaunga Street, Hastings. It is known that their father Armond was a baker prior to his retirement, so this tragedy most probably occurred in the family business. The Napier Museum has a display regarding the earthquake, and the Haxton girls' names are listed as two who were killed in this disaster.

Section of Bulls War Memorial

Acknowledgement: Ian Haxton, Paekariki (cousin)

CEDRIC GILBERT ADAMS

Lieutenant, 2/180
1st New Zealand Field Artillery Brigade, 3rd Battery
Died of wounds on 11th October 1916, aged 24

Cedric Gilbert Adams, the son of James Arthur (1848-1934) and Emma Frances, née Garland (1852-1948) was born on 1st May 1892 at Auckland. In 1914 Cedric was living with his parents at Princes Street, Northcote, Auckland and employed as a Clerk with H.M. Customs Authority. During his two years' army service he distinguished himself in such a way that he merited exceptional promotion.

Auckland Customs House (right), 1915 Auckland City Libraries, (N.Z) (Ref. W1322)

Cedric signed his Attestation Paper on 13th August 1914 and whilst in New Zealand was promoted to Corporal. He departed overseas with the main body on 16th October, and reached Alexandria on 3rd December. Training in Egypt continued until 12th April 1915 when he embarked for the Dardanelles. He was promoted to Sergeant on 26th July, and designated as Battery Sergeant Major in late August. In September he was granted the temporary rank of 2nd Lieutenant in lieu of Lt. W. E. Gardner, who was sick. On 5th October Cedric was taken on strength of the 3rd Battery, and promoted to 2nd Lieutenant in his own right on 21st October. In January 1916 he was based at Moascar until he left Egypt for France on 5th April.

Cedric was promoted to Lieutenant on 14th August. On 16th September he was seriously injured near Flers, with gunshot wounds to his right lung and spine. He arrived at No. 1 NZGH, Brockenhurst ten days later, died on 11th October 1916 and was buried two days later in Plot A, Row 4, Grave 5.

Cedric was mentioned in despatches dated 13th November 1916 by General Sir Douglas Haig, G.C.B, Commander-in-Chief of the British Armies in France, to the Secretary of State for War. This was subsequently published in the 2nd Supplement to the "London Gazette" of 2nd January 1917.

NORMAN DOUGLAS FRASER

**Gunner, 9/407
New Zealand Field Artillery
Died of sickness on 27th January 1917, aged 26**

Norman Douglas, the son of William Reynolds Falconer Fraser (1858-1936) and Jessie (1860-1912), was born on 28th March 1890 at Wyndham, near Invercargill, Southland. Norman's grandfather, William Junor Fraser, had his roots in Carlrossie, Rosshire, Scotland, and sailed from Glasgow, arriving at Port Chalmers on 8th April 1858. His son William Reynolds was born on the ship *Strathfieldsaye,* while wind bound for eight days outside Port Chalmers. After six months in Dunedin the family moved to Invercargill, where William Junor took charge of the Police force, and also escorted gold from the mines in Central Otago. William Reynolds worked his way up the banking system, and married Jessie Henderson of Bluff. There were four children:

Elsie Madeline	married William Easton of Dunedin
Muriel Grace	married Dr. Robert Callander of Melbourne
<u>Norman Douglas</u>	
Roy Henderson	who became one of Dunedin's leading architects, married Flora Campbell Menzies

The family were still living at Wyndham in 1900, with William Reynolds a Justice of the Peace and Manager of the Bank of New Zealand in the town. Norman attended Southland Boys High School in 1903, aged 12 years, before going to Waitaki Boys High School in Oamaru, from which we may assume that his father William had changed jobs within the Bank.

Norman worked for Wright Stephenson and Company, a Stock and Station Agent, before moving to the Maniototo region and being employed by Mr. A. B. Armour as a farm cadet at Closeburn Station, Gimmerburn, Central Otago.

Norman as a young man (from Shirley Skinner, Queenstown)

Gimmerburn means a young ewe, and this farming community produces fine wool from the sheep reared on very good productive soils. Spencer Clarke (whose parents bought the farm from Mr. Armour in 1923) says the Norman was a prominent Rugby player before he left for the War.

In 1914 William Reynolds, by then a widower, married Lucy J. Menzies, née Strachan (1871-1921) and the couple lived in Mosgiel, where William was the Bank Manager.

Norman enlisted with the NZEF on 21st August 1914, and initially joined the Otago Infantry Regiment as a Private. After basic military training in New Zealand he departed overseas with the main body on 16th October on board Transport ship No. 5. which arrived at Alexandria, Egypt on 3rd December. Further training followed prior to embarkation for the Dardanelles on 12th April 1915.

Four months later, on 12th August Norman was wounded in action, and transferred per H.S. *Andania* to Fulham Military Hospital, London, England for medical attention. His injuries, although unspecified, could not have been too serious because he was pronounced fit to return to active service on 12th October. His next posting was to Weymouth Camp, Dorset, where he remained until 11th January 1916 when he was posted to the Depot at Hornchurch, Essex.

Norman was posted to the New Zealand Field Artillery as a Gunner on 4th May, and went to Codford on 28th August, following its establishment in June as the Command Depot. He left for France on 24th September and marched into the base camp at Etaples. His army records indicate that he never reached the Western Front because he fell ill on 10th October suffering from influenza. A week later he was admitted to an isolation block with suspected paratyphoid and remained there for three months before arriving at No. 1 NZGH, Brockenhurst on 14th January 1917.

Norman died on 27th January 1917 of abdominal tuberculosis. He was buried on 30th January. Plot A, Row 3, Grave 7.

Norman is commemorated

> *on the war memorial gates at Gimmerburn cemetery,*
>
> *Invercargill War Memorial, and on*
>
> *his parents' grave at Andersons Bay Cemetery, Dunedin, Block 22, Plot 112.*

Gimmerburn War Memorial (from Spencer Clarke, Ranfurly)

William Reynolds, a widower for the second time, had moved to 80 Queen Street, Dunedin by the time he received his son's medals in 1922.

Acknowledgements and Source:

    Shirley Skinner, Queenstown, Otago (niece)
    Spencer Clarke, Ranfurly, Otago
    Estelle Longstaffe, Dunedin
    1900 Wise's NZPO Directory

JAMES McANULTY

Sergeant, 17/126
New Zealand Veterinary Corps,
attached to New Zealand Field Artilery, 5th Battery
Died of sickness on 29th November 1918, aged 31

James McAnulty was born on 13th November 1887, the youngest of three children of Joseph Augustus (1856-1936) and Ella May, nee Foley (1862-1939) of Hutton Street, Otahuhu, Auckland.

The McAnulty family were well established at Otahuhu, the pioneers being James's grandparents, John and Mary (née Cogan) who arrived in New Zealand on board the 801-ton vessel *Ann* in 1848. John (born 1801, Drummally, Co. Fermanagh, Ireland) married Mary in 1828 at Kampur, India where he was serving as a Colour-Sergeant in the 38th Regiment of the British Army. On return from India, and retirement from the Army he found the living conditions in Ireland unbearable, particularly as a result of the potato famine.

John decided to take advantage of the recruitment drive for soldiers to be permanently stationed in New Zealand, which Governor Grey had set up. A regiment of 721 men was formed, which became known as the Royal New Zealand Fencible Corps. They were divided into eight companies who were to ultimately settle in the four Fencible villages of Onehunger, Panmure, Howick and Otahuhu, providing a cordon of garrison settlements to protect Auckland from any Maori attack from the south. No. 6 Company, which was predominantly Irish, settled in Otahuhu. The military pensioners were required to serve for seven years for which they would receive a free passage for themselves and their family, a rent-free cottage (which would become their freehold property on completion of the seven years' service) and one acre of land. The Fencibles would support themselves and create local infrastructure e.g. roads, bridges and other public works.

John, Mary and four children left Belfast on 25th December 1847, and arrived in Auckland on 16th May 1848. A son died at sea from an influenza epidemic on board ship. The McAnulty family were allotted Plot No. 17 at Otahuhu, and later John bought several other plots in the village. The priority of the Otahuhu Fencibles was the erection of bridges across the Tamaki River and Ann's Creek to ease communication with the more populated areas towards Auckland. Sergeant-Major John McAnulty supervised the erection of the bridges and the formation of most of the original scoria (solidified lava) roads around Otahuhu. He also established Otahuhu's first postal service as the village's first postmaster (1848-1855).

John and Mary enlarged their family, and five children were born at Otahuhu; Joseph (James's father) was the second youngest.

Joseph worked as a builder, and married Ella May Foley in about 1881. They had three children, namely Cassie Mary (1882-1968), Walter George (1884-1952) and James (1887-1918).

James was a plumber who worked for Mr. W. B. Lloyd at Otahuhu. He loved horses, and volunteered for the Veterinary Corps, enlisting on 17th October 1914 at Trentham, with the rank of Trooper.

He left New Zealand with the 2nd Reinforcements on 14th December on board HMNZT No. 14 *Willochra* and reached Alexandria, Egypt on 29th January 1915.

Joseph and Ella May on their 50th Wedding Anniversary – circa 1931
(from Leo McAnulty, Rothesay Bay)

James's army records are rather spasmodic. His movements during 1915 have not been recorded, and one next hears that in March 1916 he was promoted to Veterinary Sergeant and attached to the New Zealand Field Artillery 2nd Brigade Headquarters Staff at Moascar. On 7th April he embarked for France per the *Eboe* at Alexandria.

In mid August 1917, whilst in the Basseville area James was attached to 5th Battery. After three week's leave in the United Kingdom in November, he was obviously tiring of military rules and regulations, because he was severely reprimanded for singing after "lights out", which nowadays seems somewhat harsh for such a misdemeanour.

27th October 1918 was the last day of James's active military life, when he received gunshot wounds to his left knee at Pont-à-Pierres, southwest of Le Quesnoy. That afternoon there was a heavy bombardment of shelling by the enemy, which included gas. Many of the artillery horses were killed, which, no doubt, James would have been caring for.

He was evacuated to England and arrived at No. 1 NZGH, Brockenhurst on 11th November 1918, the day of the Armistice. He was classified as Dangerously ill on 28th November suffering from bronchial pneumonia. He died the next day and was buried on 2nd December. The Reverend W. Skinner (Roman Catholic Chaplain) conducted the burial service.

Plot A, Row 1, Grave 21.

James was specially mentioned in dispatches by Field Marshall Sir Douglas Haig dated 8th November 1918 for distinguished and gallant service and devotion to duty during the period 23rd February 1918 to midnight 16/17 September 1918, in 5th Supplement to London Gazette No. 31089 dated 27th November 1918. His length of service of 4 years 44 days was much longer than the average WW1 soldier, and it is a tragedy that he met his death as a result of sickness after receiving a non-fatal wound.

James is commemorated on the McAnulty family grave at Otahuhu Public Cemetery, Section 2, Plots 346 and 347, and also on the memorial gates at Otahuhu Primary School. His father Joseph had built a house in Hutton Street for James to return to after the War, to no avail.

Acknowledgement and Source:

    Leo McAnulty, Rothesay Bay, Auckland (cousin)
    A brief history of Otahuhu

FREDERICK SELWYN FENDALL

Gunner, 11/764
New Zealand Field Artillery, 2nd Brigade Ammunition Column
Died of sickness on 8th December 1916, aged 20

Frederick Selwyn Fendall, born on 25th December 1894 at Rangiora, Canterbury, was the eldest child of the Reverend Frederick Philip Fendall (1860-1929) and Emma Florence, née York (1860-1941).

Frederick Selwyn was the fourth generation of Fendalls in New Zealand. His great grandfather the Reverend Henry Fendall, the Vicar of Crambe, Yorkshire, was a widower with 4 sons and 4 daughters. In 1850 the family applied to the Canterbury Association for the right to select a 50-acre section.

Walpole Cheshire Fendall (1830-1913), Henry's third son, left England immediately on board *Sir George Seymour*, (occupying the Chief Cabin!) leaving Gravesend on 8th September 1850 and arriving Lyttelton on 17th December. He secured his claim on Rural Section 18, between the Wairarapa and Waimairi Streams, paying £3 an acre for it. Henry and the rest of the family arrived later.

Walpole turned out to be quite a character; he set about sub-dividing his land and built a road, and the area became known as Fendall Town even though at this stage there was no church or shops to signify a town. He married Lucy Hyacinthe (née Swann) on 25th November 1854 at St. Michael's Church, Christchurch, and the couple immediately starting producing a large family. By 1860 Walpole and Lucy had left the Fendalton area for the Kowai district in North Canterbury. Walpole's great interest was in horse racing and he was an original member of the Canterbury Jockey Club. He attempted unsuccessfully to enter politics, although he did obtain a position on the Provincial Council of Canterbury. Sarah Courage, in her book describes him as being "rather stout", and "addicted to the pleasures of the table". He was apparently a martinet in his home, but he did have seven children to control. Both Lucy and Walpole Fendall are buried in the graveyard at St. Paul's, Papanui, Christchurch.

Walpole's third surviving child was Frederick Philip (1860-1929), who followed in his grandfather Henry's footsteps and entered the Church. He was educated at Christ's College and Canterbury College and qualified with B.A. in 1886. In the same year he was ordained deacon, and then priest in 1888. In 1886 he was appointed to Ross, Westland, where he was stationed for five years; this was followed by a brief period at Cust for one year before being appointed to Rangiora in November 1892 at St. John the Baptist Anglican Church.

Frederick Philip married Emma Florence York on 29th November 1893 at Rangiora, daughter of Thomas and Emma (née Edwards) of Nelson. Frederick Selwyn was born a year later, followed by three more children: Lila (b.1896), Harold (b.1897) and Hilda (b.1901).

It is an interesting coincidence that the Reverend Fendall officiated at the marriage ceremony of Captain William Charles Page, 5/563, New Zealand Army Service Corps (p. 98), who lies at Brockenhurst very near the minister's own son.

Prior to enlisting with the NZEF, Frederick (junior) worked on a farm, employed by Mr. J. G. Paterson at Manaia. (It is not known which Manaia this was, whether in the Coromandel, or Taranaki region). He signed his attestation sheet to join the Wellington Mounted Rifles on 25th October 1914 with the rank of Trooper. It is suspected that he falsified his date of birth in order to enlist earlier than allowed; his army records state that he was born in 1893, contrary to Christchurch Parish Records. Frederick left New Zealand for Egypt with the 2nd Reinforcements on 14th December 1914, on board HMNZT *Willochra*.

Frederick embarked for the Dardanelles in late June 1915, and was reported wounded at Anzac Cove at the end of August. He was evacuated per H.S. *Huntsend* and admitted to St. Patrick's Hospital, Malta for several weeks, after which it was decided to transfer him to England for further medical attention. He finally arrived at King George's Hospital, London on 4th November, having been conveyed to England per H.S. *Braemar Castle*. After four months Frederick was assessed as fit enough to rejoin his unit from the Convalescent Depot at Hornchurch, Essex. He returned to Egypt on 25th March 1916 and transferred from the Wellington Mounted Rifles to the 2nd Brigade Ammunition Column at Moascar. This was rather a fruitless exercise, because the following week he embarked on HMT *Eboe* from Alexandria, bound for France and fighting on the Western Front.

At the end of October, whilst on the Lys, near Armentières, Frederick fell ill with diarrhoea, which developed into the more serious disease of pleurisy with effusion. Evacuation to England was considered necessary, and he was admitted to No. 1 NZGH, Brockenhurst on 8th November. He survived just one month longer, dying on 8th December 1916. A comment in Fanny Speedy's diary, one of the New Zealand nurses, stated "Gunner Frederick Fendall, in 17 Sideroom who has been very ill lately died this morning, a very nice boy". He was buried on 9th December. Plot A, Row 2, Grave 7.

The death of their son obviously had a considerable impact upon Frederick Philip and Emma, because he is commemorated in several locations:

>*Christchurch Cathedral, Memorial Chapel of St. Michael and St. George*

>*War Memorial in St. John the Baptist churchyard at Rangiora*
>*NB. Herbert Joseph Baird, 2nd Battalion, Canterbury Regiment*
>*(p. 95) is also listed)*

>*On brass plaque near altar in St. John the Baptist Church, Rangiora*
>*(Note his age is stated as 22 years)*

>*Rangiora Borough and County War Memorial (also lists Herbert Baird)*

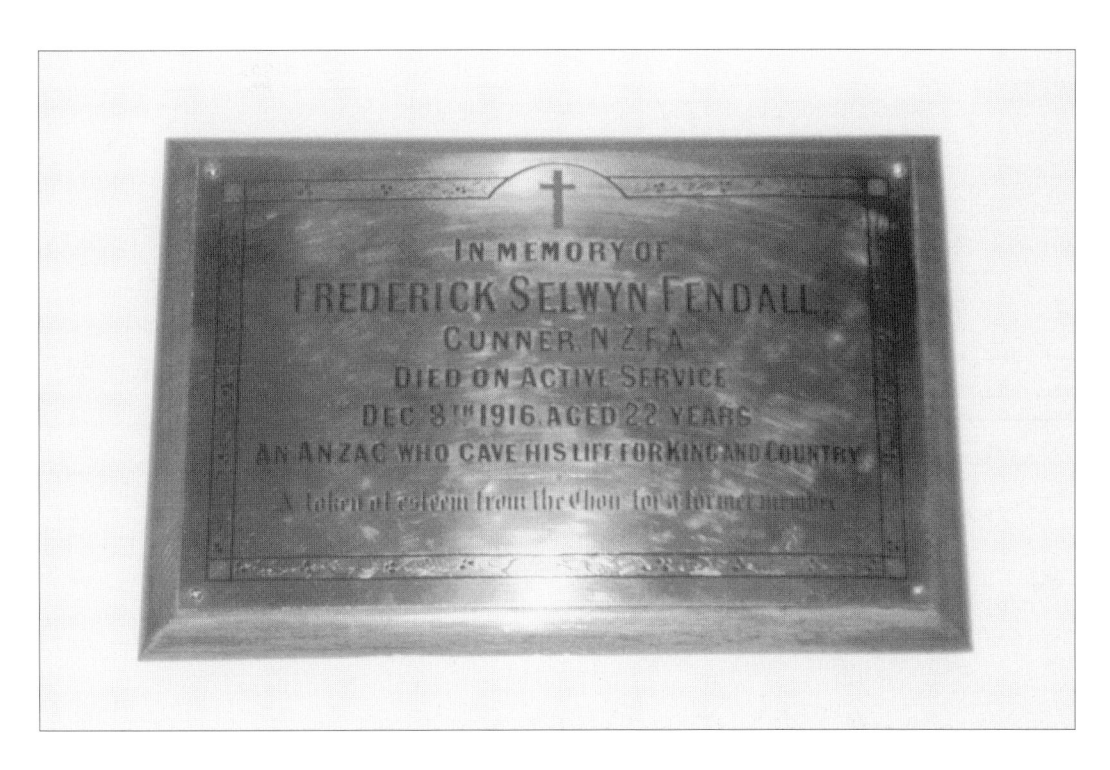

Brass plaque in St. John the Baptist Church, Rangiora

By 1921 The Reverend Frederick Fendall and Emma had moved to St. Paul's Vicarage, Glenmark, Waipara. They are buried together at Wakapuaka Cemetery, Nelson, Emma's home town. Anglican Block 33, Plot 21A.

Sources:

Christchurch Baptism Records (Rangiora)

Christchurch Local History Fact File No. 8 "Early Residents of Fendalton"

Courage, Sarah Amelia *Lights and shadows of colonial life* Christchurch (1965)

The Cyclopedia of New Zealand. Vol. 3 Canterbury. Christchurch (1903)

Speedy, Fanny Hakna Diaries 1915-1919, MS-Papers-1703,
    Alexander Turnbull Library, National Library of New Zealand,
    Te Puna Matauranga o Aotearoa

ALBERT KENNEDY

Private, 8/1272
1st Battalion, Otago Regiment, 10th Company
Died of wounds on 14th October 1916, aged 23

Albert Kennedy was the sixth son of David (1843-1909) and Jane, née Pickett (1854-1936) of Dunback, near Palmerston South, Otago.

The Kennedys came from Carrick, Ayrshire, Scotland. They were related through marriage to Robert the Bruce, titled, advisers to Kings of Scotland and holders of high office in the church. A branch of the family (which later had members emigrating to New Zealand) settled in New Luce parish in the late 1600s; later they moved south to Carscreugh in Glenluce, Wigtownshire (now Dumfries and Galloway).

In 1800 the family finally settled at a large farm at South Cairn, Kirkcolm, north of Stranraer. One of their children, James Kennedy, married Helen McClure on 15th January 1832 and they produced one daughter and six sons, who were all born at Kirkolm, namely Elizabeth, Samuel, James, William, Archibald, David and Thomas.

Besides running a farm, father James was a meteorological correspondent who regularly reported to the Scottish Meteorological Society. Owing to his efficiency he was in 1860 presented with a set of scientific instruments in recognition of his service as being "one of their most correct and comprehensive meteorological correspondents throughout the West of Scotland".

The second son, Samuel (1836-1899), lived at South Cairn all his life and remained a bachelor. At the time of his death, his sister, Elizabeth, resided with him.

Three of the brothers emigrated to New Zealand. Twins, David and Archibald, in 1864 departed for New Zealand under the government assisted immigration programme arriving at Port Chalmers on board the *Aboukir*. They initially worked on a farm on the Taieri Plains, before purchasing farms of their own, on opposite sides of the Shag River, at Dunback. David's farm was 560 acres in size. Their eldest brother, William, with his wife Margaret decided to follow suit many years later, and they and their children landed at Lyttelton on 29th October 1889.

David married Jane (born on 6th October 1854 at Dungiven, County Derry, Ireland) at the British Hotel, George Street, Dunedin, on 4th June 1875. David was then aged 32, and Jane, aged 20, was the daughter of James Pickett and Charlotte (née Cooper). The officiating Minister was the Reverend Dr. Donald M. Stuart, D.D., of Knox Church.

David and Jane subsequently produced a large family of ten children, of whom they were to lose two in the Great War.

James   m   *Helen Service (3 children)*
Helen   m   *David Philip (6 children)*
David   m   *(1) Harriett Griffen (2 children)*
                  (2) May Bradley
Elizabeth m   *Frederick Farquharson (3 children)*
William   *killed in action 15.9.1916, France, WW1*
Samuel   m   *Isabel (Bella) McLennan*
Jane   m   *Frank Deem (2 children)*
Ethel   m   *Thomas Stanley (5 children)*
Harold   m   *Barbara Alice Glover (3 children)*
Albert   *died of wounds 14.10.1916, England, WW1*

Kennedy family, approximately 1898

Standing: David, Jane, Samuel, Ethel, Elizabeth, William
Sitting: Helen, David Kennedy, Jane Kennedy, James
In front: Harold, Albert

Father David took an active part in community affairs. He represented Dunback Riding in the Waihemo County Council for a number of years after 1890. He served on the local school committee and road board, and was a member of the Palmerston Agricultural and Pastoral Association. His second son, David took over the farm probably around 1904, because when father David died on 1st October 1909 he had been suffering from chronic heart disease for five years.

When Albert signed his Attestation Sheet to join the army he stated that he was employed as a labourer for Mr. J. G. Ward at Limehills, Southland. Unbeknown to Albert, he was working at a property of Sir Joseph Ward, Bart, who was Member of Parliament for Awarua 1889-1919 and of Invercargill 1925-1930. He was also Prime Minister of New Zealand on two occasions – 1906-1912 and 1928-1930, and it was he who made an announcement in 1909 that the New Zealand Government would pay for a battleship for the Royal Navy – which, when built, was named HMS *New Zealand*. When, following the outbreak of WW1, a National Government was formed in August 1915 Sir Joseph was appointed Minister of Finance. Little did Albert know that he was working for an eminent "gentleman".

Albert enlisted with the NZEF on 28th October 1914 at Trentham. Whilst he was undertaking basic military training in New Zealand he had a photograph taken of him with a group of comrades. This was sent as a postcard (below) to his sister Ethel (Mrs. Stanley).

Albert (standing left) with comrades during basic training camp in New Zealand

Within a few weeks Albert departed from New Zealand, embarking on a troopship with the 2nd Reinforcements on 14th December 1914, bound for Egypt.

Albert was plagued with sickness for much of his army life. On 12th April 1915 he embarked at Alexandria for the Dardanelles. However, he never reached the war zone, because he fell sick just a week later and was admitted to No. 1 Australian hospital at Lemnos suffering from tonsillitis. Illness struck again in July and he spent time on the hospital ship *Neuralia* with debility, and transferred to a Cairo hospital at the beginning of August with gastro-enteritis. Eventually, in late September he was fit for duty, and a week later he was on board troopship *Simla* bound for Lemnos again, where he rejoined his unit.

In February 1916, whilst at Moascar camp, Ismailia, Egypt, Albert overstayed leave for two days, for which he forfeited four days' pay. Despite this misdemeanour, his Active Service sheet indicates that he was qualified as a stretcher-bearer. This position was usually given to the best soldiers, as the job was so important.

In April 1916 Albert embarked at Alexandria for France and the Western Front. He was ill again in June and spent time in hospital at Armentières, and then at St. Omer with mumps. In the end, his series of illnesses were not the cause of death. On 16th September whilst fighting near Flers, in the Battle of the Somme, he received gunshot wounds to both legs and was immediately evacuated to England.

Albert arrived at No. 1 NZGH, Brockenhurst on 21st September. During the next three weeks he developed cellulitis in his right leg, and never recovered from his wounds.

He died on 14th October, and was buried two days later.

Plot A, Row 2, Grave 10.

Jane Kennedy suffered a double loss because Albert's older brother, William John Kennedy, Private, 5/590 2nd Battalion, Otago Regiment, died on 15th September 1916 (the day before Albert was wounded), aged 35. He is commemorated at Caterpillar Valley (New Zealand Memorial, Somme, France (near Longueval).

William, left, and Albert, right

When Jane went to the Dunback Post Office sometime in October 1916, she received the news of her two sons' death at the same time on the same day. Not surprisingly she was in a state of shock for several days. However she obviously recovered from her trauma and lived to an old age, dying on 25th August 1936, aged 82 years.

Albert and William are mentioned on their parents' grave at Palmerston South Cemetery, Otago (Block 40, Plots 5 and 6) and also on the War Memorial at Dunback.

Kennedy family grave at Palmerston South
(note the wrong year of death for David)

Acknowledgements and sources:
    Michael and Margaret Connelly (née Kennedy - niece), Christchurch –
       information and family photographs
    Phil Haywood, Nelson (great nephew)
    Cyclopedia of New Zealand, Volume 6, 1908
    Wigtown Free Press (9.2.1860)
    Wigtown Free Press (9.2.1899)
    Probate No. 686, 1909 (Archives Ref: DAAC/D239/131)

KIRI RAPONA

Private, 16/525
New Zealand Maori (Pioneer) Battalion
Died of wounds on 29th September 1916, aged 29

Of the 12 Maori soldiers buried at Brockenhurst, Kiri Rapona is the only one who died as a result of wounds. 10 died of sickness, and one drowned.

Kiri was born in 1887, the son of Rapsana Komata and Heni Matckino, of Taikimeti. He had a brother, Pita Rapona, who lived at Mangatuna, north of Tolaga Bay, Gisborne. Kiri had been working as a labourer for Mr. D. Lysnar at Gisborne prior to enlisting on 11th January 1915 at Avondale, near Auckland.

He departed from New Zealand with the 1st Maori Contingent on 14th February 1915 and arrived in Egypt at the end of March with the 3rd Reinforcements. Initially, the Maoris were not allowed to fight with the rest of the New Zealand Force and Kiri left Egypt on 5th April and was posted to Malta for garrison duty. He embarked for the Dardanelles on 30th June, and he was one of 477 men of the New Zealand Maori Contingent who arrived at Anzac on 3rd July. They were attached to the New Zealand Mounted Rifles Brigade and were sent to No. 1 Outpost, which became known as the "Maori Pa". Their tasks entailed levelling terraces, digging roads and bringing water tanks ashore. By August the authorities had realised that the Maoris would make excellent fighting soldiers so from then onwards they were placed on reserve to fight.

In mid October Kiri was appointed as a Cook. The evacuation of the Gallipoli peninsula began on 8th December and the Maoris were withdrawn to Imbros Island (fifteen miles away) and rested. Kiri fell ill on 27th December and sailed on the *Hunstsman* from Mudros Harbour, Lemnos to Egypt for hospitalisation. In due course his unit reached the Western Front.

Kiri's days as an active soldier ended on 9th September 1916, when he received gunshot wounds to his head whilst on the Somme. The Maoris had been in this area repairing the trenches and building roads near Fricourt Wood. Kiri's injuries necessitated immediate transfer to England and he arrived at No. 1 NZGH, Brockenhurst on 14th September. He died of his wounds on 29th September and was buried the next day. Plot A, Row 5, Grave 8.

Kiri's name is listed on Gisborne War Memorial amongst hundreds of men from this region of New Zealand.

WILLIAM EDWARD JOHNSTONE

Private, 8/2020
1st Battalion, Otago Regiment, 8th Company
Died of wounds on 13th June 1917, aged 22

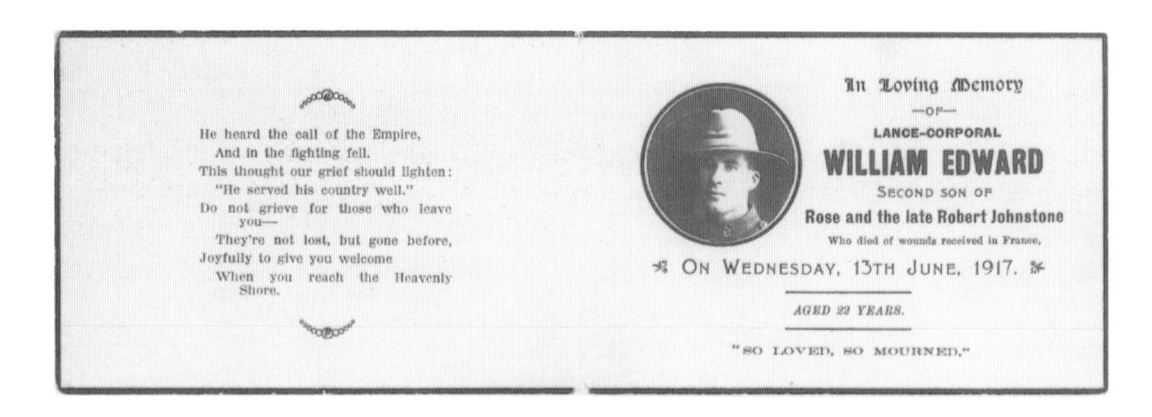

(from Russell Tavendale, Napier)

William Edward, the second son and fourth child of Robert (1859-1911) and Rose Elizabeth, née Poole (1871-1955), was born on 6th May 1895 at Isla Bank (known as Limestone Plains) near Invercargill, Southland. The area was also called Calcium, a name still retained for the district cemetery. William's father, Robert Muir Johnstone, came from Dundonald, Ayrshire, Scotland, and his parents William and Agnes (née Muir) were farmers.

In 1873 when Robert was 14 he accompanied his older brother William on a journey of a lifetime to New Zealand, and they landed at Oamaru, Otago. Their uncle, a stonemason, offered them employment, which included the construction of the bridge at Oamaru gardens. At that time the two lads were camping in a tent nearby which caught fire! Subsequently Robert and William tramped south to Isla Bank and took up working as sheepshearers and undertaking other seasonal work on farms.

Rose's roots were at Marshborough, near Sandwich, Kent, and she sailed with her family on board the *Gareloch* from London, arriving at Port Chalmers on 12th February 1875. Robert and Rose were married on New Year's Eve 1888 at Riverton. They later settled at Isla Bank, taking over the Poole family home where seven of their ten children were born. Upon Robert's death in 1911, Rose and the family, particularly William, were left to run the farm.

Johnstone family home and wagonload of firewood

William (left) enlisted with the NZEF on 12th February 1915 at Trentham, and left New Zealand on 13th June, departing with the 5th Reinforcements. Shortly after arriving at Gallipoli, Turkey, he was wounded in his shoulder in the August battles and admitted to the NZGH at Abbassia, Egypt. He rejoined his unit on 16th September from Rest Camp on the island of Lemnos, and evacuated from Gallipoli on 27th December 1915.

William embarked for France on 6th April 1916, and on 12th July he was wounded (2nd occasion) near Armentières, receiving gunshot wounds to his thigh. After a brief stay at No. 35 General Hospital at Calais, he embarked for England per H.S *Brighton* and spent time at No. 2 London General Hospital, Chelsea before admission to No. 1 NZGH, Brockenhurst.

A month later, on 26th August he was attached to strength at Codford on Salisbury Plain, where he would have undergone light training and short route marches to rebuild his fitness. He then transferred to Sling Camp on 6th October before returning to France. He arrived at the base camp at Etaples on 20th October and rejoined his regiment on 8th November near Armentières.

In March 1917 William was appointed temporary Lance Corporal. The attack and capture of the Messines-Wytshaete Ridge was planned for 7th June, with zero hour fixed for 3.10 a.m. At 12.30 a.m. all troops were in position in their trenches. The battle began with the detonation of 19 large mines under the German lines and within an hour the New Zealanders had captured Messines. William was severely injured in the process, receiving gunshot wounds to his neck and spine, resulting in paraplegia.

William embarked for England at Boulogne per *St. David* for Dover. He never saw England again because he died on 13th June 1917 on Ambulance Train No. 3 whilst travelling between Bentley and Brockenhurst. He was buried in St. Nicholas' Church cemetery on 15th June. Plot A, Row 3, Grave 5 (below).

William was the great uncle of Russell Tavendale of Napier, who was told that his grandfather, James Tavendale, a stretcher-bearer in the same Battalion and close friend of William, actually carried William from the front line. After the War, James married William's sister Elizabeth in March 1919.

The Johnstone family suffered a double loss because the third son Robert Muir, Serjeant 23/795, 1st Battalion, 3rd New Zealand Rifle Brigade, lost his life on 27th September 1918 in the Battle of the Canal du Nord (27th September-1st October). He has no known grave and is listed on the Grevillers New Zealand Memorial, Pas de Calais, France. A proud moment in his mother's life was the occasion when she received on behalf of her son Robert, from the Prince of Wales himself, the Military Medal, which was awarded posthumously.

Both William and Robert are remembered on the soldiers' memorial at Calcium Cemetery, Isla Bank, and on their parents' headstone in the same cemetery.

Soldiers' Memorial, Calcium Cemetery, Isla Bank (Russell Tavendale, Napier)

Acknowledgements and Source:
Elizabeth Beer, Invercargill (information and b/w photographs)
Russell Tavendale, Napier (great nephew)
The Isla Bank Historical Research Committee, *Images of Isla Bank* 1998

SAMUEL ALLINGTON

Private, 6/2052
1st Battalion, Canterbury Regiment, "C" Company
Died of wounds 21st November 1916, aged 27

Samuel Allington, the 7th child in a family of 13, was born at Rangiora, Canterbury on 28th November 1888. His family came from Stretton-on-Dunsmore in Warwickshire. His parents, Charles (b.1855 Stratford-upon-Avon) and Hannah, née Wright (b.1853 Towcester) emigrated to New Zealand on the *Crusader*, along with Charles's father, George (b.1830) his mother Hannah, née Robbins (b.1831), and other family members. Charles and Hannah were married at All Saints Church, Stretton-on-Dunsmore, on 21st September 1874 a few days before leaving England.

George Allington was a delegate on the Agricultural Union and travelled widely in England, Wales and Ireland, according to an article written by his son Charles many years later. George gathered about 400 agricultural labourers to accompany him to New Zealand under the "free passage and all found" system. They sailed from Plymouth on September 25th 1874, arriving Lyttelton on December 31st. [The Woodley family (see page 120) were also passengers on the same sailing and were perhaps members of this large group of agricultural labourers].

During Samuel's childhood the family moved to the Papanui area of Christchurch, and he attended Opawa School. In 1915 he worked as a chef for his father, Charles, when the family were living at 350 North Road, Papanui.

Samuel enlisted with the NZEF on 13th February 1915 and departed from New Zealand with the 5th Reinforcements on 13th June. From then on he was dogged by sickness for the rest of his short life. On 9th August he joined the 1st Battalion Canterbury Regiment in the Dardanelles, Gallipoli, but a fortnight later he fell ill and was admitted to H.S. *Ulysses*, and transferred to hospital at Abbassia, Egypt.

Samuel Allington before leaving New Zealand
(from Kath Maloney, Dannevirke)

In mid November Samuel was discharged to duty and attached to strength at Zeitoun. Illness struck again and he was admitted to NZGH, Cairo on 5th December with influenza. Convalescence followed at Heliopolis, after which he returned to the base depot at Ghezireh just before Christmas. He eventually rejoined his Battalion at Ismailia on 18th January 1916. Two days later he fell ill again and spent time at Pontak Koubbeh Hospital, and NZGH, Cairo, and at the base depot at Ghezireh.

Samuel rejoined his Battalion at Ismailia on 27th March prior to embarkation on 6th April on HMT *Franconia* at Port Said, bound for Marseilles, France.

Whilst in France, Samuel could not cope with military discipline. He absented himself from parade without leave on 1st May at Morbeque and subsequently was awarded 7 days Field Punishment No. 2 which required him to undertake extra duties for a week.

His active life ended on 27th September when he was involved in the Battle of Morval (25-28 September) on the Somme and received gunshot wounds to his right shoulder and chest.

After several weeks in France under the care of the medical authorities, Samuel transferred to England and arrived at No. 1 NZGH, Brockenhurst on 12th November. He died on 21st November 1916 as a result of his wounds and empyema, and was buried two days later. Plot A, Row 2, Grave 8.

Samuel is commemorated on Papanui War Memorial and on the Roll of Honour at Opawa School. By 1921 his parents had moved to live at 41 Leinster Road, St. Albans, Christchurch.

Acknowledgements:

    Maureen Dunlop, Springston (great niece)
    Audrey Harris (great niece)
    Kath Maloney, Dannevirke (niece)

SYDNEY ALLAN DAVIES

Sapper, 4/895
New Zealand Engineers, No. 1 Field Company
Died of sickness on 10th July 1917, aged 24

Sydney Allan Davies was born on 22nd December 1892 at Whangaroa, North Auckland (now in Northland). He was the only son of Ernest Nicholson and Eliza (née Dunne) who were married on 15th September 1888 at Kaitaia. During Sydney's early childhood his parents moved to Karangahake (below) in the Coromandel region, and he attended the local school between September 1899 and March 1904.

Overlooking the east end of Karangahake in 1914.
William A Price Collection. G-1823-1/2 (PAColl-3057). ATL

This area was renowned for gold mining, which began in 1875, and Ernest more than likely worked in the mining industry. In 1915 Sydney was a self-employed contractor and living at his parents' home at Consol Street, Waihi a nearby mining town.

Sydney enlisted with the NZEF on 17th April 1915 at Trentham, and joined the New Zealand Engineers, 1st Field Company with the rank of Sapper. He departed from New Zealand for Egypt with the 5th Reinforcements on 13th June 1915, eventually arriving at Gallipoli on 22nd August.

Sydney was ill for much of his army life. On 24th October he was admitted to St. Andrews Hospital, Malta suffering from enteritis, where he remained until 23rd December. He then transferred per H.S. *Marama* to the NZGH at Cairo, Egypt, for convalescence from dysentery. Three months later, on 24th March 1916 he was discharged to the Base Depot at Ghezireh.

Training in Egypt continued until 10th May, when Sydney embarked on HMT *Caledonia* for Marseilles. Ten days later he was attached to strength at the base camp at Etaples. However, the very next day, on 21st May he was admitted to No. 24 General Hospital at Etaples suffering from cowpox. He was back in the same hospital at the end of August, owing to acid burns on his face and hands. Ill health continued, and in December he developed acute sinusitis.

The medical authorities then organised transfer to England for treatment, and Sydney arrived at No.1 NZGH, Brockenhurst on 19th December 1916. By February 1917 he had a growth on his upper jaw and was classified as unfit by the Medical Board. He remained at Brockenhurst for the last months of his life and died there on 10th July 1917. His burial took place on 12th July. Plot A, Row 3, Grave 4.

DARCY ROYCROFT NEWELL

**Lance Corporal, 8/2687
1st Battalion, Otago Regiment, 8th Company
Died of wounds on 13th April 1918, aged 22**

Darcy Roycroft Newell, the son of Frederick Thomas (1862-1944), and Alice Maud (née Rusden, 1869-1952) was born on 22nd March 1895 at New Plymouth. Darcy's forebears left England in the early 1840s and were among the first European settlers who sailed from Plymouth, Devon to New Plymouth, New Zealand. Both sides of his family came from Cornwall. Darcy's great-grandparents on his father's side were William George (b.1813) and Ann, née Coulls (b.1811) who sailed in the *Oriental* in 1841. Their daughter, Georgina George (1837-1902) married Samuel James Newell (1829-1872) in 1856 at St. Mary's Church, New Plymouth. Samuel was a publican who had arrived on the *St. Michael* in 1852. Frederick, Darcy's father, was one of their children.

St. Mary's Church, New Plymouth
(Photograph by Des Hollard, New Plymouth, New Zealand)

On Darcy's mother's side Nicholas Julian married Eleanor James in Cornwall circa 1792. They had a son Richard (b.1793), whose eldest daughter Elizabeth (b.1817) married Thomas Rusden (b. 1811) at Helston, Cornwall in 1837. Thomas and Elizabeth sailed to New Plymouth in 1842 on board the *Blenheim* with their family, which included their three-year old son Thomas. Thomas Rusden (junior, b.1839) married Isobella Roycroft (b.1841) at Auckland in 1862. They had a daughter Alice Maud who was Darcy's mother.

Thomas Rusden (senior) was a stonemason and helped to build St. Mary's Church in 1845. The tradition must have continued because Thomas Rusden (junior) was also a stonemason as was Darcy's father, Frederick.

Frederick played a prominent role in the life of the community. He was on the committee of the New Plymouth Band, and a volunteer Private with the 11th (Taranaki Rifles) Regiment. He and Maud were married at New Plymouth in 1893, and five children followed in quick succession: Darcy (the eldest), Winnie (married Mr. C. Atkinson), Eva May (b.1900, married William Henry Quickfall), Fred and George.

Darcy was educated at West End primary school and New Plymouth Boys' High School. In 1910 he enrolled as a Bugler with the 11th (Taranaki Rifles), the same regiment that his father had been in twenty years previously. After leaving school he was employed first as a clerk with the legal firm Messrs. Roy and Nicholson, and later he joined the Bank of New Zealand at New Plymouth.

On 19th April 1915 Darcy left the family home in Powderham Street, New Plymouth, and enlisted with the NZEF at Trentham. He departed from New Zealand on HMNZT No. 27 *Willochra* with the 6th Reinforcements on 14th August. On 1st October he joined the 4th Company of the Otago Infantry Battalion, at Mudros, on the island of Lemnos.

Then on 27th December he was posted to Egypt for further training prior to his promotion to Lance Corporal in early February. He formed part of the major transfer of troops from Egypt to France at the beginning of April 1916, and joined 1st Battalion, Otago Regiment.

Darcy Newell in Taranaki Regiment, July 1915 (from Derek Quickfall, New Plymouth)

71

There is a gap in Darcy's army records until 11th July 1917 when he was sick in hospital for one month, after which he marched into base camp at Etaples. He was attached to strength near Eecke on 7th October and posted to 8th Company two weeks later.

The 1st Otago Regiment was involved in the attempt to take Polderhoek Chateau, set high on a promontory between two streams (Reutelbeek and the Scherriabeek) surrounded by a swamp of mud and putrefaction. Although the attack was a failure and losses were severe, the British had managed to gain high ground nearby. Darcy was wounded in the face by a sniper on 3rd December 1917, the bullet passing through both cheeks.

He transferred to England and arrived at No. 1 NZGH on 12th December. On 26th February 1918 he was discharged to duty at the hospital, but this was just for a few days. By 18th March Darcy was on the Seriously Ill list and he died of his wounds on 13th April 1918. The burial was officiated by the Reverend A. Jacob.

Plot A, Row 4, Grave 13.

Derek Quickfall, Darcy's nephew says that he was told by his mother Eva, that his grandmother (Alice) woke during one night from a most vivid dream shortly after news had arrived in New Zealand that Darcy had been wounded. In the dream she had a vision of a figure lying in bed, head swathed in bandages. A few days later, a telegram arrived informing the family Darcy had died of his wounds.

Some time later, Alice received a letter from one of the nursing sisters who had cared for Darcy at No. 1 NZGH, Brockenhurst. She described his injuries, and the bandaging around his head was exactly as Alice had seen it in her dream even though she was unaware of the nature of Darcy's wounds, and the time he died. Taking into account the twelve-hour time difference between New Zealand and England, the time of her dream coincided with the time of Darcy's death. Maybe this was something more than a mother's intuition?? Who knows!

A long obituary in the *Taranaki Herald*, 18th April 1918, ends with the comment,

"Darcy was a popular young fellow of a type we can ill afford to lose".

Darcy is commemorated on the memorial gates at New Plymouth Boys' High School. A member of the Newell extended family is also remembered with Darcy on a brass plaque inside St. Mary's Church, New Plymouth. He was Frank <u>Leslie</u> Newell, Rifleman, 56825, 1st Battalion, New Zealand Rifle Brigade, who died on 2nd May 1918, aged 20. Leslie is buried at Louvencourt Military Cemetery, Somme, France. Plot I, Row D. Grave 40.

Darcy's parents, Frederick and Alice, lived until old age. They are buried at Te Henui Cemetery, New Plymouth, Row 6, Block F. Unusually, their son Darcy is not mentioned on their headstone, a practice that has been noticed on several family graves.

Grave of Frederick and Alice Newell, Te Henui Cemetery, New Plymouth

Acknowledgements and Source:

    Lawrie Geden, New Plymouth
    Derek Quickfall, New Plymouth (nephew)
    Taranaki Herald, 18th April 1918

ANDREW GILBERT

Driver, 2/1975
New Zealand Field Artillery, Divisional Ammunition Column
Died of sickness on 28th February 1917, aged 22

Andrew Gilbert, the son of George and Edith Mortimer, was born on 7th June 1894 at Gapes Valley, Geraldine, South Canterbury. This area is sheep farming territory, and George was most probably farming here before moving to Little River (Banks Peninsula) shortly after Andrew's birth. Three siblings have been identified, Samuel William (1885-1917), Edith Sarah (b.1896) and Harold Charles (b.1899). Before leaving home Andrew was working for his father on the farm at Little River.

Andrew signed his attestation sheet on 19th April 1915 at Trentham. He was initially ranked as a Gunner, but he later transferred to Driver. He left New Zealand on 14th August with the 6th Reinforcements, which included a draft of 48 New Zealand Field Artillery soldiers. Nine of these men were from Canterbury and would have been 'cobbers' i.e. friends. These reinforcements embarked upon HMNZT No. 27 *Willochra* (below) bound for Egypt.

After arrival, on 25th September Andrew was posted to the 2nd Brigade Ammunition Column at Zahirieh, Alexandria. On 1st March 1916 he transferred to the 4th Brigade Ammunition Column at Moascar and the following month, on 8th April, this contingent embarked for France on board *Haverford*.

It appears that at this time Andrew's health was failing and on arrival at Marseilles he went immediately to No. 2 Australian General Hospital. By the end of June he was seriously ill, suspected of having enteric fever. He made a brief recovery and was reported as convalescent in mid July. However, he never fully recovered, and by November he was classified 'C' by the medical board, suffering from anaemia and debility following bronchial pneumonia and arthritis of the left hip.

It was thus decided that he should be transferred to No. 1 NZGH, Brockenhurst, where he was admitted on 29th November. By the beginning of February 1917 Andrew was classified as unfit by the Medical Board and placed on the nominal roll. He died of bronchial pneumonia on 28th February 1917.

Fanny Speedy, one of the New Zealand nurses working at the Brockenhurst, wrote in her diary "Andrew Gilbert died this morning. One can only feel it is better so, it is doubtful if he could ever have been less than a misery to himself". Andrew had been hospitalised for ten months, and Fanny Speedy's wording is surely most appropriate. He was buried on 2nd March 1917.

Plot A, Row 3, Grave 6.

George and Edith suffered a double loss because an elder son, Private Samuel William Gilbert, 17067, N.Z. Machine Gun Company died on 5th June 1917, aged 32 and is buried at Trois Arbres Cemetery, Steenwerck, Nord, France. Plot I. Row Q. Grave 5. He was the husband of Sarah Gilbert, of Te Kiri, Taranaki.

Acknowledgement and Source:

    John Hall, Bombay

    Speedy, Fanny Hakna Diaries 1915-1919, MS-Papers-1703,
    Alexander Turnbull Library, National Library of New Zealand,
    Te Puna Matauranga o Aotearoa

WILLIAM MUNRO DUNCAN

Lieutenant, 3/667
New Zealand Medical Corps
Died of sickness on 15th July 1918, aged nearly 25

William Munro Duncan was born on 20th July 1893 at Petone, Wellington, son of George and Alexanderina. After leaving school, William worked as a Shorthand Typist for the New Zealand Government Railways Department at Wellington, and commuted from the family home at 160 Hutt Road, Petone.

Railway Offices, Wellington
J. N. Taylor Collection. F-104795 (PAColl-5310). ATL

William enlisted with the NZEF on 19th May 1915 at Trentham and departed from New Zealand with the 5th Reinforcements on 13th June 1915 with the rank of Sergeant. His promotion to Warrant Officer, Class I took effect from 15th September 1915 after arrival in Egypt. He spent the next nine months working at the New Zealand Auxiliary Hospital at Moascar and the NZGH at Cairo. He must have carried out his tasks beyond the call of duty in order to be mentioned in the Despatch of General J. G. Maxwell of 16th March 1916.

On 2nd June 1916, William was posted to England and left Alexandria on board the *Dover Castle* bound for Southampton. By 25th June he was on the staff of No. 1 NZGH, Brockenhurst.

William remained at Brockenhurst until the beginning of May 1917 when he was attached to the strength of No. 4 New Zealand Field Ambulance, which spent brief periods in several training camps in England – Sling, Blackpool and Codford.

On 29th May, William left for France for duties in the Field at Messines. He received a second accolade on 7th August when he was brought to the notice of the Secretary of State for War "for valuable services rendered in connection with the War".

During the early months of 1918 William visited the United Kingdom and Paris on leave, after which he worked for a short spell with No. 1 New Zealand Field Ambulance in France. In mid May he returned to No. 1 NZGH, Brockenhurst, was promoted to Lieutenant and given the position of assistant quartermaster.

New Zealand Medical Corps Cap Badge (from Ken Treanor, Burnham, Canterbury)

William's duties as assistant quartermaster would have involved overseeing hospital orderlies in the carrying out of their tasks such as sorting out the clothing for men being discharged the next day, and also carrying out the unpleasant task of handling battle stained boots and clothing that had been stripped from patients on admission.

After so long a period caring for others, William succumbed to serious illness himself and on 1st July he was admitted as a patient to No. 1 NZGH, Brockenhurst with influenza which soon developed into tubercular meningitis. A week later he transferred to the Royal Victoria Hospital at Netley, near Southampton and was considered to be Dangerously Ill.

William died on 15th July 1918. His body was taken to Brockenhurst, for the burial ceremony, which was officiated by The Reverend W. R. Hutchinson on 18th July.

Plot A, Row 4, Grave 18.

ALFRED BENJAMIN BOOKER

MILITARY MEDAL

Rifleman, 23/77
1st Battalion, 3rd New Zealand Rifle Brigade, "A" Company
Died of wounds on 31st October 1917, aged 22

Alfred Benjamin Booker was born on 6th August 1895, at Mangatoki, near Eltham, Taranaki, and son of dairy farmers Benjamin and Caroline (née Sambrook). He was the eldest child of a family of three, with a brother William, and a sister May.

Alfred worked as a farm labourer for Mr. T. J. Wills at Lowgarth, near Eltham prior to enlisting with the NZEF at Trentham on 28th May 1915. He departed from New Zealand with the Advance Party, 1st New Zealand Rifle Brigade on 18th September 1915 on board *Waitemata* and disembarked at Suez on 26th October. In December he sailed to an army base on the extreme western coast of Egypt at Mersa Matruh for action against the Senussi tribe. He left Egypt on 6th April 1916 for Marseilles, France, and proceeded onward to the Western Front.

Alfred was appointed Cook in the Field on 12th May 1916 near Armentières. Later in the year he was injured whilst involved in the assault from Longueval to Flers on the first day of the Flers-Courcelette Battle (15th-22nd September). He received gunshot wounds to his ear and scalp, which were not serious, because a fortnight later he was back on duty as a cook. By April 1917 Alfred obviously decided a break was called for because he absented himself without leave, for which he was awarded 28 days Field Punishment No. 2 (extra duties) and he also he forfeited three days pay. Presumably he never completed his punishment because he was in hospital again on 19th April, suffering from mumps.

His next few months were spent in Reinforcement and Rest Camps until he was sent back to the Field on 9th September 1917 to play his part in the 3rd Battle of Ypres (Passchendaele). However, his days at the front were short-lived because he was wounded on the second occasion, this time in the neck, on 12th October, just three days after returning to the Field. His injuries were severe and he transferred to England and arrived at No. 1 NZGH, Brockenhurst on 28th October. Alfred survived three days longer and died on 31st October. His burial took place on 3rd November.

Plot A, Row 1, Grave 12.

On 21st November 1917 Alfred was posthumously awarded the MILITARY MEDAL for acts of gallantry in the field.

Alfred's parents in later life lived in Westown, New Plymouth. On Caroline's death, the family placed the following obituary in the Taranaki Herald.

BOOKER, Caroline – (221 Tukapo Street, New Plymouth).

On November 9, 1956, at New Plymouth Public Hospital,

Beloved wife of Benjamin Booker, and loved mother of May

(Mrs. R. G. Uncles, Okato), and the late Alfred and William,

and loved grandmother of Benny; aged 86 years.

Benjamin died on December 11th, 1960, in his 95th year, and a similarly worded obituary appeared in the Taranaki Herald.

Husband and wife lie side by side in Te Henui Cemetery, New Plymouth, Plot No. B1.B/Lot 44 and 45. No headstone was erected in their memory.

Acknowledgements:

    Lawrie Geden, New Plymouth

    Phyllis Booker, New Plymouth (nephew's wife)

    Stuart Scarre, Parkscape Services, New Plymouth

WILLIAM LESLIE MORICE

Private, 23/831
New Zealand Machine Gun Corps
No. 3 New Zealand Machine Gun Company
Died of wounds on 4th February 1917, aged 23

William Leslie Morice was born on 10th October 1893 at Gisborne, the fourth child of 10 of William and Sarah. He belonged to a large extended family that is still well represented in the Opotiki area, Bay of Plenty, where the family settled.

The Morice family originally came from Elgin, near Inverness, Scotland. James Morice (b 1801) married Murray Innes (b.1815). Their children, George, David, William, Frank and Charles all went together to New Zealand in the mid 1870s. Later their mother and her two unmarried daughters joined them and they lived at Aberdeen Road in Gisborne at one time.

The Morice brothers managed farming stations in the East Cape area of Gisborne. In 1876 they went into partnership at Te Aroha Station, 28 miles from Gisborne towards Wairoa. They purchased a block of land at Whakapunake and also took on a 50-year lease of Okahuatini No. 2 Block, but left this area after 30 years probably due to the remote location. The partnership was dissolved in 1906.

William Morice married Sarah Allen in New Zealand and had ten children, namely James (b. 1887), Allen, Emily, William Leslie (b. 1893), Archibald, Dora, Isobel, Frances, Elsie and Walter (b. 1905). Dora was born at Te Aroha Station, and the children were educated with a governess at home.

William Leslie was about aged 14 when his family moved to the Opotiki area. He worked as a station hand for his father. They had a property at Awaawakina Bay, which is still often called Morice's Bay, with views of the Bay of Plenty and White Island. The family called their place Oroi homstead, and the original building is still standing.

William Leslie enlisted with the NZEF at Trentham on 29th May 1915, as a Rifleman with the 1st New Zealand Rifle Brigade and was posted overseas, departing from Wellington on 9th October, and disembarking at Suez six weeks later.

William Leslie Morice (from Sonia Edwards, Opotiki)

The Senussi Muslims of Libya, inspired by Turkish propaganda, attacked the British on Egypt's Western frontier in November 1915. The 1st New Zealand Rifle Brigade went to support a mixture of largely untried troops (Egyptian, Sikh, Australian and New Zealanders) known as the Western Frontier Force. On 19th December William left Alexandria by ship bound for Mersa Matruh, 200 miles west along the Egyptian coast. On Christmas Day the Brigade took part in the "affair of the Wadi Medwa" – none of the actions in the Senusssi War received higher rating than "affair" in the Official History – driving back a large force of Senussi and preventing their advance beyond Matruh. The loss on the British side was 13 killed and 51 wounded, among whom was William, with severe wounds to his left forearm and chest.

Immediate medical attention was administered at the Notts and Derby Field Ambulance, after which William was admitted to No. 21 General Hospital at Alexandria on 11th January 1916. He was altogether out of action for two and a half months, and transferred to the New Zealand General Hospital, Cairo, followed by a stay at the Convalescent Home at Luxor.

On 6th March William was considered to be fit enough for light training and thus was posted to the base depot at Ghezireh. Whilst there he absented himself for 1½ hours without leave, for which he was required to forfeit one day's pay. The punishment seems harsh, but on the other hand, rules were to be obeyed! On 25th March he was posted to "C" Company and transferred to the camp at Moascar.

William was one of the many soldiers in the main transfer of troops to the Western Front in France, and departed from Alexandria on 6th April. His army record states that he contracted influenza on 22nd May whilst on the River Lys, near Armentières. After four days at No. 3 New Zealand Field Ambulance, he was back with his unit.

One next hears about William towards the end of August when he was reprimanded for the second occasion and deprived of one day's pay for being improperly dressed on parade. He then transferred to No. 3 Company New Zealand Machine Gun Corps on 31st August. On 27th December, again around Christmastime, he was wounded in action whilst in the Cordonnerie subsector on the River Lys near Armentières, with gunshot wounds to his leg and a compound fractured femur. Immediate evacuation to England took place and he was admitted to No. 1 NZGH, Brockenhurst on 11th January 1917. William died as a result of his wounds on 4th February and was buried two days later.

Plot A, Row 1, Grave 5.

William is commemorated on the memorial plaques at St. Andrews Presbyterian Church in Gisborne and, at St. John's Union Church, Opotiki as well as on the cenotaph in the town.

In 1921 the Morice family land was reclaimed for Maori Reparation, for the wrongful confiscation of lands in the Wars of 1860. The family was barely compensated and walked off. Letters show they auctioned all their property before leaving, even "my lovely pullets must go, for four shillings and sixpence".

William (senior) and Sarah lived to an old age; William died on 15th June 1937 aged 85 years, and Sarah died on 5th October 1952 aged 87 years. They are buried at Opotiki Cemetery.

Acknowledgement:

Sonia Edwards, Opotiki

WILFRED BLYTHE KIRK

Lance Corporal, 24/484
N.Z. Machine Gun Corps, No. 3 Company (2nd Battalion 3rd NZRB)
Died of sickness on 18th February 1917, aged 22

Wilfred Blythe Kirk, born on 1st February 1895 was the second of six children of William (1866-1947) and Emma, née Wood (1870-1949), of Eccles Street, Gore, Southland.

It is believed that Wilfred's grandparents, John and Margaret Kirk, and their five children, which included Wilfred's father, William, emigrated to New Zealand in 1870 on the ship *Otago*. Other children were born to John and Margaret in New Zealand.

William's roots were in Scotland, and Emma came from Australia. Besides Wilfred, their children were:

Mervyn William   *(1893-1918)*
Margaret Mataura   *(1896-?)*
Ralph Clifford   *(1903-1908)*
Ewin Rex   *(1909-1980) and*
Kathleen Mavis   *(1912-?)*

Wilfred attended Gore Main School (Register No. 877), and later worked as a Clerk for Gore Borough Council.

He enlisted with the NZEF on 29th May 1915 and departed overseas with the 2nd New Zealand Rifle Brigade on 9th October on the same day as his brother, Mervyn Kirk, Rifleman 24/207, New Zealand Rifle Brigade, thus implying that the two brothers enlisted within days of each other. The troopship arrived at Egypt on 18th November and shortly afterwards Wilfred joined the Western Frontier Force that was sent to Mersa Matruh. In January 1916 he proceeded to Ismailia and then at the beginning of March he transferred to No. 3 Machine Gun Company. He gained the promotion to Lance Corporal, which took place before being posted to France in early April.

From early August onwards, Wilfred's health deteriorated rapidly. Whilst he was in the Field in the Armentières area, he was sent to the nearest New Zealand Field Ambulance suffering from neurasthenia and loss of memory. After a few days he rejoined his unit, but a fortnight later he was ill again, this time suffering from influenza. He was back with his unit for just one week when, on 9th September he was ill again with catalepsy, shell shock and no longer in a fit state to fight for his country. Such a catalogue of traumas well illustrates the consequences of daily life in the trenches.

The rest of Wilfred's life was spent in England, firstly at No. 1 NZGH, Brockenhurst, followed by a month at Hornchurch Convalescent Depot, a spell at Codford Command Depot, in hospital in Edinburgh, and finally back at Brockenhurst. By early January 1917 the medical authorities had diagnosed that he was suffering from hysteria epilepsy. The cause of his death on 18th February was cerebral tumour, which explains his rapidly deteriorating condition.

Wilfred was buried on 20th February. Plot A, Row 2, Grave 6.

William and Emma's lives must have been shattered when they learned that three of their children had not outlived them. Their youngest son, Ralph, had died aged five in 1908. A decade later Wilfred and Mervyn (who served in Egypt and on the Western Front) died as a result of the War. Mervyn died the year after his brother, on 15th November 1918 and is buried at Gore Cemetery, Section 5. Block I. Lot 37 in the family grave plot. This indicates that he was repatriated to New Zealand before the War ended, but did not survive long after.

Both Wilfred and Mervyn are commemorated on their parents' headstone at Gore Cemetery and on Gore War Memorial.

Kirk family grave, Gore Cemetery

Gore War Memorial

Acknowledgements:

    Graeme Middlemiss
    Ron Kirk

THOMAS CYRIL BROADBRIDGE

Rifleman, 24/693
2nd Battalion, 3rd New Zealand (Rifle) Brigade, "C" Company
Died of wounds on 11th November 1916, aged 25 or 28

Thomas Cyril was the son of George Howard and Lilian Mary (née Weir). There is a discrepancy regarding Cyril's birth date. His army record states he was born on 5th April 1889, yet the births indexes indicate that it was 1892. It is suspected that the latter is correct, because a son George Howard Weir was born in 1889, a year after George and Lilian were married. Other children were Muriel Agatha (b.1893) and Mary Louisa Lilian (Maimie) (b. 1898).

The family came from the Wairau Valley, to the west of Blenheim, in the Marlborough region of South Island. Cyril's father, George Howard, came from England, possibly from the south, because many Broadbridge's are listed in the International Genealogical Index (IGI) from Sussex and Kent.

In 1893 George Howard was listed in the Electoral Roll as employed as a station hand at Hillersden, a few miles west of Wairau Valley Township. By 1897 he had opened the general store at Wairau Valley, and was assisted by his wife Lilian, and later by their two daughters. George Howard Weir delivered goods by horse and cart as far away as Tophouse (a hotel), about 50 miles one way, across wild streams, the Wairau River, and mountainous country.

Tophouse, near St. Arnaud, Nelson Lakes

Tophouse is still a hotel; the building was built by Ned James, an ex ships' carpenter and master of cob constructions (building material consisting of a mixture of clay and chopped straw) for Mr. Nat Longney in 1887.

Cyril attended the small Wairau Valley School before going to work as a labourer for a Mr. McLaughlin at Kaikoura. It is not known whether he was employed in sheep farming or whaling, Kaikoura being a major whaling centre from 1843 until 1922.

On 29th May 1915 Cyril enlisted with the NZEF. Within a week he was posted to "C" Company, 2nd Battalion of the Trentham Regiment as a Rifleman, and he left New Zealand on 9th October on board *Tahiti*. The ship reached Egypt on 18th November, whereupon he transferred to the 2nd Battalion, 3rd NZRB. He proceeded to Ismailia on 17th January 1916 to undertake further training. Shortly after arrival at camp he was admitted to the 1st Australian Stationary Hospital with conjunctivitis. He had two periods of this eye problem and was not fit for active service until March.

Cyril left Alexandria for Marseilles on 6th April. On eventual arrival in the Field on the Western Front, he obviously found the conditions unbearable because his army record mentions three bouts of disobedience for which he was appropriately reprimanded. He absented himself on two occasions without permission, and was caught being drunk whilst on duty!

By 15th September, Cyril's luck had run out and he was wounded in action, with gunshot wounds to his left thigh. This happened on the first day of the Flers-Courcelette Battle on the Somme (15th-22nd September) when his Battalion's task was to capture a sector of the Flers Trench System, then to take Flers village. After a period in France receiving medical attention, he was transferred to England, and arrived at No. 1 NZGH on 27th September.

Six weeks later, on 11th November 1916, Cyril died as a result of his wounds, and was buried two days later. Plot A, Row 3, Grave 10.

In 1921 George Howard (Senior) sold the store at Wairau Valley and he and his son George Howard Weir had adjoining farms in the valley. The latter married Alice Mary Timms, and they had two sons, Cyril Desmond and Noel Weir (b.1927). Cyril Desmond started a road cartage company, which Noel helped create. The company now has a large fleet of trucks, with Broadbridges still involved.

Acknowledgements and sources:

Noel Weir Broadbridge, Blenheim (nephew)
Harry Wright, Blenheim
J. E. Tomlinson (1968) *Remembered Trails* printed by Timaru Herald Co. Ltd.
Lott, Murial I. *Old Hillersden*

HERBERT LIONEL EDMAN

**Private, 6/3007
2nd Battalion, Canterbury Regiment, 13th Company
Died of wounds on 11th November 1916, aged 23**

Herbert Lionel Edman was born at Christchurch on 3rd August 1893, the son of Mrs. Katie Monson, of Hawkhurst Road, Lyttleton. In 1915, Herbert had left home and was residing c/o Mrs. Beaumont of Stafford Street, Timaru, South Canterbury, and was employed as a Packerman for W. Evans in the same town.

Herbert enlisted on 12th June 1915 at Trentham, but shortly afterwards was admitted to hospital with influenza. He departed from New Zealand on 9th October with the 7th Reinforcements and disembarked at Suez six weeks later. His health was not A1 because he had another spell in hospital at Choubra Isolation Hospital with diphtheria. Upon recovery he went to the base depot at Zeitoun. On 8th March 1916, whilst at Moascar, he joined the 2nd Battalion, Canterbury Infantry Brigade, and in April he arrived in France. Herbert's ill luck continued as he was reported missing on 21st September whilst in Goose Alley, near Flers on the Somme. He was found two days later with gunshot wounds to his back and immediate transfer to England and No. 1 NZGH, Brockenhurst took place per H.S. *Maheno*.

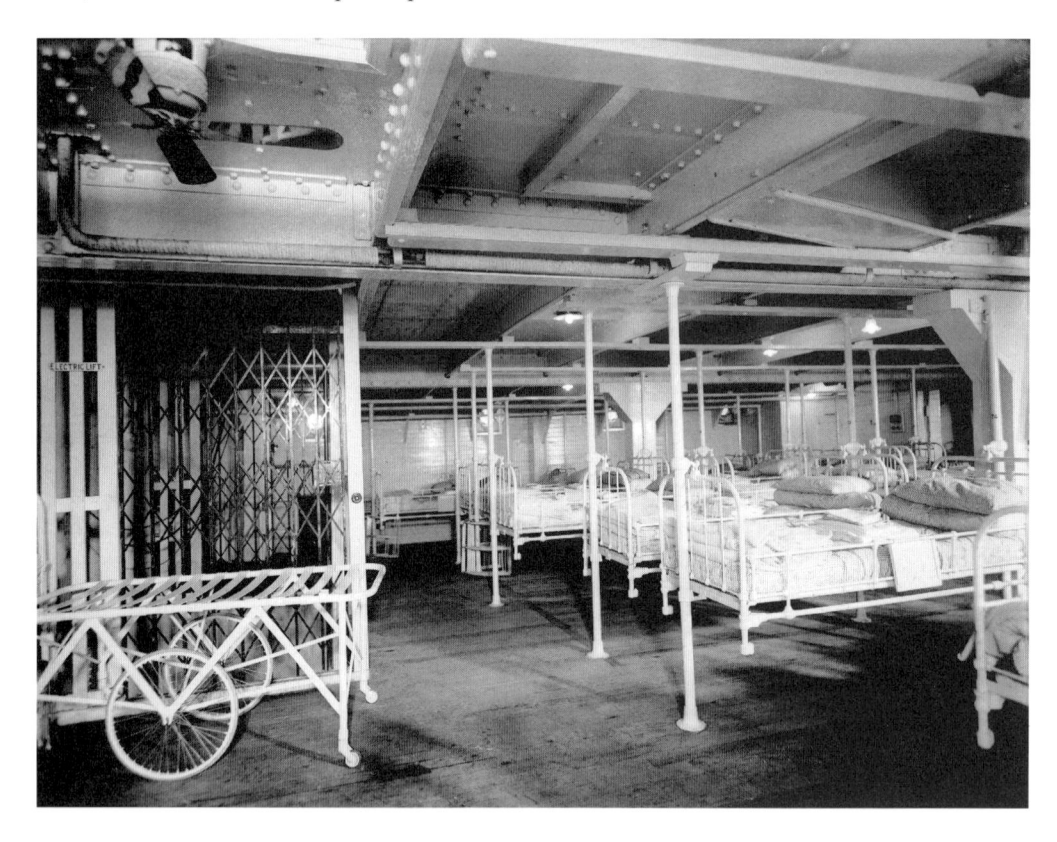

Interior view on board the *Maheno*
John Dickie Collection. G-002218-1/1 (PAColl-3037). ATL

Herbert survived a further six weeks and died on 11th November 1916. He was buried on 13th November. Plot A, Row 1, Grave 7.

ALEXANDER MILES STIRRAT

Private, 8/3081
1st Battalion, Otago Regiment, 8th Company
Died of wounds on 19th January 1919, aged 32

Alexander Miles Stirrat was born on 16th November 1886, the youngest child of John (a builder) and Elizabeth (1846-1919) of 52 Venus Street, Georgetown, Invercargill. Other members of the family were John (1881-1889), Robert (b.1882) and Lizzie (b.1885). Alexander was a pupil at Invercargill South School from 1892 until 1900. Prior to enlisting with the NZEF on 12th June 1915 at Trentham, he worked as a carpenter for Mr. W. Falconer of Rodney Street, Trafalgar, Invercargill.

Alexander departed from New Zealand with the 7th Reinforcements on 9th October for training in Egypt before transfer to France in April 1916. He found it difficult to cope with army discipline and committed a series of offences such as breaking out of barracks and absenting himself from water-carrying duty in the trenches, for which he received the appropriate punishments.

In September 1917 Alexander fell ill with pyrexia and was a patient at 26th General Hospital, Etaples before transferring to Tooting Military Hospital, London. He convalesced at Grey Towers, Hornchurch, Essex, and then transferred to Codford Camp for light training. Sling Camp was his next base before returning to France on 2nd June 1918.

On 5th September Alexander was wounded in his chest and pharynx near Havrincourt Wood.

He arrived at No. 1 NZGH, Brockenhurst on 19th September. He died on 19th January 1919, with his burial two days later. Plot A, Row 1, Grave 22.

Alexander is remembered on the Stirrat family grave (above) at Eastern Cemetery and on the War Memorial, Invercargill. There is a street named after the Stirrat family but no one of this name lived in Invercargill in 2001.

Acknowledgement: Elizabeth Beer, Invercargill

JAMES HAYTER BARTER

Lance Corporal, 10/2852
1st Battalion, Wellington Regiment, 11th Company
attached to N.Z. Provost Corps
Died of sickness on 3rd August 1918, aged 34

James Hayter Barter was born on 16th April 1884 at Manor Park, Essex, England. His parents, Edwin James and Mary Maria, in 1881 were living at 26 Quadrant Grove, St. Pancras, London, with their older children Frances (b.1873), Edwin (b.1876) and Edgar (b.1879).

In 1915 James was a seaman on Troopship 17, working for the New Zealand Government. His parents then lived at 25 Baxter Avenue, Southend-on-Sea.

James signed his attestation sheet at Trentham on 14th June 1915, and departed overseas with the 7th Reinforcements on 9th October. After arrival in Egypt he joined his Battalion at Ismailia on 9th January 1916. Transfer to France began on 6th April and three months later, on 6th July, he fell ill with pneumonia and was repatriated to England for medical attention. After a spell at No. 5 General Hospital, London he then convalesced at Hornchurch in Essex.

In September 1916 James was posted to Codford Command Depot. He remained in England for the rest of his time, and on 11th June 1917 was taken on strength of the Anzac Provost Corps (Military Police) with rank of Lance Corporal. In February 1918 he transferred to No. 1 NZGH, Brockenhurst staff, and was often a patient himself. He had contracted meningitis on his final admission on 25th July and died on 3rd August. He was buried three days later.

Plot A, Row 5, Grave 16.

After WW1 James's mother moved house several times, and her last known address in 1923 was 20 Britannia Road, Westcliff-on-Sea, Essex.

Source: 1881 UK Census, FHL Film 1341047, PRO Ref RG11,
    Piece 0214, Folio 111, Page 27

JOHN JAMES MONAHAN

Private, 10/3035
1st Battalion, Wellington Regiment, 7th Company
Died of wounds on 25th September 1917, aged 27

John James Monahan, the son of John and Helena, was born on 22nd April 1890 at Kumara, south of Greymouth, Westland. John (junior) became a letter carrier for the General Post Office at Wellington whilst he was living at Lyall Bay, on the outskirts of the city. Meanwhile his father was employed at the Defence Stores at Wellington.

John enlisted with the NZEF on 14th June 1915 and departed from New Zealand with the 7th Reinforcements on 9th October. He disembarked at Suez on 18th November and joined the Wellington Infantry Battalion at Ismailia on 9th January 1916. After training in Egypt the Battalion left for France on 6th April.

John was injured on 31st July 1917 at Basseville, southeast of Messines, receiving gunshot wounds to his scalp. He received medical attention in France for three weeks before admission to No. 1 NZGH, Brockenhurst on 24th August. By 19th September the medical authorities realised he would not return to duty and he was "placed on the New Zealand Roll" which we may assume was the way of listing such personnel. He died on 25th September and was buried on the 27th. Plot A, Row 2, Grave 2.

John's parents are buried at Karori Cemetery, Wellington (Area 3, Block C, Plot 23). Their grave (below) does not mention John, but two other members of the family are commemorated: Mary (died 1st April 1977) and James Patrick (died 15th July 1979).

RAKAPA AKENA

Private, 16/598
New Zealand Maori (Pioneer) Battalion
Died of sickness on 16th June 1918, aged 21

Rakapa Akena, who was born at Port Awanui in 1897, was the son of Patio and Mere Akena of Rangitukia, near Tikitiki, on the east coast of North Island. He worked as a labourer for George Smith at Tolaga Bay.

Rakapa enlisted with the NZEF on 28th June 1915 at Tolaga Bay, and departed from New Zealand with the second Maori contingent on board the troopship *Waitemata* on 18th September. Regrettably his army records are scant and there is little detail of his movements. However, it is recorded that he spent time in Egypt undertaking training before transferring to France in 1916. He arrived at the New Zealand Base at Etaples on 28th June.

Rakapa had several spells in hospital in France, the final period being in March 1918, when he was suffering from tuberculosis of the lungs. He was evacuated to England straightaway and admitted to No. 1 NZGH, Brockenhurst.

He died on 16th June 1918 and was buried the next day.

Plot A, Row 2, Grave 17.

Rakapa's name is listed on Gisborne War Memorial and also on the war memorial tablet inside St. Mary's Church at Tikitiki.

Note that POTENE TUHORO (p. 97) is also listed on this memorial tablet.

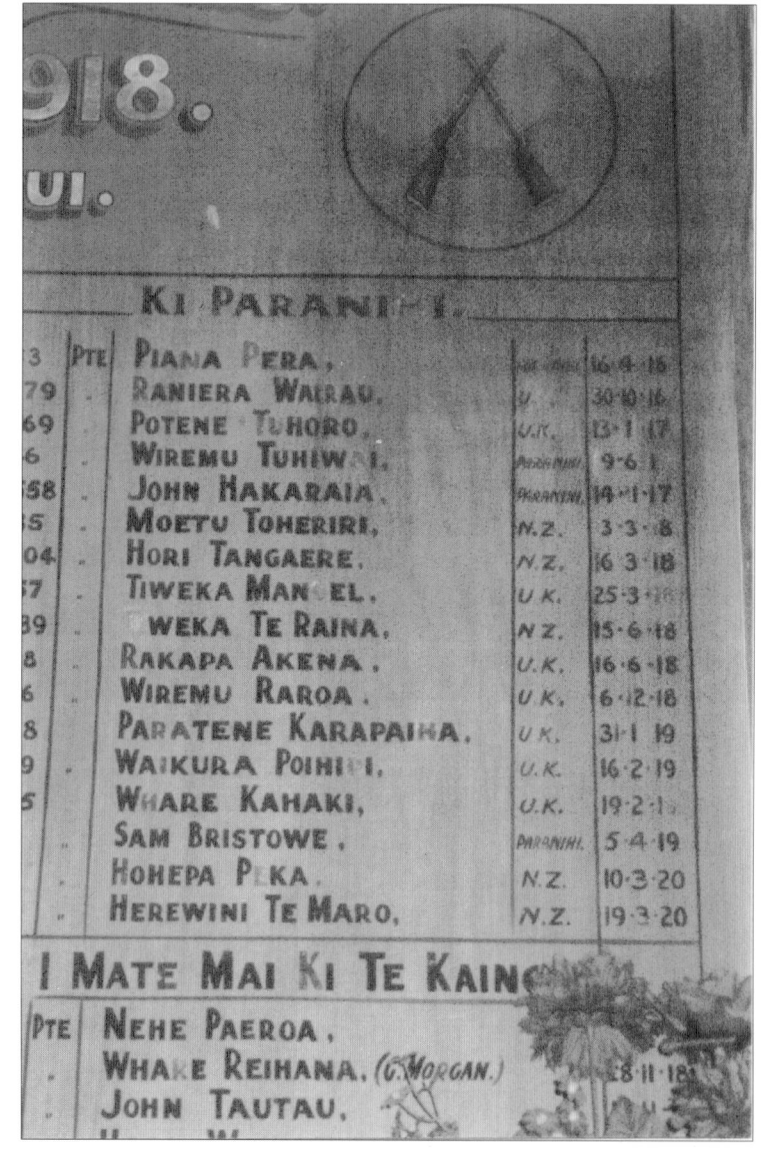

TUHEKE TUI MATENGA

Private, 16/810
New Zealand Maori (Pioneer) Battalion
Died on 14th May 1918, aged 23

Tuheke Tui Matenga was born in 1895 at Muriwai, Poverty Bay, Gisborne, the son of Karepa Tui Matenga (1869-1913) and Matire Bartlett (1880-1932). Karepa's immediate family lived in the Wairarapa region, whereas Matire was born at Mahia and lived all her life in Wairoa County, near Gisborne.

Tuheke enlisted with the NZEF on 30th June 1915 and departed from New Zealand with the 2nd Maori Contingent on 18th September, disembarking at Suez, Egypt on 26th October. He is next recorded as being posted to the Otago Infantry Battalion at Moascar on 20th January 1916.

Along with other members of the recently formed Maori (Pioneer) Battalion, he embarked for France from Port Said on 9th April. On 29th May he was wounded in action, receiving gunshot wounds to his head, arms and legs. This happened in an area that was supposedly the "quiet" sector near Armentières. After a week at No. 22 General Hospital at Camiers, Tuheke was evacuated to England on 6th June per H.S. *Newhaven*.

He spent the next two months at hospitals in Lincoln, Woodcote Park (below) and Walton-on-Thames, prior to transferring to the Convalescent Hospital at Grey Towers, Hornchurch, Essex. He was eventually attached to strength at Codford (Command) Depot on Salisbury Plain for light training before joining the Reserve Group at Sling Camp on 13th November. He was then sent back to Codford in early January 1917.

Tuheke was still stationed at Codford the following July, and he somehow received a gunshot wound to his finger, which required amputation. After a spell in hospital he returned to Hornchurch for convalescence. He was back at Codford in November but was still having problems with the scar on his finger.

WW1 Army hut at Codford (now used as a Scout hut)

Tuheke's final posting took place on 24th April 1918 when he marched into the New Zealand Engineer Reserve Depot at Christchurch, near Bournemouth. One will never know what happened during his final hours, but he was found drowned in the River Stour at Christchurch on 14th May.

His body was taken to Brockenhurst and the Reverend P. Wainohu officiated at his burial on 16th May.

Plot A, Row 1, Grave 17.

Acknowledgement:

Ani Hine Terekia, Waihirere, Gisborne

HERBERT JOSEPH BAIRD

Lance Corporal
7/1440
2nd Battalion Canterbury Regiment, 13th Company
Died of wounds on 1st November 1916, aged 21

Herbert Joseph Baird was born at Ashley, Canterbury on 21st December 1894, the son of Joseph (1867-1901) and Annie, née Croft (1869-1951). Joseph was born on 24th May 1867 at Balcairn, Canterbury and he married Annie, a local girl, in 1893. Joseph's parents were John Wallace and Matilda (née Bolton), and Annie's were Thomas and Mary (née Furby).

In 1915 the family were living at 76 Percival Street, Rangiora, Canterbury. Herbert was employed as a Shepherd, working for an uncle Mr. J. Croft of Loburn, near Rangiora.

Herbert had a brief but varied life with the NZEF. After enlistment on 1st July 1915 at Trentham as a Trooper he departed from New Zealand on 14th August with the 6th Reinforcements, bound for Egypt. A few days after disembarkation, he fell ill on 4th October with diphtheria and was admitted to the Infections Hospital at Choubra. On 13th November, he was considered fit enough to return to duty, and was posted to Anzac, Gallipoli to join the 1st Canterbury Mounted Rifles. However, Herbert can have played only the briefest part in this campaign since he arrived back at Alexandria, Egypt on 26th December 1915, following the evacuation of troops from the Gallipoli peninsula.

In March 1916 Herbert was posted as a Gunner to the New Zealand Field Artillery, 3rd Brigade Ammunition Column at Moascar, near the Suez Canal. Later that month he joined the 2nd Battalion, Canterbury Infantry Regiment, as a Private and he left Egypt for France on 7th April with the transfer of troops to the Western Front. On 24th August 1916 he was appointed Lance Corporal whilst training for fighting on the Somme.

Regrettably, Herbert's promotion to Lance Corporal did not last long. A month after joining his Battalion he was wounded in action on 24th September. On the night of 21/22nd September the 2nd Canterbury Regiment had been relieved from the trenches on the line near Flers, and went back to trenches just north of the Longueval-Bazentin le Grand road. It was during this period that Herbert received shell wounds to his leg, which resulted in a compound fracture of the femur.

Herbert was immediately evacuated to England, and arrived at No. 1 NZGH, Brockenhurst on 27th September. He was reported as being seriously ill on 13th October. He died on 1st November 1916 and was buried two days later.

Plot A, Row 2, Grave 9.

Herbert is commemorated on Rangiora War Memorial (above left) and on the cross in the churchyard at St. John the Baptist Anglican Church, Rangiora (above right).

Note that F. S. Fendall (p. 53), the son of the vicar, is also mentioned on this cross.

POTENE TUHORO

Private, 16/769
New Zealand Maori (Pioneer) Battalion
Died of sickness on 13th January 1917, aged 21

Potene Tuhoro was born in 1896 at Rangitukia, Waiapu, near East Cape, North Island. His parents, Raniera Tuhoro and Heni Kohao, née Manuel were married at Te Arero, between Tokomaru and Tolaga Bays.

Potene worked as a self-employed farmer in his home area. He enlisted with the NZEF on 6th July 1915 at Takapuna, Auckland, departed from New Zealand with the 2nd Maori Contingent on 18th September on board the troopship *Waitemata* and arrived at Suez on 26th October. In the first week in December he was admitted to the New Zealand General Hospital in Cairo suffering from enteritis. A month later he transferred to a convalescent home at Alexandria for a few days before being posted to the army base at Ghezireh, Cairo, for light training. On 19th January 1916 he was attached to the Canterbury Infantry Battalion at Moascar.

In April the newly formed Maori (Pioneer) Battalion embarked for France from Port Said. Potene was ill again at the end of October with debility and diarrhoea. This developed into tuberculosis and pneumonia, and after a month in hospital in St. Omer, he was evacuated to England and arrived at No. 1 NZGH, Brockenhurst on 3rd December. He died six weeks later on 13th January 1917 of tubercular peritonitis and was buried on 16th January. Plot A, Row 3, Grave 8.

Potene's name is listed on Gisborne War Memorial. He is also commemorated on the memorial board inside Tikitiki Church, near Rangitukia (below) a few names above Private Rakapa Akena, 16/598, Maori (Pioneer) Battalion (p. 92).

WILLIAM CHARLES PAGE

Captain
5/563
New Zealand Army Service Corps, No. 3 Company
Died on 27th May 1918, aged 43

William Charles Page was born on 27th February 1875 at Ashburton, Canterbury, the son of William Charles (a builder) and Rebecca Selina (née Kemp).

William (junior) was working as a carpenter at Rangiora, Canterbury when he married Amy Florence Harrison Stephens on 21st October 1897 at St. John the Baptist Church, Rangiora. An interesting connection is the fact that the Reverend F. P. Fendall, the father of Gunner Frederick Selwyn Fendall (p.53), conducted William and Amy's marriage ceremony. Amy's parents were Solomon (a nurseryman) and Selina (née Harrison) from Rangiora.

St. John the Baptist Anglican Church, Rangiora

The couple soon produced a family:

Amy Dorothy	*born 9.11.1898*	*at*	*Stratford, Taranaki*
Elma Rita Selina	*born 21.11.1899*	*at*	*Rangiora, Canterbury*
Huia	*born 7.8.1903*	*at*	*Eltham, Taranaki*
Roy Anderson	*born 16.4.1906*	*at*	*Island Bay, Wellington*
Riri	*born 22.8.1907*	*at*	*Wellington*

From the above birthplaces, it is apparent that William and his growing family lived in several different locations during his early married life.

Prior to enlisting with the NZEF in 1915, William had served as a Territorial soldier with the New Zealand army for many years:

30th October 1900   *Enlistment in Eltham Rifles (Taranaki Region)*
13th February 1907   *Transferred to Zealandia Rifles (based at Wellington)*
12th November 1908   *Transferred to Masterton Mounted Rifles*
date not known   *Transferred to 9th (Wellington East Coast) Mounted Rifles*
30th October 1911   *Transferred to Reserve of Officers (as Lieutenant)*
27th October 1914   *Transferred to New Zealand Army Service Corps (NZASC)*
                                    (as Captain)

William was the Assistant Director of Supplies and Transport, Auckland District, prior to enlisting with the NZEF on 16th July 1915 at Palmerston North. On this date he transferred to command No. 5 Company, New Zealand Army Service Corps. The family home at that time was at Milford, Takapuna, Auckland.

By the time he departed from New Zealand with the New Zealand Rifle Brigade on 9th October 1915 he had transferred to NZASC, No. 3 Company. After disembarkation at Suez, Egypt he was initially based northeast of Cairo at Zeitoun.

On Christmas Day, 1915 No. 3 Company NZASC invited No. 5 Company NZASC to Christmas Dinner, at 5.30 p.m. at the nearby Aerodrome Camp, Heliopolis, Egypt, with the President named as Captain W. C. Page. This invitation card can be seen at Auckland War Memorial Museum (Te Papa Whakahiku) in the WW1 section of the "Scars on the Heart" exhibition.

William left Egypt for France on 9th April, as one of the many troops transferring to the Western Front. He is next recorded as being admitted to the 2nd Anzac Officers Rest Home on 18th October owing to contusion in his leg. Then on 13th December he was evacuated from the Divisional Area and struck off strength of No. 3 Company, Army Service Corps owing to neurasthenia and suspected shell shock. He spent time in St. Omer and Boulogne Stationary Hospitals and after examination by a nerve specialist he was recommended for three weeks sick leave in England. This took place at Brighton Convalescent Hospital, commencing on 21st March 1917.

One consolation for William was that during these difficult months he was recognised for his long-standing service with the New Zealand Territorial Force and was awarded the New Zealand Territorial Service Medal on 27th November 1916, which he eventually received on 10th April 1917.

RECEIPT FOR NEW ZEALAND TERRITORIAL SERVICE MEDAL.

I, William Charles Page, N.Z.A.S.C. hereby acknowledge to have received from the Commandant, New Zealand Forces, a **NEW ZEALAND TERRITORIAL SERVICE MEDAL** awarded to me for long and efficient service in the New Zealand Territorial Force.

Signature of Recipient:

Witness:

Dated at London, this tenth day of April, 1917

William's time at Brighton was extended until 8th May when he went on further leave in England, with instructions to report to the New Zealand Reserve Group at Sling Camp on 23rd May. The next day he returned to France and departed from Southampton, disembarking at Le Havre. Three days later, on 27th May, he was in Marseilles where he joined No. 3 New Zealand Depot Unit of Supply. He assumed command of this unit on 6th June. William spent the next year at Marseilles during which time he had another period of leave in England and transferred to the Field Butchery in February 1918.

William was admitted to hospital in France in early April 1918, suffering from inguinal hernia. After several weeks the medical authorities decided to transfer him to England and he was admitted to No. 1 NZGH, Brockenhurst, Forest Park Section, on 20th May 1918. He died unexpectedly a week later on 27th May and was buried by the Reverend Jacob on 30th May. Plot A, Row 5, Grave 14.

After WW1 Amy was living at 11 Alten Road, Auckland, and later at Moyola House, Hinemoa Street, Birkenhead, Auckland.

Sources: Christchurch Marriage Records, Register SJR3, 2330
          New Zealand Gazette (various dates)

WILLIAM DAVID DUNBAR

Private, 8/3434
2nd Battalion, Otago Regiment, 10th Company
Died of wounds on 8th March 1917, aged 29

William David Dunbar, the son of William and Eliza Jane, was born at Napier on 8th February 1888. Prior to his enlistment with the NZEF he worked for Mr. J. R. Clark of Balfour, northwest of Gore, Otago, in the capacity of labourer. His mother at this time lived at Dickens Street, Napier, and his father was deceased.

William attested under the name of DAVID WILLIAMS when he signed on at Trentham on 23rd August 1915. He departed from New Zealand with the Otago Infantry Battalion, 8th Reinforcements on 13th November, and arrived at Suez, Egypt on 20th December. A month later William was admitted to No. 1 NZGH, Cairo with ear trouble where he remained for ten days.

The middle of April 1916 saw him embarking on *Kinfauns Castle* bound for France and the Western Front. He joined the 2nd Battalion, Otago Regiment near Armentières on 18th May and was posted to 14th Company. On the night of 14th May the 4th and 8th Companies of the 2nd Battalion, Otago Regiment had relieved the 12th Manchester Regiment on the front line immediately east of Armentières. William would have joined the 14th Company at Houplines where the men were held in reserve.

William's army records indicate that he could not cope with the rigid military discipline that was enforced, because he absented himself from Tattoo Roll Call and failed to comply with an order, for which he was given the appropriate punishments. He also suffered from further illness, this time influenza and deafness.

He found himself back at the base camp at Etaples towards the end of August, and on 8th September he returned to the Front on the Somme and transferred to 10th Company. On 11th September the Battalion was camped outside Mametz Wood. Less than a week later, on 16th September, William received gunshot wounds to his back, arms and legs. On that day the New Zealand Division had received orders to occupy the line of Grove Alley and capture Goose Alley, which stretched from Flers Trench to Gird Support. However, there were heavy casualties and the intended attack on Goose Alley (timed for 1.00 p.m.) was postponed until 18th September owing to the lack of backup support on the right of the line.

William was immediately evacuated to England and arrived at No. 1 NZGH, Brockenhurst on 20th September. He was a patient at this hospital for six months. In the end his injuries proved fatal and he died on 8th March 1917. His burial took place on 9th March in Plot A, Row 2, Grave 5.

CHARLES FREDERICK GAME

Gunner
2/2127
New Zealand Field Artillery, 12th Battery, 3rd Brigade
Died of wounds on 20th December 1916, aged 32

Charles Frederick Game was born on 15th May 1884 at Te Kopuru, near Dargaville, Northland, son of Charles John Game. Charles (junior) was employed as a Butcher for Corkill Brothers of Aratapu, just north of Te Kopuru.

He enlisted with the NZEF on 24th August 1915 at Trentham. Prior to departure from New Zealand he married Margaret Millie Glink at Red Hill, near Te Kopuru on 29th September; the marriage ceremony was officiated by W. H. Speen. He also wrote a Will - his wife was to have his house and property and all moneys due, and his mother to have effects in the house.

Charles left New Zealand with the 7th Reinforcements on 9th October and disembarked at Suez on 18th November. He then spent several months in Egypt prior to posting to France and fighting on the Western Front. He left Alexandria on 7th April 1916 per the *Menomenu*.

His movements are next recorded when he was fighting on the Somme on 25th September. He was wounded in his head with the consequence of a depressed fracture to his neck and back. After medical attention in France, he arrived at No. 1 NZGH, Brockenhurst on 28th October.

Charles died of his wounds on 20th December 1916. The burial ceremony was held on 22nd December.

Plot A, Row 1, Grave 6.

CHRISTOPHER ROY TAIT

Gunner, 2/2557
New Zealand Field Artillery, 15th Howitzer Battery, 1st Brigade
Died of wounds on 5th October 1916, aged 21

Christopher Roy Tait was the fourth child of a family of six of John and Lavinia née Chandler (b.1868), who married on 31st May 1888 at Masterton and lived there during their children's youth. Christopher was born on 4th June 1895.

His siblings, all born at Masterton, were:

James	*b. 28th April 1888*
Madelene	*b. 25th September 1889*
Lavinia Chandler	*b. 1st September 1892*
John Chandler	*b. 16th July 1898*
Douglas Sinclair	*b. 23rd May 1904*

In 1915 John and Lavinia were resident at Rautangi Road, Mount Eden, Auckland, whilst Christopher was living at Hamilton and employed as a Clerk for Hamilton Furnishing Company.

Christopher enlisted with the NZEF on 24th August 1915 at Trentham. His army records state that he was born in 1894, but he must have falsified his age to gain entry. He left New Zealand with the 8th Reinforcements on 13th November and disembarked at Suez on 20th December. On 25th February whilst at Moascar camp, he was transferred temporarily to 4th Brigade Ammunition Column.

Posting to France commenced on 5th April when Christopher embarked at Alexandria on board HMT *Minnewaska*. He was one of the many soldiers to be injured on the Somme, receiving gunshot wounds to his chest, left arm, and left thigh on 21st September. He was immediately evacuated to England and arrived at No. 1 NZGH on 27th September. Christopher survived just a few days more and died on 5th October, with his burial two days later.

Plot A, Row 5, Grave 5.

Christopher is commemorated on the wall plaque in Hamilton Memorial Park. After WW1 his parents moved to live at Victoria Street West, Hamilton.

Acknowledgement: Molly Gallagher, Hamilton

WILLIAM AINSLIE

Sapper, 4/1323
New Zealand Engineers, Tunnelling Company
Died of wounds on 22nd September 1917, aged 37

William Ainslie was born 29th July 1880, the son of Mrs. A. Ainslie of Black River, North West Coast, Tasmania. Prior to enlisting with the NZEF he was working as a bushman for T. T. T. Company, Mokai (north of Lake Taupo). On his Attestation Sheet he stated that he was not married, yet his History Sheet states that his next of kin was Mrs. B. J. Ainslie, who he must have married after enlisting.

William volunteered for the NZEF on 1st October 1915, in response to the request for New Zealand to provide one Company to dig tunnels between the opposing lines under "no man's land" in order to charge the enemy's line with high explosives. There was an appeal for recruits in September 1915 for mature men whose previous jobs had been bushmen, miners and navvies. There was no difficulty in filling the places, and training took place on Avondale Racecourse, near Auckland prior to overseas posting.

The Tunnelling Company left New Zealand on the *Ruapehu* (below) on 18th December 1915, and reached Plymouth, England on 18th February 1916.

On arrival in England, the Tunnelling Company stayed for a month near Pendennis Castle, Falmouth, Cornwall, before being sent to France.

In France the Company was initially based at Arras under the command of Major J. E. Duigan. The men's services were highly regarded by those in command, as displayed by letters of appreciation sent by Lt. General A. Haldane, Commanding VI Corps, and Major-General C. J. Deverell, Commanding 3rd Division.

William attended the 3rd Army Mine School in February 1917 for two weeks which included instruction on the use of mine rescue apparatus (known as the Proto).

On 15th August William's active service ended because he was wounded in his back near Basseville with the consequence of paraplegia. He straightaway transferred to England for medical attention. On arrival at No. 1 NZGH, Brockenhurst on 29th August he was classified as Seriously Ill. He never survived his substantial injuries and died on 22nd September 1917, with his burial on 25th September.

Plot A, Row 1, Grave 2.

On William's death, his widow's address was c/o Mrs. Giles? of "Ennismore", Park Close, Brockenhurst, Hants. She had remarried by 1921, to a Mr. Hendria, and their last known address was "Tolcarne", Fitzroy Street, Abbotsford, Sydney, Australia.

JOHN BLACKHAM

Rifleman, 25/948
3rd Battalion, 3rd New Zealand Rifle Brigade, "C" Company
Died of wounds on 26th September 1916, aged 32

John Blackham was born on 14th May 1884 at Invercargill. His parents, Richard (1837-1912) and Elizabeth, née Webb (1855-1924) were married in the same town in 1875, and the family lived in Dee Street. John was one of many children; three who died in infancy are mentioned on their father's grave at Eastern Cemetery, Invercargill. Older known siblings were Elizabeth (1879-1955) and William (1882-1951).

By 1915, Richard had passed away, and the family had moved to 26 Preston Street, Timaru. John was then aged 31 and employed by Brebant Brothers as a Cycle and Motor Mechanic. He had previously been apprenticed to P. H. Vickers at Invercargill.

John joined the New Zealand Army on 13th October 1915 at Trentham and departed overseas on 5th February 1916 with the 3rd Battalion, New Zealand Rifle Brigade, "C" Company. The troopship on which he travelled arrived at Suez, Egypt on 13th March. John had barely recuperated from the long sea journey when he was on board ship again, bound for France, this time on the *Alaunia*, departing from Alexandria on 7th April.

During his time in France John did experience a diversion from the horror of trench warfare, for during the summer of 1916 he spent some weeks training as a pigeon handler at the Pigeon School. However, in the autumn, whilst on the Somme he was injured with multiple gunshot wounds. This happened on 15th September, the first day of the Battle of Flers-Courcelette, when the Battalion's task was to capture Flers.

The seriousness of John's injuries meant that he should be evacuated to England as soon as practicable. He arrived at No. 1 NZGH, Brockenhurst on 24th September, but died two days later on 26th September from multiple gunshot wounds and tetanus. He was buried the next day. Plot A, Row 5, Grave 9.

John wrote his Will in his Pay Book, leaving all his New Zealand belongings to Sarah, Siss, Lizzie, Willie, George and Harry Blackham. One can assume that they were siblings owing to the mention of Elizabeth and William above. Also Elizabeth is named on her mother's grave at Timaru Cemetery as being the third daughter of Richard and Elizabeth.

John is commemorated at St. Mary's Anglican Church, Timaru, which is located at the intersection of Church and Sophia Streets, perched on a hill.

> Their name liveth for evermore
> To the Glory of God and in proud
> And grateful memory of those from this parish
> who gave their lives in the Great War 1914-1918

John is also commemorated on the family grave at Eastern Cemetery, Invercargill, Southland, Block 4, Plot 139 (below), and on Invercargill War Memorial.

Acknowledgement: Elizabeth Beer, Invercargill

RICHARD WILLIAM LYNCH

Rifleman, 26/965
4th Battalion, 3rd New Zealand Rifle Brigade, "D" Company
Died of wounds on 30th September 1916, aged 25

Richard William Lynch was born at Timaru on 23rd September 1891. Prior to joining the army he worked as a compositor for G. Stone Printing Company, Wellington and he was resident at 396 Taranaki Street in the same city. His brother Arthur Thomas, a picture dealer and framer at Takaka, Nelson was nominated as next-of-kin. Another brother, Albert Dennis Lynch lived at Parkstone, Holme Street, Ngaio, Wellington.

Richard enlisted with the NZEF on 15th October 1915 at Trentham. He left New Zealand with the 4th Battalion, NZRB, "D" Company on 5th February 1916 on *Mokoia* bound for Suez. After a brief spell in Egypt he transferred to France on 7th April. Whilst near Flers on the Somme on 12th September, he was wounded in both his arms and right thigh and was immediately transferred to No. 1 NZGH, Brockenhurst. He died on 30th September and his burial on 2nd October was conducted by Father J. J. McNemamin, Roman Catholic priest.

Richard is commemorated on the war memorials at Anzac Park, Nelson and at Motueka (below) near Takaka, his brother's home.

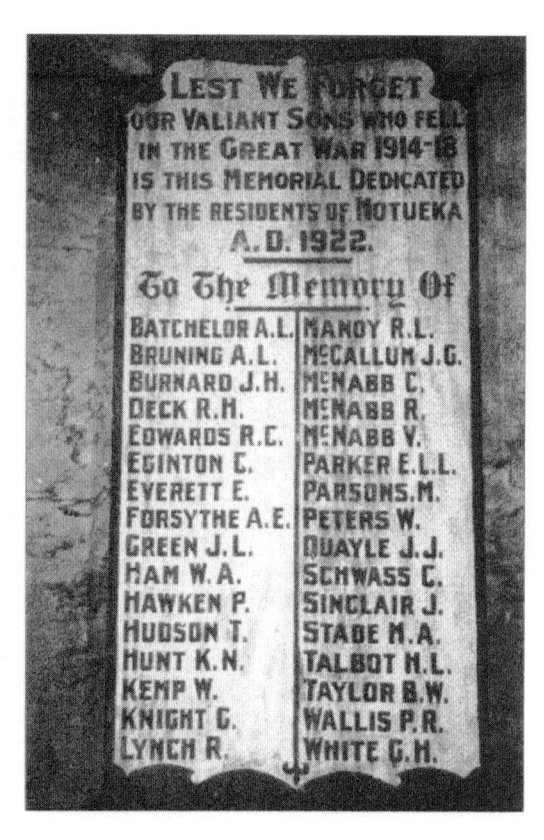

Acknowledgements and Source:
Allan Pope, Motueka
The Guardian – Motueka, Tasman and Golden Bays 15 April 2002 pp. 1 & 3
Motueka Branch, NZSG (information and photographs)

ALFRED LEONARD HARRIS

Private, 6/3729
2nd Battalion, Canterbury Regiment, 12th Company
Died of wounds on 17th October 1916, aged 27

Alfred Leonard Harris, born on 24th December 1888 at Christchurch, was the fourth child of Alfred William (1855-1933) and Maria Jane (1865-1939). Alfred William, whose roots were in Oxford, England, arrived in New Zealand (with two brothers, George and Harry) prior to 18th October 1883, when he married Maria Jane (née Prebble) from Christchurch.

Leonard's great-grandparents (on his mother's side), the Prebbles, originated in Kent, England and they arrived at Petone, Wellington in 1840 on the sailing ship *Aroroa*. They had a baby two days old when they landed, so mother and baby were carried ashore and hidden amongst beer barrels in a tent, away from the Maoris. After a time, the Prebbles moved to the Christchurch area and were amongst the first Canterbury settlers at Prebbleton (named after the family).

Alfred William and Maria Jane (left) had seven children -

Mary Ann   (b. 1.6.1884)
Elsie   (b. 15.8.1885)
James (Jim)   (b. 3.4.1887)
Alfred Leonard   (b. 24.12.1888)
Albert   (b. 1893)
 – who named a son Leonard, after his brother,
Henry Cecil   (b. 1896) and
Harold Walter   (b. 1900)

The following story has been written by Mary Ann Ensor (née Harris), Leonard's eldest sister:

"My parents, with their children, left Christchurch when I was 6 ½ years old. We left Lyttelton in a little steamer called *Rotomahana* for Poverty Bay. We had to go the whole way by boat in those days.

We left Gisborne for Tiniroto, 45 miles distant, where my father had got a sheep and cattle run. The most part was bush country. We travelled in a wagonette drawn by four horses, travelling up a hill called "Gentle Annie" – for why, I do not know as it was anything but gentle. The adults all got out to walk. The driver lost control of the horses, and the children and the wagonette all dropped right down over a steep bank. My mother thought we had been killed. As soon as the wagonette was lifted, I let her know differently, for we were all sitting in the middle of a bed of Scotch thistles!"

After a time the family moved into Gisborne so that the children could get schooling. The four eldest children, including Leonard, upon leaving school went to work at a big dairy farm. Many years later Leonard and his brother Cecil had a farm of their own at Paenga, near Murchison, Nelson region. Then in October 1915 Leonard enlisted with the NZEF.

Leonard's father, Alfred William, also signed up, and falsified his date of birth in order to be eligible. Apparently he had very dark hair, which fortunately aided the deception. He spent most of his service life on board the ship *Ulimaroa* employed as a Baker/Cook, which had also been his civilian trade when he lived at Matawai, midway between Opotiki and Gisborne.

Leonard signed up to join the New Zealand army on 19th October 1915 at Trentham. In November he spent several days at Tauherenikau Hospital with influenza. He left New Zealand with the Canterbury Infantry Regiment "C" Company, 9th Reinforcements on board *Tahiti* on 8th January 1916, and disembarked at Suez a month later.

In March he joined the 2nd Battalion at the Reserve Camp prior to posting to France in early April.

On 12th April Leonard was ordered to pay 7s. 6d. because he had lost his hat and pugaree (a scarf around crown of hat), which was the Quartermaster's replacement cost, to discourage loss of kit.

Leonard as a young man

21st September saw the end of Leonard's time on the Western Front when he received gunshot wounds to his left thigh. This happened in Goose Alley, near Flers. The severity of his injuries necessitated his transfer to England, and he arrived at No. 1 NZGH, Brockenhurst on 9th October. He died on 17th October 1916, and was buried two days later.

Plot A, Row 1, Grave 11.

Leonard is commemorated on Murchison War Memorial (below).

After WW1, his father Alfred William was allocated a farm on the Remuera Estate, Ohaeawai, northwest of Whangarei, in recognition of his war service. He lived there until his death on 13th July 1933. Henry Cecil inherited his father's farm and he remained there until after his mother's death on 4th June 1939. Both parents are buried in the cemetery at St. John's Church, Waimate North.

Acknowledgements:
    Brenda Jenkins, Kaikohe (great nephew's wife) –
        information and family photographs
    Mary Ann Ensor, née Harris (sister)
    Gaylene Harrison (great-great niece)
    Leonard Harris, Palmerston North

WILLIAM COLLETT COOPER

Private, 15/149
2nd Battalion, Otago Regiment, 14th Company
Died of wounds on 1st October 1916, aged 32

William Collett Cooper was the son of Charles Alfred and Mary Jane (née Beighton), who were married at Dunedin in 1883. William was born on 26th August 1884 at Te Aroha, situated in the south of the Coromandel region.

Prior to enlistment with the NZEF William was employed as a farmer for W. T. Wells at Glen Murray in the Waikato region. At this time his parents were living at 15 St. Stephens Avenue, Parnell, Auckland.

He signed his attestation sheet on 20th October 1915 at Trentham. Basic training in New Zealand took place for the next few months, and he was posted overseas on 8th January 1916 with the New Zealand Divisional Headquarters Staff, 9th Reinforcements, "A" Squadron. The troops disembarked at Suez on 12th February and training in Egypt continued until early April. During this time William was posted to the 2nd Battalion, Auckland Infantry Regiment at Moascar.

William embarked for France at Alexandria on 8th April but there are no details of his life on the Western Front until 27th August, when he transferred to the 2nd Battalion, Otago Infantry Regiment, which was then camped at Airaines, southeast of Abbeville. He was immediately subjected to training in preparation for action on the Somme, and on 2nd September the troops were on the move towards the battle zone.

On 11th September the Battalion was camped outside Mametz Wood, southwest of Bazentin-le-Petit. The next day orders were given that the enemy was to be attacked, simultaneously by the Fourth Army and the Reserve Army, together with the French. The aim was to capture Morval, Guedecourt and Flers. On 12th September the 2nd Otagos took up a position near High Wood, northeast of Bazentin-le-Petit. Zero hour was 6.20 a.m. on the 15th September, and early that morning all ranks had been issued with a tot of rum (good, for morale, perhaps, and helps keep out the cold, but not the ideal drink to keep the senses alert!).

Three days later, on 18th September, William's period in the field came to an abrupt halt. The 2nd Otagos had been ordered to contribute to the attack on the enemy at Flers Trench and Flers Support near Goose Alley. During this encounter William was wounded in his head and back, after having endured 60 hours of incessant rain and mud up to his knees.

By 23rd September William was a patient at No. 1 NZGH, Brockenhurst, but his wounds were so severe that he died a week later, on 1st October 1916. His burial took place on 3rd October. Plot A, Row 5, Grave 7.

SAMUEL BENNETT

Gunner, 2/2575
New Zealand Field Artillery, 5th Battery, 2nd Brigade
Died of sickness on 6th October 1916, aged 21

Samuel Bennett was born on 3rd March 1895 at Auckland, son of Thomas and Polly. The family home was at Tirohanga, a small seaside settlement near Opotiki, Bay of Plenty. There are family members still living in the area, belonging to the Whakatohea Iwi (tribe). Samuel had younger brothers and sisters: Iris (b.1897), Victoria (b.1899), Thomas (b.1901) and Reginald (b.1904). Samuel probably attended Opotiki Primary School, but records for the first few years are lost. His siblings attended this school in 1910 and they also attended the Tirohanga School, which served a small country area and shared a teacher with Otara East School. Prior to joining the army, Samuel worked as a shipwright for J. J. Craig of Auckland.

Samuel's voluntary military service had entailed Garrison Duty at Fort Takapuna with No. 7 Company. He enlisted with the NZEF on 20th October 1915 at Trentham and departed from New Zealand with the 9th Reinforcements on 8th January 1916, disembarking at Suez on 14th February. After nearly two months training in Egypt, Samuel was at sea again, departing from Alexandria on *Eboe*, bound for France, where he joined the 5th Battery.

On 6th September Samuel fell ill with appendicitis and immediately transferred to No. 1 NZGH, Brockenhurst. He survived less than a month and died on 6th October of appendicitis and intestinal obstruction. His burial was on 9th October. Plot A, Row 4, Grave 6.

Samuel is commemorated on Opotiki War Memorial (above)

Acknowledgement: Sonia Edwards, Opotiki

ANTHONY ARROWSMITH

Private, 6/3609
2nd Battalion, Canterbury Regiment, 13th Company
Died of wounds on 21st October 1916, aged 42

Anthony Arrowsmith was born on 20th November 1873 at Milton, near Dunedin, Otago. He married Emily Latham (a widow), at Wellington on 10th March 1904. Prior to enlisting with the NZEF at Trentham on 23rd October 1915, his address was 645 Moorhouse Avenue, Christchurch and he worked for Christchurch Tramways as a labourer. Meanwhile, his wife, Emily, was living at 3 Sand Hills, Petone, near Wellington.

Sumner tram outside depot, Moorhouse Avenue, Christchurch
G-7753-1/1. ATL

Anthony departed from New Zealand with the Canterbury Infantry Battalion, No. 3 Company, 9th Reinforcements on 8th January 1916, disembarking at Suez on 8th February. A month later he was posted to the 2nd Battalion Canterbury Infantry Regiment at Moascar. He sailed for France on 7th April, and whilst there he forfeited two days pay for neglect of Government Property in losing one pair of putties, and also falling out of ranks without permission! Anthony was injured on 16th September whilst on the Somme, with gunshot wounds to his chest and shoulder and by 28th September he was at No. 1 NZGH, Brockenhurst. He died of his wounds and an aneurysm on 21st October and was buried two days later in Plot A, Row 1, Grave 10.

After the War Emily relocated to Waimata, Taihape, then c/o H. Odlin at Tomoana, Hastings.

HARRY RHOADES

Sapper, 8/3745
New Zealand Engineers, No. 3 Field Company
Died of sickness on 24th June 1918, aged 29

Harry Rhoades was born in England in Spitalfields, London, not Westcott, near Dorking, Surrey as stated on his NZEF History Sheet. (NB. He signed his attestation sheet for the NZEF stating that he was born in 1882, but the UK censuses indicate that this should be 1888). He was the fourth child of Fred (b.1846 at Coningsby, Lincoln) and Emma, née Cole (b.1847 at Hainton, Lincoln).

In 1881, Harry's father, Fred was a grocer in London, living at 6 Hanbury Street, Spitalfields with his wife and a family of three children. Harry's older siblings were Joseph (b. 1875/6), Jessie (b.1878/9) and Amy (b. 1879/80). The family was not at this address in 1891.

The Rhoades family most probably moved to Westcott, near Dorking, Surrey in 1895. Henry (Harry), born 14 December 1888 and Elsie, born 24 June 1890 were both admitted to the village school on 28th October 1895, the school register noting that their previous school was "Orby Bd". This implies that the family had either moved from London to Lincolnshire, or that the children had temporarily been living with relatives. The 1901 Census lists Fred as a retired grocer, aged 55, with his wife Emma and five children living at Orby Villa, Westcott Road with all the children shown as having been born in Spitalfields, London. Westcott Road probably refers to Guildford Road, Westcott; the main (A25) road that passes through the village

The family movements after 1901 have not been ascertained, but Westcott Local History Group archives reveal that in May 1911 "Mr. Rhoades was abroad". The appropriate authority had contacted all owners and occupants of properties that were situated within 100 yards of a proposed new burial ground, and initially Fred did not reply to the correspondence. However, later in the year his solicitors confirmed that he had been away from Westcott.

It is not known when Harry arrived in New Zealand. Prior to his enlistment with the NZEF he was employed as a carpenter for Binny at Wellington and was resident c/o Mrs. Jew of 144 Lambton Quay, Wellington.

Harry signed his attestion sheet on 29th October 1915 at Trentham, and joined the Otago Infantry Battalion with the rank of Private. Following basic military training, he was posted overseas on 8th January 1916, departing with "D" Company, 9th Reinforcements, and he arrived at Suez on 14th February. On 8th March he was given the rank of Sapper and transferred to No. 3 Field Company, New Zealand Engineers at Moascar (along with George William Haxton, 10/3592, p. 43). Both men then were posted to France on 7th April and embarked on *Alaunia* at Alexandria bound for Marseilles.

The army records state that Harry was "awarded 21 days Field Punishment No. 2 on 19th February 1917, for drunkenness". Despite this misdemeanour he did not forfeit his period of a fortnight's leave in late July, which no doubt was justly earned after more than a year in France. He fell ill with diarrhoea towards the end of August and spent a week in hospital recovering. In the middle of November he was detached to the Royal Engineers Workshop for one month and then on 15th December he rejoined No. 3 Field Company.

Harry fell ill again on 25th April 1918, suffering from trench fever. He transferred to England and was admitted to No. 1 NZGH, Brockenhurst on 13th May. At the beginning of June he was considered to be "Seriously Ill", by which time he was diagnosed as having lobar pneumonia and pernicious anaemia. He died on 24th June, and was buried two days later, with the officiating clergyman the Reverend Hutchinson.

Plot A, Row 4, Grave 16.

Harry is commemorated on a magnificent WWI War Memorial inside Holy Trinity Church at Westcott.

Holy Trinity Church, Westcott

The memorial depicts the regimental badges of the soldiers who died, which is a rare embellishment. A cross, situated in the churchyard is a further memorial to the thirty-six Westcott men who lost their lives in this War.

Sections of WW1 memorial inside Holy Trinity Church, Westcott

Harry's parents had moved back to Lincolnshire in the early 1920s, and his older sister Jessie was living at 3 Linden Road, Cranley Gardens, Muswell Hill, London in 1921. Terry Wooden from Westcott Local History Group has confirmed that the Rhoades family retained an interest in the property (Little Bay Tree Cottage, known previously as Tweenway and presumably before that as Orby Villa) until at least the 1950's, with Ralph F Rhoades listed in the 1951 Kelly's Directory.

Acknowledgement and Sources:

Terry Wooden, Westcott, Surrey
UK 1881 Census, FHL Film 1341094, PRO Ref. RG11, Piece 0434, Folio 83, Page 11
UK 1891 Census for 6 Hanbury Street, Spitalfields, London
UK 1901 Census for Westcott
Westcott Local History Group (2000) *The History of Westcott and Milton*
1951 Kelly's Directory for Surrey

CHARLES JAMES LANKEY

**Private, 24/2019
2nd Battalion, Canterbury Regiment, 10th Company
Died of wounds on 22nd October 1916, aged 38**

Charles James Lankey was born on 7th October 1878 at Masterton. When he enlisted with the NZEF, his eldest brother John of Dannevirke was named as nearest relative, and his next-of-kin was a friend Dorothy Maren Pederson of Club Hotel, Marton. Another brother, Robert of Te Waitere, Kawhia County was the designated legatee.

Charles's previous occupation was that of Bushman, employed by John D. Piper near Coonor in the Puketoi Range. He enlisted on 16th November 1915 at Trentham and during his basic military training period he suffered from influenza, like so many of his comrades and was admitted to Wairarapa hospital. He was posted overseas on 4th March 1916, departing from New Zealand with F Company, New Zealand Rifle Brigade, 4th Reinforcements. He disembarked at Suez on 10th April, and three days later embarked on *Kinfauns Castle* from Port Said, for France.

He joined the 2nd Battalion, Canterbury Infantry Regiment on 26th May at Armentières.

Charles was wounded in action on 21st September near Flers on the Somme with gunshot wounds to right leg. It was necessary for his leg to be amputated below the knee, and immediate evacuation to England was arranged for him.

He arrived at No. 1 NZGH, Brockenhurst on 28th September but died on 22nd October 1916, the cause of death stated as popliteal aneurysm (behind his knee). Charles had been in the Army less than a year. He was buried on 25th October in Plot A, Row 1, Grave 9.

Original grave marker (from Margaret Curry)

Acknowledgement:
    Margaret Curry, Dannevirke (great niece)

WILLIAM HENRY STEELE

Private, 6/4148
2nd Battalion, Auckland Regiment, "C" Company
Died of sickness on 26th April 1918, aged 27

William Henry Steele was born on 18th December 1890 at Christchurch, the youngest child of George (1843-1904) and Sarah, née Jackson (b.1853). Their family were:

William	*b. 23 Feb 1869*	*bap 22 Jan 1871*	*(mother aged 16)*
Elizabeth Ann	*b. 2 Aug 1870*	*bap 22 Jan 1871*	
James George	*b. June 1872*	*buried 9 Dec 1872 age 6 months*	
Henry Arthur	*b. 24 July 1873*	*buried 3 Feb 1874 age 6 months*	
Charlotte Mary	*b. 25 Nov 1876*	*bap 31 Dec 1876, buried 21 Oct 1885 age 8.*	
Jane	*b. 21 July 1878*		
James George	*b. 5 April 1880*	*d. 28 June 1916 2nd Bn. Canterbury Regt.*	
Charles George	*b. 5 Jan 1882*	*bap 26 Feb 1882*	
Eleanor Mary	*b. 27 May 1883*	*bap 26 Aug 1883*	
Alice Adelaide	*b.18 June 1885*	*bap 30 Aug 1885*	
Sarah Ann	*b. 20 Oct 1886*	*bap 5 Dec 1886*	
2nd Henry Arthur	*d.o.b not known*	*next-of-kin of William Henry,*	
William Henry	*b. 18 Dec 1890*	*bap 8 Feb 1891*	*(mother aged 37)*

The first William must have died prior to 1890 in order for a second William to be named. The family lived at South Town Belt, followed by Hazeldean Road, Christchurch. William's occupation was that of hotel porter at Southbridge, Canterbury, his employer named as G. H. Piper.

William enlisted with the NZEF on 18th November 1915 at Trentham. Whilst at Featherston Camp he found regulations irksome and overstayed his leave period, thus forfeiting concessions. He left New Zealand with the Canterbury Infantry Battalion, "C" Company, 11th Reinforcements on 1st April 1916, and disembarked at Suez on 3rd May. A week later he was on board ship again, bound for France where he joined the 2nd Battalion, Auckland Regiment. He contracted bronchitis in February 1918, which developed into pleurisy and was admitted to No. 1 NZGH, Brockenhurst on 3rd April. William died on the 26th from pleurisy pneumothorax. The burial took place on the 29th; officiating clergyman, the Reverend A. Aust. Plot A, Row 4, Grave 14.

The executrix of William's Will was a friend Lucy Mary Allen Of 51 Mays Road, Papanui, Christchurch, and all his property was bequeathed to her, including his medals. She married Alexander James Grant on 3rd January 1917 at Knox Church, Christchurch, and they lived at Colombo Street, Frankton Junction. Henry Arthur, William's next-of-kin, in 1921 was County Foreman, at Buckland, Auckland.

The family suffered another tragedy as a result of the War. A brother, Private James George Steele, 7/1006, 2nd Bn. Canterbury Regt. died on 28th June 1916. He is buried at the Cite Conjean Military Cemetery, Armentières, Nord, France, Ref 11.B.6.

Source: Christchurch Parish Records

# ANDREW WOODLEY

Private, 10/4218
2nd Battalion, Wellington Regiment, "B" Company
Died of wounds on 22nd September 1916, aged nearly 21

Andrew Woodley was the first NZEF serviceman to die at Brockenhurst. He was born on 19th November 1895 at Cheviot, Canterbury, the son of Albert (1869-1946) and Ann Ethel, née Neville (1871-1904).

The Woodley family had lived in West Hagbourne, Berkshire (now Oxfordshire), since at least 1672, the first known members of the family being Anthony, who married Anne that year. Their house, which was reputedly built in 1688, is still standing (2001) and called "Woodleys" (below).

Joan Snow, Andrew's niece, has told the following story of the family's emigration to New Zealand.

Three Woodley brothers, John (b. circa 1848), Caleb (b. circa 1852) and Charles (b. circa 1859) worked for the local squire. John and his family lived in Main Street, West Hagbourne, and one day when John was walking home through the orchard for lunch, he picked up a windfall apple and ate it as he carried on his way. But one of the squire's servants saw him and reported him to the squire, who at once sent for John and sacked him on the spot. John said, "OK, I'll work elsewhere". "No you won't" retorted the squire "I'll see to it", and he rode his horse in a radius of 20 miles and forbade anyone to employ John. So the three brothers made arrangements at once to set sail for New Zealand. John and Caleb were married, but Charles was only 16. John, his wife Martha, and their family of four children, Caleb and family and Charles sailed from Plymouth on the *Crusader* (photo page 6), a 1058-ton ship, departing on 25th September 1874 and arriving at Lyttelton on 31st December.

On the way the ship sprung a leak after a gale in the Bay of Biscay, and all toiled at the pumps to prevent the vessel from sinking. The leather used for the diaphragm of the pumps gave out owing to continual pumping. All reserves were used up, so a passing vessel was signalled for a fresh supply, to no avail. However, another vessel came to the rescue and provided sufficient leather, so all was not lost.

On the same ship was George Allington, executive of the National Union of Agricultural Labourers (see page 66), who was in charge of a great number of immigrants. Perhaps the Woodley family were part of this large group.

John's son, Albert, was Andrew Woodley's father. Albert was born at Woodcote, Berkshire on 10th September 1869, and was five years old when he arrived in New Zealand. In due course, he met and married Ann Ethel Neville. Albert worked as a labourer on the land and also helped to build the railway up the coast of South Island. The children kept coming, and over the years the following were born: Ethel, Albert, Cecil, Walter, Lottie, Myrtle, Millie, Andrew, Leo, and from Albert's third marriage, George.

In 1900 the whole family moved up to the North Island and settled in the Wairarapa region, and Albert worked on a dairy farm. Once again Ann was pregnant, the year 1904. She was terrified of earthquakes, and that August there was a bad one. She was paralysed with terror and it is the belief that this caused the haemorrhage for which nothing could be done in those days. She took three days to die, the children creeping around in terror. She is buried in Featherston cemetery.

The following tale, involving Andrew was related by Cecil to the latter's daughter, Joan, many years later after the event.

In 1905, a sailing vessel came to grief on the sand bar, which formed a barrier between Lake Onoke and Palliser Bay, to the southeast of Wellington. Cecil, one of the sons borrowed a rowing boat and he and Andrew, then aged nine, set out to see it. Cecil rowed down the huge Wairarapa Lake and by evening had come to the channel, which ran between it and the smaller Onoke Lake. They landed and Cecil knew a Maori who had a hut nearby. They went to his door but he was not there, so they moved in. Cecil lit the open fire and made some scones. Next morning the boys left everything as they had found it and set out once more. They made one more camp that night, then next day arrived at the sand bar and there was the "Addenda" still fairly upright. With Andrew left on the sand, Cecil scrambled up a rope and forgot Andrew. When he looked over the side "there was a tearful little face looking up". So Andrew was hauled up and the boys explored the vessel for a long while.

Then a southerly wind came in and the boys rigged a sail and this took them swiftly back, and at dark they heard the seven o'clock steam train whistle coming over the hills. So they knew the time!!

Albert moved his family further north to another dairy farm at Mangatainoka, near Pahiatua. There he met and married a "good woman" who was kind and loving to all the little motherless children. But all must not have been well as after two years she took rat poison and died in agony. The children were utterly lost, so Albert moved again, this time onto a few acres of his own at Nireaha near Eketahuna. By this time some of the older children had left home.

Once again, Albert met another Ann, a "decent little widow woman" with three children. They married and they lived on "the old farm" a poor and windswept place. Andrew had to help in the cowshed, as did his younger brothers and sisters, for which they received no remuneration.

The War came, and Andrew by now had met a girl he loved, and the story is that he told his father, Albert, he wanted to marry, and father no doubt seeing a free helper getting away, refused. "I'll go to the War then" Andrew said. He joined up, so did his brother Albert, as later did Cecil.

George, the half brother, was about four when Andrew went off to War, and he remembered the huge send off that Andrew was given with a party and music. This was held in the big loft of the farm's hay barn and George recalled seeing the piano being swung up and into the big doorway into the loft.

Andrew enlisted on 14th December 1915, and left New Zealand with the Wellington Infantry Battalion "B" Company, 11th Reinforcements on 1st April 1916 on board *Maunganui*.

Andrew Woodley (from Joan Snow, Masterton)

Whilst at sea, Andrew wrote a letter home to his sisters, Millie, Rose, and Myrtle.

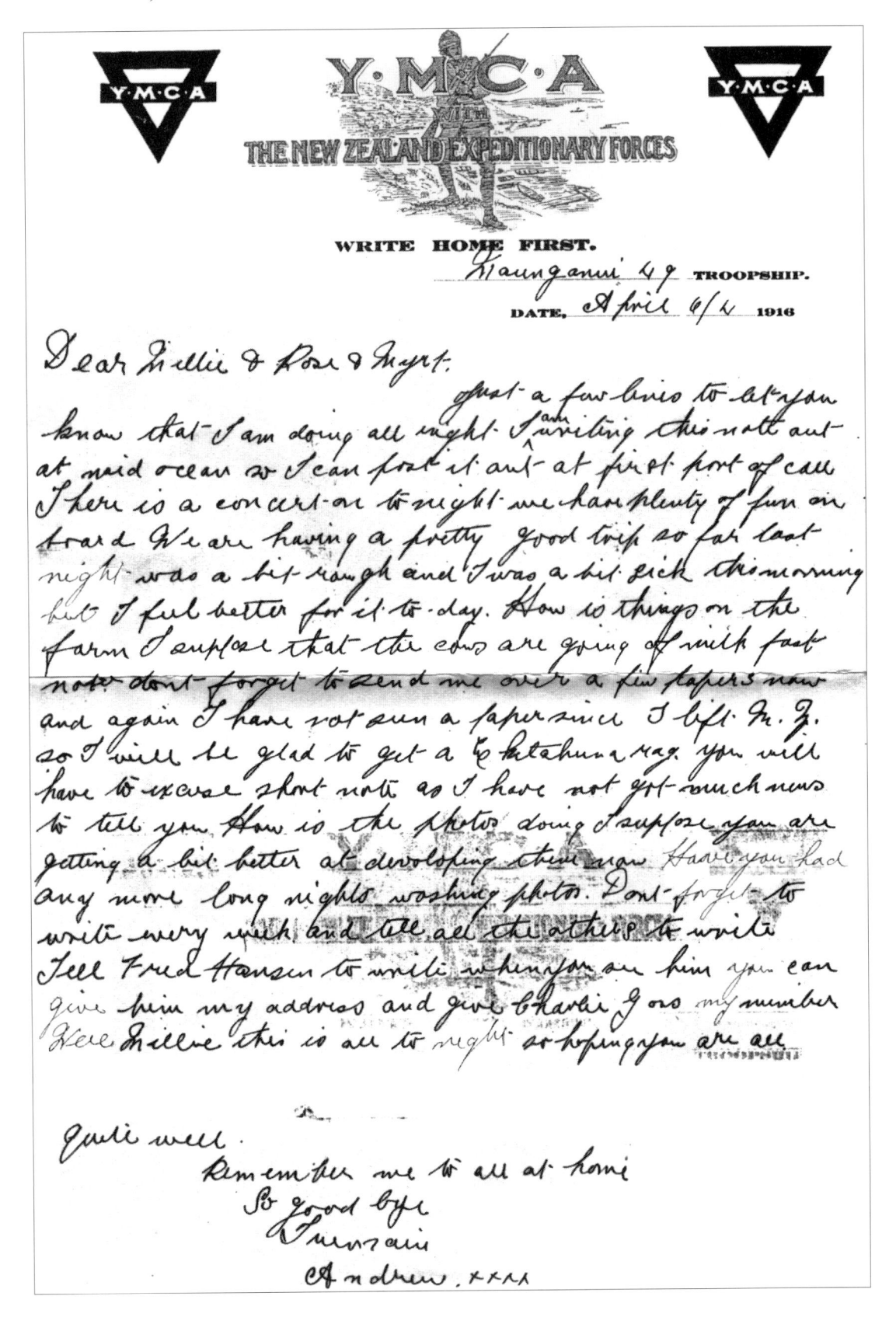

> **Y.M.C.A WITH THE NEW ZEALAND EXPEDITIONARY FORCES**
>
> WRITE HOME FIRST.
>
> Waunganui 4 9 TROOPSHIP.
>
> DATE April 6/4 1916
>
> Dear Millie & Rose & Myrt.
>
> Just a few lines to let you know that I am doing all right. I am writing this note out at mid ocean so I can post it out at first port of call. There is a concert on to-night we have plenty of fun on board. We are having a pretty good trip so far last night was a bit rough and I was a bit sick this morning but I feel better for it to-day. How is things on the farm I suppose that the cows are going off milk fast now. Dont forget to send me over a few papers now and again I have not seen a paper since I left N.Z. so I will be glad to get a Ketahuna Mag. You will have to excuse short note as I have not got much news to tell you. How is the photos doing I suppose you are getting a bit better at devoloping them now. Have you had any more long nights washing photos. Dont forget to write every week and tell all the others to write. Tell Fred Hansen to write when you see him you can give him my address and give Charlie Goss my number. Well Millie this is all to night so hoping you are all quite well.
>
> Remember me to all at home
> So good bye
> from
> Andrew. xxxx

His letter home implies that he is coping with sea life, despite suffering from seasickness. He enquires how things are on the farm, and how his sisters are

123

progressing with their photographic developing. He hasn't seen a paper since he left New Zealand so he requests the Eketahuna 'rag' to be posted to him, and asks that his friend Fred Hansen write him a letter. The wording in Andrew's letter is no doubt typical of what many of the NZEF soldiers wrote home, whilst they were on their way to the other side of the world, many of them never to return to their loved ones.

The troopship *Maunganui* arrived at Suez on 3rd May and three weeks later Andrew was at sea again, this time on the *Ivernia* bound for France. On 27th June he joined the 2nd Battalion, Wellington Regiment in preparation for the Battle of the Somme.

On 14th September, Andrew was wounded in the head, whilst near Flers. He immediately transferred to England, and arrived at No. 1 NZGH, Brockenhurst on 20th September.

He died two days later on the 22nd September, and was buried the next day.

Plot A, Row 6, Grave 5.

Andrew is commemorated on the War Memorial in the porch at Eketahuna Memorial Hall (above right). After WW1 his father, Albert, was living at 5 King Street, Lansdowne, Masterton, suggesting that he had given up the farm at Eketahuna.

Acknowledgements and Sources:

      Joan Woodley Snow, Masterton (niece)
      Richard Woodley, Chilton, Oxon, UK
      UK 1871 Census, PRO Ref. RG10, 1271, page 29
      Timms, J. H. (1925) in "Lyttelton Times", February 3rd
      West Hagbourne Village History Group (2000)
          Windsor Hakebourne: The Story of West Hagbourne

RAUKAWA HURA

Private, 16/1339
New Zealand Maori (Pioneer) Battalion
Died of sickness on 10th April 1917, aged 23

Raukawa Hura was the son Takitahi Hura and Mere Rumaki Pirihi. He was born in December 1893 at Ruataniwha, near Waipawa, Wairoa. Prior to enlisting with the NZEF he worked for Mr. McMillam at Ohinepaka Station, Tiniroa as a labourer.

Raukawa signed his attestation sheet on 16th December 1915 at Narrow Neck Camp, near Auckland. His army record indicates that even before he left New Zealand he was in trouble with the authorities on several occasions and found it difficult to obey orders. Such misdemeanours amounted to overstaying leave, drunkenness, insolence and breaking out of camp. Punishments amounted to confinement to barracks and fines.

Raukawa departed from New Zealand with the 4th Maori Contingent on 6th May 1916 and disembarked at Suez on 23rd June. After a month's stay in Egypt at Tel-el-Kebir Camp he left Alexandria on 26th July, bound for Southampton, England. He followed the usual pattern of further military training at Sling Camp on Salisbury plain before being posted to France early in September. He was attached to strength of the New Zealand Infantry at the New Zealand General Base Depot at Etaples until 27th September when he joined the Maori (Pioneer) Battalion on the Somme. The new advance on Flers with the aim of capturing Factory Corner had begun on 25th September. The Pioneers were required to construct various advanced lines of communication trenches, so on arrival Raukawa was in the midst of hard work.

On October 31st General Godley, Commander-in-Chief of the New Zealand Division inspected the Maori (Pioneer) Battalion, accompanied by Mr. Massey, Prime Minister of New Zealand, and Sir Joseph Ward.

During November the Pioneers worked on erecting barbwire entanglements, but on the 19th, Raukawa was evacuated to hospital sick, suffering from conjunctivitis. His health did not improve so it was decided to transfer him to England. He arrived at No. 1 NZGH, Brockenhurst on 3rd December, by which time he was also suffering from debility. He was a patient at Brockenhurst for four months, during which time he had developed lobar pneumonia. Raukawa died on 10th April 1917 and was buried two days later in Plot A, Row 1, Grave 3.

Two brothers also served in WW1:

Private George Hura, 16/610, departed from New Zealand with the 2nd Maori Contingent on 18th September 1915, and

Private Teo Hura, 16/1298 departed from New Zealand with the 3rd Maori Contingent on 5th February 1916.

EWEN DONALD CAMPBELL

**Sapper, 4/2060
New Zealand Engineers, No. 2 Field Company
Died of sickness on 2nd October 1918, aged 27**

Ewen Donald Campbell, born on 24th March 1891, was the third in the family of five sons of Duncan (1857-1938) and Mary, née McFadzien (1865-1921).

This branch of the Campbell family arrived in New Zealand in 1846 when Duncan's father, Duncan (senior) left Scotland for a new life on the other side of the world. His wife Sarah (née Cameron) arrived in New Zealand with her parents in 1840.

Duncan (junior) was born at Lawrence, Central Otago where his father was a schoolteacher. Upon reaching maturity, Duncan moved to Wyndham, in eastern Southland and worked with a Mr. R. A. Elliot as a builder. Later he settled in Fortrose and established his own business.

Mary and Duncan Campbell

Duncan married Mary McFadzien, and as time went by, she was kept busy caring for her sons:

Andrew James "Jim"   *(1886-1974)*
Alfred Duncan "Alf"   *(1887-1967)*
Ewen Donald   *(1891-1918)*
Colin McGregor   *(1897-1978)*
Clive Cameron   *(1898-1973)*

Ewen attended Fortrose School from 1896 until 1905.

Campbell family (l-r): James (Jim), Alfred, Clive, Colin, Duncan, Ewen

Duncan was a man of many talents. He erected his own carpentry shop, in Fortrose main street. He was the local funeral director, and he helped with making coffins for the victims of the *Tararua* shipwreck in 1881, in which 65 persons perished. He was also an insurance agent for the National Insurance Company and the South British.

Duncan Campbell's shop (from *A History of Fortrose*)

When the sons were old enough they all helped Duncan in his family business until they married and moved further away, or in Ewen's case, went to War.

Jim, the eldest son, became a photographer in Invercargill, and many of the photographs reproduced in *A History of Fortrose* were his work, as the district was very loyal to its sons and daughters. Later another son, Duncan Ewen, was born of Duncan's second marriage to Bessie Findlater. (NB. Mary had left the family home in about 1902, but in later years the boys all boarded with her while working in town as builders).

When War came, the men of Fortrose showed great enthusiasm for serving their country overseas, and altogether 21 men signed up from the township. The training camps were much in need of horses and Ewen took his horse along to sell it. The set pattern was for the Sergeant in charge of buying the horses to check the animal over, and automatically offer half of what the seller wanted. Because Ewen had trained his horse and dog to do many tricks, e.g. showing its teeth on command, he made sure that his horse performed to perfection so that the Sergeant offered him the best bargain of the day!

Ewen's dog (Toss) and Horse

Ewen enlisted with the NZEF on 17th December 1915 at Trentham, and departed overseas with the New Zealand Field Engineers, No. 1 Field Company, 11th Reinforcements on 1st April 1916. He arrived at Suez, Egypt on 2nd May and only spent a week there before he was at sea again, leaving Alexandria on board the *Caledonia* bound for Marseilles.

As mentioned by Joan Macintosh in the *A History of Fortrose*, "When overseas, Ewen's brother, Colin, went enquiring for him at his unit and no one seemed to know the name at all. So Colin said, "D'you know a Doc Campbell?" Recognition was immediate, for Ewen's old township name had followed him. He had been the Doctor in a school play and as children will, the "Doc" nickname stuck for his lifetime."

On arrival in northern France Ewen went to the base camp at Etaples before marching out to Armentières and joining No. 2 Company. His movements are next recorded on 14th April 1917 when he was slightly wounded whilst in the Messines area, and spent a few days in hospital.

In February 1918, towards the end of a harsh winter in the Ypres area, Ewen contracted dermatitis to his left leg and the medical authorities decided that he should be evacuated to England. He initially went to No. 2 NZGH, Walton-on-Thames, and from there he transferred temporarily to Hornchurch Convalescent Depot, and then to Codford, on Salisbury Plain.

Ewen was never considered fit enough to return to France and fatal illness struck him during the summer months.

He was admitted to No. 1 NZGH, Brockenhurst on 24th July, with tuberculosis of the lung. He rapidly deteriorated and died as a result of this disease on 2nd October.

Ewen was buried on 4th October 1918 in Plot A, Row 4, Grave 20. The officiating clergyman was the Reverend Hutchinson, New Zealand Chaplains Department.

Ewen had built a home in Lorn Street, Fortrose to return to after the War. Regrettably this did not happen and his brother Colin bought it off Ewen's estate.

Ewen is commemorated on Invercargill War Memorial along with many other men from this region. He is also remembered on the War Memorial in the school grounds at Fortrose. The names of 15 men who returned are recorded and also the 1914-18 THE FALLEN lists six names of which Private E. D. Campbell is one. (Note that according to the NZEF records he was a Sapper). In 1921 Ewen's medals and scroll (below) were sent to his father, Duncan at Fortrose. Mary died that year in Invercargill. Duncan lived to an old age, and died in Timaru in 1938.

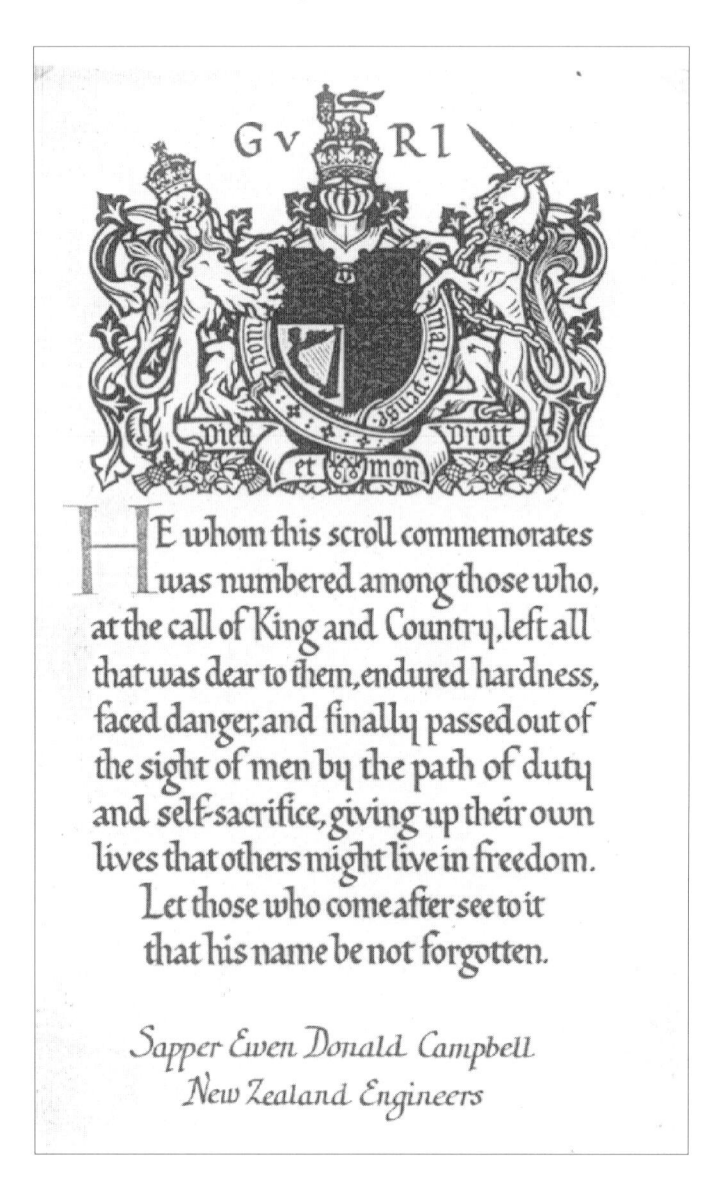

> HE whom this scroll commemorates was numbered among those who, at the call of King and Country, left all that was dear to them, endured hardness, faced danger, and finally passed out of the sight of men by the path of duty and self-sacrifice, giving up their own lives that others might live in freedom. Let those who come after see to it that his name be not forgotten.
>
> *Sapper Ewen Donald Campbell*
> *New Zealand Engineers*

Acknowledgements and Source:

  Margarita Field, née Campbell (niece, Clive's daughter), Invercargill
  – Information and family photographs
  Elizabeth Beer, Invercargill
  Macintosh, Joan (1975) *A History of Fortrose* Times Printing Service,
      Invercargill - pages 134, 136, 163, 201, 317

EDWARD PERCY MEEK

Private, 11896
1st Battalion, Wellington Regiment, "B" Company
Died of sickness on 19th February 1919, aged 35

Edward Percy Meek (known as Perce) was born on 27th May 1883 at Wellington. He was the eldest son of Edward Percy (1858-1939) and Lilian (née Remmington).

The Meek family, probably in the early 1900s
(l-r) standing: John (Jack), Perce, Dallimore (Dal)
sitting: Edward, Dorothy (Dos), Florence

Father Edward had an interesting life and the following is an extract from his Obituary published in the local press in 1939.

"The many friends of Mr. Edward Meek, L.R.I.B.A., of Khandallah, will regret to learn of his death recently, in his 82nd year, after a short illness.

The late Mr. Meek was born at Brighton, Sussex, England in 1858. At a very early age he was taken to New York, where he attended school for a time, but his parents returned to England after a year or so. The sailing vessel on which they returned caught fire on the voyage, but succeeded in reaching England without loss of life. For a time the family settled at Brighton again and Mr. Meek commenced to study architecture under his grandfather, Mr. John Dallimore, but the urge to go abroad again took possession and the family came to New Zealand in about 1875, when Mr. Meek was seventeen years of age. A few years later, in the middle eighties, he joined a small party, which proceeded to the gold fields at Kimberley, Western Australia. This proved a disastrous adventure, and the party eventually found its way back to New Zealand in a penniless condition.

Mr. Meek was articled to Mr. Toxford, architect, well known in Wellington and Wairarapa in the seventies and eighties, and eventually became a Licentiate of the Royal Institute of British Architects. In 1891 he went to Perth, Western Australia, where he was appointed architect in the Marine and Architectural Departments of the Government. Some of the time he was employed at Coolgardie during the gold rush, but when, in the middle and later nineties, great difficulties overtook the Government of Western Australia, and heavy retrenchments were made, Mr. Meek returned to New Zealand and soon found employment in the architectural branch of the New Zealand Railways, where he remained until his retirement in 1926. Among the many works in which he had a part was the erection of the Dunedin Railway Station, which took two years to build, and at which Mr. Meek was the resident supervising architect until its completion."

Dunedin Railway Station (below), built between 1904 and 1906 is in the Flemish Renaissance Style, and the entrance hall has a Royal Doulton mosaic floor.

Perce's daughter, Peggy Irvine, has provided interesting information about him. Lilian died when she was having her second baby (Doris, known as Dos), so Lilian's family then looked after Perce. His father, Edward, remarried, to Florence Hislop, a manufacturing jeweller's daughter from Dunedin, when Perce was about seven years old. From then on he lived with his father and Florence. She was very kind to Perce and he thought the world of her. In due course, Dallimore (Dal) and John (Jack) were born.

Perce was educated in Wellington and later worked for the engineering firm of Cables. He then went out into the country at about the age of 25 and worked in a creamery at Paraparaumu.

He first met his wife, Annie Winnifred Cornor (known as Win), when she was sixteen and went home and told Florence he had met the girl he was going to marry. When he told her who it was, her reply was, "I think you had better wait until she grows up". Four years later, on 14th May 1913 he did marry her at the Anglican Church, Paraparaumu, the ceremony officiated by the Reverend Edwin Jones – she was 20 and he was 30.

Perce and Win on their Wedding Day

Their first child Winifred Mary Isabel (known as Peggy) was born on 22nd September 1914. Peggy recalls that Win said that Percy was a very bright and happy person, full of fun and he always came in with a smile and a loving greeting. He had a very pleasant singing voice and sometimes sang in local concerts. Win was an excellent pianist so was able to accompany him.

In 1915 Perce, Win and Peggy moved to Piopio where Perce was the manager of the creamery at Paraparaumu in charge of the butter making.

He enlisted with the NZEF on 10th January 1916, and departed overseas at the beginning of May. At that time, Win moved back to her parents' farm near Paraparaumu and their second child, Percy Robert (known as Bob) was born there on 12th January 1917.

Win Meek and her two children Peggy and Bob
(with inset of Perce)

Perce left Wellington with the Wellington Infantry Battalion, "B" Company, 12th Reinforcements, (First Draft) on HMNZT *Ulimaroa*.

Perce's granddaughters have chosen a page from his diary (below), written shortly after his departure from New Zealand. His mention on 2nd May to the "signal with the window blind" would refer to the fact that when the ship was leaving Wellington Harbour, he would have been able to look up and see his parents' house on the hillside in Khandallah. Perhaps he had a premonition that he would never return to his homeland to view this scene again? One will never know.

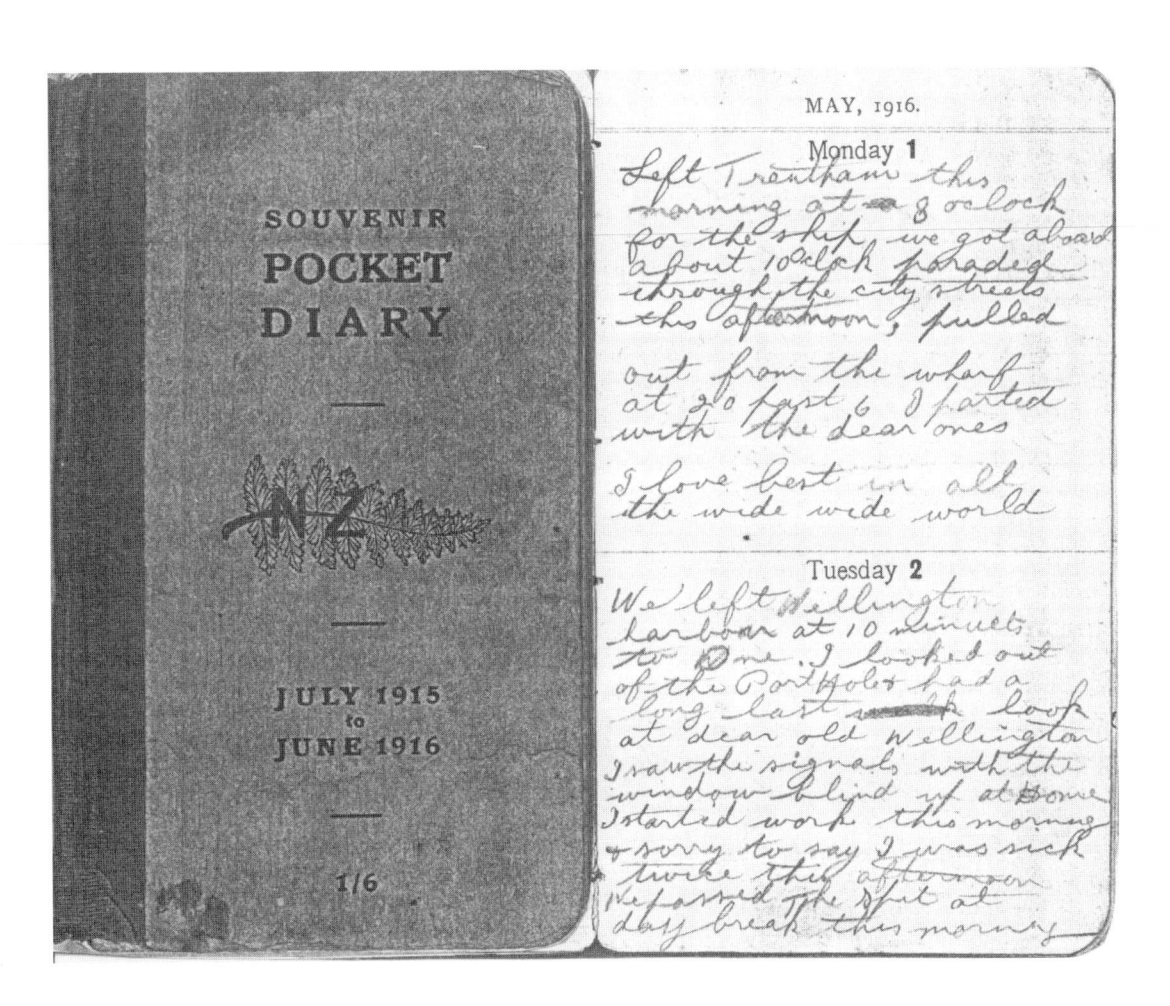

Suez was reached on 9th June, and after a few weeks of further training in Egypt, Perce was on his way again, this time embarking on HMNZT *Ivernia* at Alexandria, bound for Southampton on the south coast of England. Sling Camp was not far away, and Perce found himself training there until 5th September when he was posted to France. He joined the 1st Battalion, Wellington Regiment in the Field on 30th September at Mametz Wood on the Somme.

During his military life Perce moved around considerably. He was based at the reinforcement camp at Morbeque in June 1917, was awarded "Blighty" leave in the United Kingdom in October, and trained to become a Batman in May 1918. On 4th October that year, whilst in the Crèvecoeur area near the Scheldt Canal, he was wounded accidentally in his right leg. The injury resulted in his evacuation to England and admission to Southwark Military Hospital, London on 12th October.

Perce transferred to No. 1 NZGH, Brockenhurst on 20th December. His injury was not the cause of his death, but the conditions under which he was living when he received it no doubt contributed to the development of phthisis pulmonalis (tuberculosis of the lung). He died on 19th February 1919 from this disease.

Perce was the penultimate NZEF soldier to die at Brockenhurst.

He was buried on 21st February, the ceremony conducted by the Reverend A. J. Jacob.

Plot A, Row 3, Grave 22.

Peggy Irvine has described that her mother, Win, learned of Perce's death in a very tragic manner. One day she was driving home from an outing and called into the little local Post Office to arrange for some money to be sent to him in Brockenhurst, and the Postmistress, who must have been a very callous women, replied,

"Oh you can't sent money to your husband Mrs. Meek, he is dead".

It is a wonder Win ever recovered from the shock. She was faithful to his memory and never married again.

Acknowledgements:

    Peggy Irvine, Te Puke (daughter)
    Margaret Downey, Auckland (granddaughter)
    Janet Rochfort, Auckland (granddaughter) – diary extract
    John Irvine, Wainuiomata (grandson) - photographs

ERNEST GUY GIBLIN

Sapper, 12032
New Zealand Engineers, No. 2 Field Company
Died of wounds on 3rd October 1916, aged 23

Ernest Guy Giblin was the second of seven sons of David and Mary Phoebe (née Taylor). David's parents, Frederick (1819-1881) and Mary Ann (1829-1912), came from the Cambridge area of England. Shortly after their marriage in 1850, Frederick and Mary Ann emigrated to New Zealand on board the *Mariner* with Frederick's mother, Elizabeth (a widow) and two of her sons, Daniel and William, leaving behind other members of her family.

The Giblins arrived in New Zealand in September 1850 and settled at Stoke, Nelson. Frederick was very much involved with the original Building Committee for St. Barnabas Church at Stoke, which was completed in August 1866. He was responsible for the carting of the stones from Marsden Valley, situated nearby, to the building site.

St. Barnabas Church, Stoke, Nelson with grave of
Frederick and Mary Ann Giblin (right hand)

David was the youngest son of Frederick and Mary Ann, and he married Mary Phoebe on 11th September 1890 at Richmond, nearby. Just over two years later, on 10th December 1892, their second son, Guy, was born. David, with his brother Thomas, owned orchards, and were two of the earliest fruit growers in Stoke.

Four of the seven Giblin brothers served overseas in WW1:

Louis Hubert	born 1896	fought at Passchendaele
Maurice		wounded France
<u>Guy</u>	(1892-1916)	wounded on the Somme
Wilfred	(Dorothy Giblin's father)	wounded Gallipoli and invalided back to New Zealand before finally being discharged

(l-r): Louis Hubert, Maurice, Guy and Wilfred (from Dorothy Giblin, Nelson)

Guy attended Stoke Primary School, which then had about 50 pupils on the school roll. At that time Stoke, situated approximately 4 ½ miles from the town of Nelson, was just a small rural township. Along with his brothers he spent many hours tramping and shooting in the hills behind Stoke. The boys were also keen cricket and hockey players. Prior to joining the army, Guy was employed as a carpenter by Mr. W. E. Wilkes of Richmond, a building firm that is still in operation in the 21st century.

He enlisted with the NZEF on 11th January 1916 at Trentham, and was placed in the 12th Reinforcements of the New Zealand Engineers, No. 2 Field Company. On 1st May the Company embarked at Wellington on HMNZT *Ulimaroa* for Suez, and disembarked on 9th June. Shortly after arrival in Egypt, Guy embarked on the *Ivernia* at Alexandria, and the ship docked at Southampton, England on 7th August. He was posted to Sling Camp for 10 days before transferring to France.

Guy's period on the Western Front was very brief because on 10th September, whilst on the Somme, he received gunshot wounds to his back and a fractured spine. He had been involved in the laying of a railway line from Longueval to Delville Wood for the purpose of running up shells for the heavy artillery, and he received his injuries during this operation.

Guy transferred to No. 1 NZGH, Brockenhurst on 29th September. He never recovered from his injuries and died on 3rd October 1916 with his burial two days later. Plot A, Row 5, Grave 6.

One of Guy's younger brothers once visited the graves at Brockenhurst, according to his niece Dorothy.

Guy's mother, Mary Phoebe died on 24th November 1934, aged 64 years, and father David died on 22nd September 1956 in his 94th year. At the time of his death he was the oldest Stoke born resident. They are buried in Richmond Cemetery, Nelson.

Guy is commemorated on the war memorial gates at Stoke (below) along with fellow men from his home township.

Guy (from Dorothy Giblin, Nelson)

REMEMBER AND HONOUR

A.E. CRESSWELL
L.C. CHING
S.G. DAVIS
E.G. GIBLIN
H.B. JELLYMAN
L.F. SMITH
W.S. BOVEY

Acknowledgement and Source:
    Dorothy Giblin, Nelson (niece)
    Nelson Evening Mail, 28th Sept. 1956

THOMAS CHARLES ADAMS

Private, 11589
2nd Battalion, Canterbury Regiment, 2nd Company
Died of wounds on 7th February 1917, aged 36

Thomas Charles Adams was born on 15th March 1880 at Shirley, Canterbury (north of Christchurch), the son of farmers Thomas and Isabella, née Kelly (1864-1935). Other members of the family were an elder brother, William Alexander, and two sisters, Jane (married Adam Reid in 1910), and Margretta.

Prior to enlisting with the NZEF Thomas (junior) was living at Radcliffe Road, Belfast, Canterbury, with his parents. He was employed as a wool sorter for William Nicholls at the Kaputone Wool Works, Belfast. His work would have involved spreading the sheep's wool on the ground to dry in the sun before it was bundled into bales for transportation elsewhere.

Men working with large bundles of wool in a field at
William Nicholls' Woolscour, Kaputone, Belfast.
G-3945-1/1. Steffano Webb Collection (PA Coll-3061). ATL

Thomas signed his attestation sheet for the NZEF at Trentham on 12th January 1916. He departed from New Zealand with the Canterbury Infantry Battalion "C" Company, 12th Reinforcements (first draft) on 1st May 1916 on board *Ulimaroa*, disembarking at Suez on 9th June.

The 26th July saw him on the *Ivernia* at Alexandria, bound for England and Southampton. The ship docked on 7th August and Thomas marched into Sling Camp where he joined the 2nd Canterbury Company. He left for France on 20th August and joined the 2nd Battalion, Canterbury Regiment on 1st September, which was preparing for fighting on the Somme.

Thomas survived the Somme battle but was injured on 2nd January 1917 whilst on the Lys, near Armentières. He was wounded the day after the 2nd Canterbury Battalion returned to the line, receiving gunshot wounds to his left thigh. It was necessary for his left leg to be amputated and he remained at No. 1 Australian Casualty Clearing Station for over three weeks before transfer to a stationary hospital at Wimereux on 29th January.

The next day Thomas embarked on a hospital ship, destination Southampton, and was admitted to No. 1 NZGH, Brockenhurst on 1st February. His injuries proved to be fatal and he died on 7th February 1917.

He was buried the next day in Plot A, Row 1, Grave 4.

Isabella, Thomas's mother, died in 1935 at the age of 71 and was buried on 3rd July in Sydenham Cemetery. Just prior to her death she lived at Wordsworth Street, Christchurch.

Acknowledgement and Source:

    Evelyn Robertson, Christchurch (cousin)
    Christchurch Parish Records, Burial Register SSS-1

GEORGE HURRELL

Gunner, 10603
New Zealand Field Artillery, Divisional Ammunition Column
Died of sickness on 2nd December 1918, aged 23

George Hurrell, born on 1st April 1895, was a Tongan, the son of James of Haapai, Tonga, Friendly Islands. George lived c/o Mrs. Phelan at Great North Road, Grey Lynn, Auckland, and worked as a boat builder for Charles Bailey (Junior), who also employed Private Frank Clark, 12/2183, 2nd Battalion, Auckland Regiment (p. 42). Charles's father established this ship, yacht and boat building business in 1870.

View of Auckland Waterfront with C. Bailey (Junior) boatyard
Auckland City Libraries (N.Z.).   Ref. W.1524

George enlisted with the NZEF on 12th January 1916 at Trentham, and departed from New Zealand with the NZFA, No. 6 Howitzer Battery, 12th Reinforcements (Second Draft) on 6th May. After a spell in Egypt he arrived in England on 7th August, marched into Sling Camp and was taken on as a Gunner. During the last week in September he proceeded overseas to France, and in October he was posted to the Divisional Ammunition Column.

His army records are scant and nothing is known of his movements until 13th July 1918 when, whilst serving in France, he fell ill with influenza. This developed into pleurisy with effusion so he was admitted to No. 1 NZGH on 3rd August. George never recovered and died of tuberculosis of the lung on 2nd December. His burial took place on 5th December. Plot A, Row 2, Grave 21.

Source: Cyclopedia of New Zealand, Auckland District (1902)
           re Bailey's boatyard

JOHN GEOFFREY

Rifleman, 13000
3rd Battalion, 3rd New Zealand Rifle Brigade, "A" Company
Died of Sickness on 17th June 1917, aged 32

John Geoffrey was born on 11th June 1885 at Wedderburn, Otago, the son of Dominick (1843-1920) and Johannah, née Hanrahan (1852-1912). Dominick came from Messina, Sicily. He arrived in New Zealand when he was a young lad and joined the gold seekers of Central Otago. Johannah's roots were in County Cork in Ireland. The couple were married on 8th June 1879 at Omakau Roman Catholic Church, Otago, and Dominick was granted New Zealand citizenship on 8th August 1883. They settled in Wedderburn and raised a family of two boys, Joseph and John, and two girls, Kate and Margaret.

Prior to 1900 the family ran a hotel at Eden Creek. The Cobb and Company coaches that had a service from Dunedin through Central Otago to the gold mining town of Cromwell used to break their journey for an overnight stop at Geoffrey's Hotel. It was the job of the two young lads, Joseph and John to feed, groom and stable the team horses from the coaches and have them ready the next morning to continue the journey. Although the photograph (below) was taken at Roxborough, the scene is typical of the circumstances outside Geoffrey's Hotel. This particular coach was carrying gold, which required an escort of policemen and Bank of New Zealand staff.

Gold escort, Roxburgh, Central Otago.
Making New Zealand Collection. F-1736-1/2-MNZ. ATL

In 1900 Dominick was listed as a farmer at Wedderburn, so it is presumed that the family had left the hotel by then. Sister Mary Basil O.P. (a niece of John Geoffrey) states that the family bought land on which they built their house and developed a sheep and cattle farm. Johannah died on 8th September 1912, aged 60 years.

John was a self-employed farmer when he enlisted with the NZEF at Trentham on 13th January 1916. He departed overseas on the *Navua* with the 3rd Reinforcements to the 4th Battalion, "H" Company, New Zealand Rifle Brigade on 6th May 1916. The troops disembarked at Suez on 22nd June, and after a month spent in Egypt John embarked on the *Ivernia* at Alexandria. On arrival at Southampton, England on 7th August he was then posted to "C" Company and based at Sling Camp. Here he undertook a Signallers course and passed the examination, being graded a 1st Class Signaller. He left for France on 7th January 1917 with the 5th Reserves Battalion, 3rd New Zealand Rifle Brigade. A month later he joined the 3rd Battalion, and was posted to "A" Company.

In June he fell sick suffering from acute lymphatic leukaemia and immediately transferred to England and No. 1 NZGH, Brockenhurst. He died on 17th June and was buried two days later in Plot A, Row 2, Grave 4.

His older brother, Joseph, later ran the farm at Wedderburn. One of the girls, Margaret (Maggie) by 1916 was married to a Mr. Smith, and living at Glenledi, via Milton, Otago. Later she lived at 196 Melbourne Street, South Dunedin.

John is commemorated on the Geoffrey family grave (right) at Ranfurly, Otago. Sadly the lettering is much worn, but the names can just be recognised.

In 2001, Gerrard Geoffrey, great-grandson of Dominick, owned the farm at Wedderburn.

Acknowledgement and Source:

Sister Mary Basil O.P.
(Mary Teresa Geoffrey)

List of persons naturalised in New Zealand, pre 1948
(File No. 1883/3346,
Cert. Register 16, page 102)

WILLIAM HOLT

Private, 11167
2nd Battalion, Otago Regiment, 14th Company
Died of sickness on 16th October 1918, aged 24

William Holt was born on 27th August 1894 at Lake Dunstan, near Clyde, Otago, the son of William John (1866-1914) and Christiana, née Raper (1868-1927). Christiana's parents were Francis Raper and Hannah (née Foulstone) from near Doncaster, Yorkshire. In 1874 Christiana, her parents and two sisters arrived in New Zealand on board the *Atrato*. William (junior) came from a large family and had 5 sisters and 2 brothers (possibly 3). His siblings were Thomas?, Ellen, Christiana, Emmy, Julia, John, Annie, and James.

William worked as a draper at Hallensteins, the store in Dunedin, which at that time sold mainly men's and boys' wear. Bendix Hallenstein (1835-1905), the founder of the retail "empire" had his roots in Germany, and had arrived in New Zealand in 1863, via Australia.

Exterior of Hallenstein Bros. Ltd. building, Dunedin in 2001

Hallenstein opened his first store in Invercargill in 1863, which was not successful so he moved to Queenstown to try his luck there. In a short while he established other shops in neighbouring towns. Owing to the difficulty in stocking his stores (especially with men's clothing) due to irregular shipments of goods from Britain, he decided to manufacture his own clothes. The first factory was set up in Dunedin in 1873, with the obvious consequence that he established a store in the town. The retail store in the Octagon, Dunedin originally consisted of three shops with offices above. Over the years the Hallenstein "empire" expanded and by 1900 there were 34 shops throughout New Zealand. After Bendix's death in 1905 a limited company was formed known as Hallenstein Bros. Ltd. The present building was erected in 1913.

When William enlisted with the NZEF on 13th January 1916 at Trentham, his father was deceased and his mother, Christiana, lived at Prendergast Street, South Dunedin. He departed from New Zealand on 1st May, embarking on the *Ulimaroa* at Wellington with the Otago Infantry Battalion, "D" Company, 12th Reinforcements (First Draft). The ship reached Suez on 9th June, and after a brief spell in Egypt, William was on board ship again, this time on the *Ivernia* from Alexandria to Southampton, England, disembarking on 7th August. Training at Sling Camp followed, during which time William was appointed Acting Corporal.

He left for France on 28th August and three weeks later he joined the 2nd Battalion, Otago Regiment, 14th Company near Flers on the Somme, the same day as Private William Healey, 11279, 2nd Battalion, Otago Regiment (p. 147).

Christiana and William Holt
(from Lynette Walsh, Dunedin)

By mid November William's health was failing, to the point of requiring hospitalisation to cure enteritis. He did not recover, however, because on 3rd December he was admitted as a patient at No. 1 NZGH, Brockenhurst. His army records state that when he was assessed as fit on 28th January 1917, he was employed at the hospital (capacity not known) on and off for the rest of his service. However, during this period he was often a patient himself, suffering from pleurisy, hammertoes, and influenza, which developed into bronchial pneumonia.

William died of this latter disease on 16th October 1918, and was buried two days later in Plot A, Row 1, Grave 20. The officiating clergyman was The Reverend Jacob.

Acknowledgements:

      Terry Holt, Caversham, Dunedin (nephew)
      Lynette Walsh, Dunedin (cousin)
      Estelle Longstaffe, Dunedin

WILLIAM HEALEY

Private, 11279
2nd Battalion, Otago Regiment, 4th Company
Died of sickness on 18th March 1918, aged 30

William Healey, born on 21st November 1887, was the oldest of eight children of John and Christina, of Dipton, a farming area 37 miles north of Invercargill. His siblings were Annie (b.1889), Dennis (b.1890), Thomas (b.1891), Henry (b.1893), David, Magnus (b.1896) and Christina Martha (b.1900). Their parents were pioneer settlers at Dipton where the family were farming from the 1880s until 1941. John Healey owned a property south of the School Lane and also had a property on the hills of 260 acres. In 1891 John was listed as a Carrier and when the Dipton dairy factory opened in October 1894 he was the first supplier of two cans of milk. Many of the farmers had small herds of less than twelve cows that were milked by hand, and the milk was taken to the dairy factory where there were two vats for cheese making.

John Healey was one of Dipton's characters and he took many of his arguments to court, without success. Court officials used to try and discourage him but to no avail. On one occasion while riding into Dipton a local farmer encountered John who had had more than enough to drink and was beating his wife. Jumping off his horse the farmer went to the assistance of the lady, whereupon both set upon him and he was glad to remount in haste and escape! William's education began on 14th July 1893 at Dipton School and it is likely that was where he received all his primary schooling. For the celebrations of King Edward VII Coronation the Healey boys helped the Superintendent of the Presbyterian Sunday School to build a bonfire. Being the oldest child, it is likely that he began farming work in his very early teens.

Prior to his enlistment with the NZEF, William worked for Mr. P. Begg of Woodlaw as a labourer. He signed his Attestation Sheet on 14th January 1916 and left New Zealand from Wellington on 1st May 1916 with the Otago Infantry Battalion, "D" Company, 12th Reinforcements (First Draft) on board the *Ulimaroa*. [His comrade William Holt, 11167 (p. 145) was also on this posting].

After reaching England, the two Williams trained together at Sling Camp until 20th August when William Healey left for France. William Holt joined him a week later at Etaples, and they both were assigned to the 2nd Battalion, Otago Regiment on the Somme on 22nd September and were among a group of welcome reinforcements, amounting to 8 officers and 140 other ranks. On 24th September the Battalion took up its quarters at Carlton Trench for the task of attempting to capture Gird Trench and also to take over the village of Guedecourt.

Whilst in France, William spent two periods with other regimental companies. In mid March 1917 he was attached to the 3rd Canadian Tunnelling Company, then on 4th June he transferred temporarily to No. 1 Field Company of the New Zealand Engineers. Eventually he rejoined the 2nd Battalion, Otago Regiment at the end of June. By October he had earned a two-week period of "Blighty" leave in the United Kingdom.

William rejoined his Battalion on 19th October, and a few days later undertook a fortnight's training near Lumbres. He then proceeded to Ypres, and on 16th November the command of the whole Divisional Front passed to the New Zealanders. Divisional Headquarters were established at Chateau Segard, two miles southwest of the town. The winter of 1917/18 proved fatal for William as he fell sick on 11th January 1918, suffering from bronchitis. On January 8th the 2nd Battalion, Otago Regiment had taken over the Reutel sector, immediately east of Polygon Wood. The weather was atrocious, with heavy snow, and the trenches were in a terrible condition, either flooded or fallen in. No wonder William and many others succumbed to illness.

William was classified as seriously ill so he immediately transferred to England and was admitted to No. 1 NZGH, Brockenhurst on 25th January. By now his bronchitis had developed into tuberculosis of the lung. He survived barely two months longer and died on 18th March 1918. He was buried two days later in Plot A, Row 3, Grave 4, officiated by the Reverend Hutchinson.

William is listed on the War Memorial outside Dipton Memorial Hall (right). Three of his brothers, T. Healey, H. Healey and D. P. Healey are mentioned as "served faithfully" on a different plaque, which implies that they survived the War.

William's next-of-kin was named as Mrs. Charlotte Walker of Dipton.

Acknowledgement and Sources:

    Elizabeth Beer, Invercargill
    Milligan, D (1977) *"Moonlight Ranges" The Story of Dipton 1877-1977*
        The Dipton Centennial Committee
    Southland Branch of the New Zealand Society of Genealogists
        (School Records)

JAMES ERNEST CLIFF

Lance Corporal, 17697
1st Battalion, Wellington Regiment, 9th Company
Died of sickness on 7th July 1918, aged 31

James Ernest Cliff was a son of farmers Richard (1847-1897) and Elizabeth, née Sykes (1858-1947). Richard and Elizabeth were married on 26th February 1878 at Kaipara, Auckland and James was born on 1st January 1887 at Paparoa, Otamatea.

Five other children have been identified: Fanny Louisa (1879-1888), Bertha Arnold (1880-1888), Mary (1885-1888), Ina (1894-1925) and Richard Leonard. When James was one year old in 1888, fatal illness struck the family, because three sisters died within one week in April 1888. James was admitted to Paparoa School (Register No. 38) on 4th April 1892. Richard (senior) died in 1897, so Elizabeth was left to tend the family farm on her own.

Like his parents, James was a farmer; he worked for Mr. William Alison at Titoki, Whangarei. He enlisted with the NZEF at Trentham on 7th February 1916. In May he transferred to Featherston camp but immediately absented himself without permission for three months. He was apprehended in August and punished by forfeiting 90 days pay. He therefore remained in New Zealand for a longer period than the average recruit and was not posted overseas until eight months after joining the army. Despite his misdemeanour he was promoted to Lance Corporal shortly before leaving New Zealand. He embarked at Wellington on board *Tofua* on 11th October with the 12th Reinforcements to the 1st Battalion "E" Company of New Zealand Rifle Brigade and reached Plymouth, England on 29th December.

James went immediately to Sling Camp and was posted to 1st Wellington Company. After six weeks in England he was sent to France on 11th February 1917 and joined the 1st Battalion, Wellington Regiment in mid March where the troops were billeted at Pont de Nieppe, near Armentières. Later in the month the Battalion was inspected by Brigadier-General C. H. J. Brown, D.S.O, Commanding, 1st New Zealand Infantry Brigade.

In December 1917 James was detached to the II Anzac Lewis Gun School for training in the handling of these weapons. He was awarded leave in the United Kingdom at the end of the course.

James fell ill with influenza towards the end of June 1918, and was sent to hospital in France. He did not recover quickly so it was decided to transfer him to England for further treatment. He never reached England, because he died of pneumonia on board H.S. *Grantully Castle* on 7th July 1918. His body was taken to Brockenhurst, where he was buried on 10th July. Plot A, Row 4, Grave 17.

After the War James's mother, Elizabeth moved to live at 141 Crummer Street, Grey Lynn, Auckland. All children except Richard Leonard are commemorated on the family grave at Paparoa Methodist Cemetery.

HUGH O'CONNOR

Private, 24215
1st Battalion, Canterbury Regiment, 2nd Company
Died of sickness on 6th January 1917, aged 26

Hugh was born at Geraldine, South Canterbury on 7th October 1890, the son of Eugene O'Connor. Before joining up Hugh worked for a J. O'Connor, at Temuka (presumably a family member) as a farm labourer. Eugene was also living in this area in 1916.

Hugh's time with the NZEF lasted less than a year. He enlisted on 10th February 1916 at Trentham, and left New Zealand with the Canterbury Infantry Battalion, "C" Company, 13th Reinforcements on 27th May. Even by this time his health was failing; his Statement of Services states he disembarked at Devonport on 26th July sick. Despite this, he was sent to Sling Camp for further training, and left for France a month later, on 28th August.

After a month at the army base camp at Etaples Hugh joined the 1st Battalion, Canterbury Regiment near Flers on 22nd September. His active service was brief. In the middle of October he caught dysentery and spent three weeks at the British Isolation Hospital at Bailleul. After several weeks receiving medical attention in France, his condition deteriorated and he developed empyema. Immediate transfer to England took place and he arrived at No. 1 NZGH, Brockenhurst on 12th December.

Regrettably Hugh's illness was beyond recovery and he died on 6th January 1917 as a result of acute nephritis and pleurisy.

Fanny Speedy, one of the nursing sisters, wrote in her diary "A sad death in the Ward this morning, quite a young man O'Connor, came to us from France two or three weeks ago had had 2 or 3 complaints at the same time and has never made any headway. A very good patient and a general favourite in the Ward."

Hugh was buried on 8th January. Plot A, Row 3, Grave 9.

He is commemorated at St. Joseph's Church, Wilkin Street, Temuka, alongside several other O'Connors. Surprisingly, his name is not on the Temuka War Memorial. The reason may be because after the War his father, Eugene, had moved from Temuka to 66 College Road, Timaru.

Source: Fanny Hakna Speedy Diaries, MS-Papers-1703,
           Alexander Turnbull Library, National Library of New Zealand,
           Te Puna Matauranga o Aotearoa

FRED HALLETT BROWN

Private, 13406
1st Battalion, Canterbury Regiment, 1st Company
Died of wounds on 16th October 1917, aged 22

Fred Hallett Brown was born on 4th February 1895 at Christchurch. His parents John and Annie lived at 133 West Belt, Lower Riccarton, Christchurch. Fred's occupation prior to joining the NZEF was that of carpenter for William Stephens. He enlisted on 11th February 1916 at Featherston (below).

Featherston Military Camp (circa 1915) F-008217-1. ATL

Fred left New Zealand with the Otago Infantry Battalion, "J" Company, 13th Reinforcements on 27th May on board HMNZT No. 55 *Tofua*. After arrival at Plymouth, Devon on 27th July he proceeded to Sling Camp.

He was posted to France on 16th November and marched out to "C" Division at the beginning of December and joined the 1st Battalion, Canterbury Regiment in the Lys valley. During December and January he twice absented himself from Tattoo Roll Call so was confined to barracks for 7 days and forfeited 7 days' pay.

There are no details of his movements until 12th October 1917 when Fred was wounded in the 3rd Battle of Ypres (Passchendaele). He received gunshot wounds to his abdomen and transferred to No. 1 NZGH, Brockenhurst on 15th October. He died the next day and was buried on 18th October.

Plot A, Row 5, Grave 4.

PERCY LAWRENCE WILLIAMS

Corporal, 20271
3rd Battalion, 3rd New Zealand Rifle Brigade, "D" Company
Died of wounds on 19th August 1918, aged 22

Percy Lawrence Williams was the son of Charles Henry (1865-1945) and Mary Ann, née Blatchford (1866-1956). Charles's parents were William John (an occasional carpenter) and Catherine Jane (née Andrews). Charles Henry married Mary Ann (nicknamed Dolly) on 26th April 1891 at the Congregational Church, The Terrace, Wellington. They had six children

Cyril Ernest   b. 21 February 1892
Percy Lawrence   b. 9 October 1895
Eric Robin   b. 24 November 1899
Jessie   b. 8 July 1901
Martin Juffs   b. 20 May 1905
Myra (or Marion)   b. 3 September 1906

The family lived in Campbell Street, Karori, Wellington.

The Williams' house at Campbell Street, Karori, Wellington

(l-r): Unknown, Charles (father), Cyril, Mary Ann (mother), Jessie and Percy.

Percy attended Karori Primary School. Then in 1913 the family moved to Kaitoke, to farm 600 acres near the main highway from Upper Hutt to Featherston, and he worked as a farm hand for his father. Their new house was two-storeyed, but is no longer standing, as it was demolished when the road was upgraded in later years.

Whilst the family were living at Kaitoke the brothers often went tramping in the Tararua Forest to Otaki, hunting for deer and pigs. Later, whilst Percy was in France with the NZEF he wrote home saying he disliked shooting because he was being ordered to kill people (Fritz) rather than pigs.

CORP. P. L. WILLIAMS, of Kaitoke.

Percy enlisted with the NZEF on 30th April 1916 at Trentham, and departed from New Zealand with the 10th Reinforcements to the 2nd Battalion, NZRB, "F" Company. He embarked on HMNZT 61 *Aparima,* which sailed on 19th August from Wellington. The ship arrived at Devonport on 25th October and Percy marched into Sling Camp. He was not long there, however, for on 15th November he was posted to France. Eventually he joined his Battalion in the field on 7th December, on the River Lys.

Nothing further is recorded until nearly a year later, when on 29th November 1917 Percy was promoted to Corporal. He was granted a period of leave in the United Kingdom when he visited relatives in Edinburgh.

On return to France at the end of January 1918, Percy rejoined his unit. Then on 13th March he was sent to the Corps Bombing School for a fortnight's instruction. At the beginning of April he marched into camp at Abeele for one week, prior to returning to the Front in the Upper Ancre valley. He remained in the Field until 26th July, when he was wounded in action, receiving gunshot wounds to his right arm, legs and buttocks.

Evacuation to England immediately took place, and Percy arrived at No. 1 NZGH on 8th August. The operation on his wounds was successful but shortly afterwards he developed lobar pneumonia and died on 19th August 1918. His burial ceremony was officiated by the Reverend A. J. Jacob, on 21st August.

Plot A, Row 2, Grave 18.

Percy's older brother, Cyril, also enlisted with the NZEF, and the brothers ensured they went into the same unit. In the event this was unwise, and the practice was discouraged in WW2 as too many families lost all their sons in WW1.

Cyril Ernest Williams, Lance-Corporal, 20269, 3rd Battalion, 3rd NZRB was killed in France the same week that Percy died in Brockenhurst. Cyril died at No. 56 Casualty Clearing Station on 23rd August 1918 and was buried at the Bagneux British Cemetery, Gezaincourt, Somme. Grave reference: IV.D.29.

The "boys" parents retained each letter and postcard that was sent from France and Britain, which have been handed down to the present Williams generation via the youngest brother, Martin (1905-1988).

L.-CORP. C. E. WILLIAMS,
of Kaitoke.
Died of wounds.

Amongst the archives are bereavement cards written by their father, Charles with the following wording:

> *He died that we might live in peace*
> *He fought for freedom, not for fame,*
> *Yet on New Zealand's Roll of Honour*
> *Stands inscribed our hero's name.*

Glenn Williams, the great nephew of Percy and Cyril, and grandson of Eric, relates that his grandfather never spoke about the two brothers being killed. No doubt this was because the family tragedy was too traumatic to mention.

The two brothers are commemorated in several locations:

On the Roll of Honour at the Returned Services Association building at Karori, Wellington

At Upper Hutt, on a memorial at St. John's Anglican Church, Trentham Road (opposite the Primary School), and

Karori Cemetery memorial

Acknowledgements: Roberta Cooper, Auckland (information and photographs)
Glenn Williams, New Plymouth (great nephew)

WILLIAM JAMES MOGG

Private, 26129
New Zealand Machine Gun Battalion, "A" Company
Died of wounds on 16th September 1918, aged 29

William James Mogg's parents lived in Warwickshire, England. Although the Commonwealth War Graves Commission (CWGC) states that William was the son of John James (b. 1853) and Lily Mogg, of Wolverton, near Stratford-on-Avon, Lily was his stepmother. James Mogg was the son of Henry and Elizabeth (née Waters) from Inkberrow, Worcestershire.

On 10th June 1873 James married a local girl, Sarah Ann Job (1855-1900) at Claverdon. She was the daughter of Edgar and Maria (née James) who were married on 3rd November 1851 in the same village.

William was born on 15th August 1889. In 1891 he was the youngest child of a large family living at Church Lane, Claverdon (near Wolverton).

James Mogg	*Head*	*38*	*General Labourer*	*born Little Alne, Warwick*
Sarah Mogg	*Wife*	*38*	*Washing Woman*	" Claverdon "
Charles	*Son*	*13*	*General Labourer*	" " "
Ellen	*Daughter*	*11*	*Scholar*	" " "
Rose	"	*9*	*Scholar*	" " "
Edith	"	*7*	*Scholar*	" " "
Harry	*Son*	*4*		" " "
William	*Son*	*1*		" " "

At that time two older daughters, Eliza Jane (17) and Mary Ann (15) were no longer living at home.

Two further children completed the family: Hilda Lucy and James Henry (1896-1915). Like their father, the children regularly alternated their first and second names, which was certainly the case with the youngest child, as will be noted below.

William's mother, Sarah, died early in 1900 (GRO Ref. 6d, 1253) and James sought another wife to care for himself and his family. He found Lily, and married her early in 1903 (GRO Ref 6d, 777).

In due course the Moggs moved to Wolverton and (according to a local resident) they lived in the main street opposite the rectory in a three-storey house. James is listed in Kelly's Directory of Warwickshire as Parish Clerk for Wolverton, so the house (below), now called "Wayside" was most probably their home.

It is not known when, and why William went to New Zealand, but in 1916 he was working as a painter for Mr. C. E. Daniell at Masterton, Wairarapa. When he enlisted with the NZEF on 30th May 1916 he named a friend Charles Humphries of Marton Road, Carterton as next-of-kin in New Zealand.

William departed from New Zealand on 25th September with the 11th Reinforcements to the 2nd Battalion, New Zealand Rifle Brigade "F" Company on board the *Devon*. The ship docked at Devonport, England on 21st November and William marched into Sling Camp. In June 1917 he transferred to the Machine Gun Depot at Grantham, Lincolnshire. He left for France on 23rd July and joined his unit at Passchendaele on 10th October.

On 13th April 1918 William made a Will in favour of Miss Elsie Abbott (Domestic) Lanesborough House, 27 Dale Street, Leamington Spa, Warwickshire. One can assume that she was his sweetheart, and that he feared he might never return to England to see her again.

No other movements are recorded until 2nd July 1918 when William succumbed to a bout of influenza. Then towards the end of August, whilst fighting in the Battle of Bapaume, he was seriously wounded in action, receiving gunshot wounds to his right buttock and suffering from the effects of gas. He transferred to England immediately and arrived at No. 1 NZGH, Brockenhurst on 30th August. His injuries never healed and gangrene set in, resulting in his death on 16th September 1918. William was buried on 18th September, the officiating clergyman the Reverend Archibald J. Jacob. Plot A, Row 2, Grave 19.

438 men from WW1, including MOGG, W. J. are commemorated on the War Memorial in Queen Elizabeth II Park at Masterton.

An inscription on the memorial reads:

> THEY WHOM THIS MONUMENT COMMEMORATES, WERE NUMBERED AMONG THOSE WHO AT THE CALL OF KING AND COUNTRY, LEFT ALL THAT WAS DEAR TO THEM, ENDURED HARDNESS FACED DANGER AND FINALLY PASSED OUT OF SIGHT OF MEN, BY THE PATH OF DUTY AND SELF SACRIFICE, GIVING UP THEIR OWN LIVES THAT OTHERS MIGHT LIVE IN FREEDOM LET THOSE WHO COME AFTER SEE TO IT THAT THEIR NAMES ARE NOT FORGOTTEN

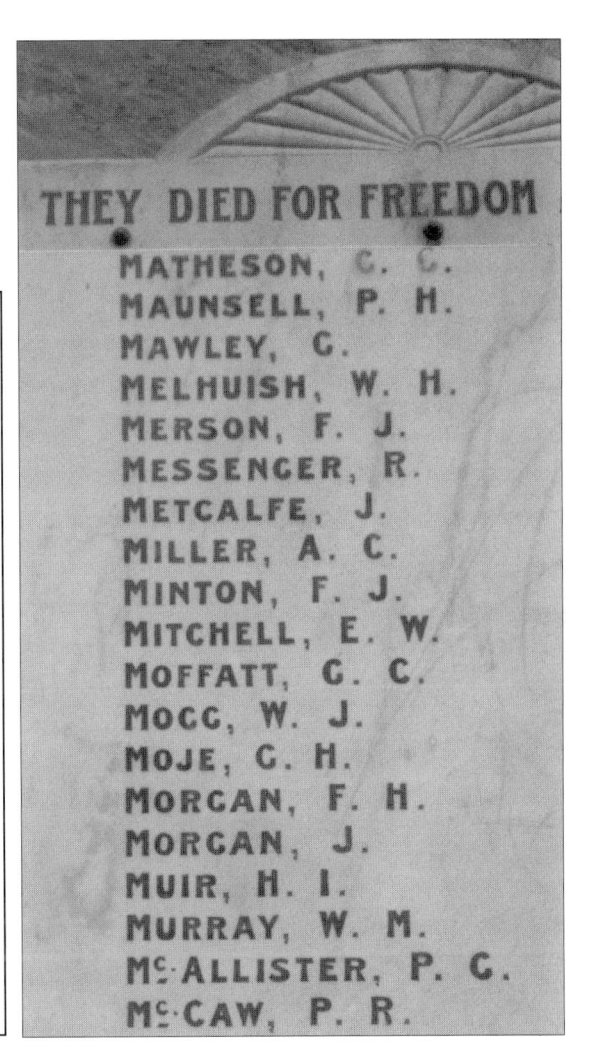

THEY DIED FOR FREEDOM
MATHESON, C. C.
MAUNSELL, P. H.
MAWLEY, G.
MELHUISH, W. H.
MERSON, F. J.
MESSENGER, R.
METCALFE, J.
MILLER, A. C.
MINTON, F. J.
MITCHELL, E. W.
MOFFATT, G. C.
MOGG, W. J.
MOJE, G. H.
MORGAN, F. H.
MORGAN, J.
MUIR, H. I.
MURRAY, W. M.
McALLISTER, P. G.
McCAW, P. R.

Two other sons of the Mogg family died as a result of WW1.

The CWGC lists:
Henry James Mogg, Driver, 65045, Royal Field Artillery, died on 23rd February 1915, aged 19, son of James John Mogg. This person is James Henry Mogg, the youngest member of the family. He is buried in the churchyard at St. Mary's Wolverton, northwest part, and has a CWGC headstone.

The eldest son, Charles Edward Mogg, Private, 32036, 6th Battalion, Somerset Light Infantry, died on 27th January 1917, aged 38. Charles was killed in action in France and is buried in Wanquetin Communal Cemetery Extension, Pas de Calais. Grave Ref. I.B.8. Wanquetin is a village approximately 12 kilometres west of Arras and 6 kilometres north of Beaumetz. Charles was the husband of Charlotte Mogg of 65, Cromwell Street, Nechells, Birmingham.

William and Henry James (James Henry) are commemorated on the War Memorial inside St. Mary's Church, Wolverton, yet Charles is not. The reason is probably because he was no longer living in his home village and had moved to Birmingham.

**WITH HUMBLE THANKSGIVING TO
ALMIGHTY GOD FOR VICTORY AND PEACE
AND IN MEMORY OF THOSE
WHO GAVE THEIR LIVES FOR RIGHT
THIS RECORD OF THEIR NAMES IS MADE
BY THE RECTOR OF WOLVERTON
THAT ALL WHO COME MAY KNOW THE
COST OF LIBERTY AND MAY SEEK TO
LIVE FOR THIS FOR WHICH THEY DIED**

1914 – 1919

**DRIVER HENRY JAMES MOGG. R.F.A.
DRIVER HENRY MORRIS VERNEY. R.F.A.
SERGEANT WALTER NEALE. 4TH WORC. R.
PRIVATE EDWIN WASHBURN. 101ST L. CORPS
PRIVATE WILLIAM JAMES MOGG. N.Z.M.G.C.
PRIVATE PERCY HENRY WOODFORD. 10TH R.W.R.**

Copy of WW1 Memorial in St. Mary's Church, Wolverton

Acknowledgement and Sources:

    Ben Wright
    1881 UK Census, PRO Ref RG11, Piece 3104, Folio 23, Page 1
    1891 UK Census, PRO Ref RG12, Piece 2479, Div. 396, Sub Div No. 3
    Kelly's Directory of Warwickshire, 1912 and 1924

WILFRED CECIL BEDFORD

Corporal, 27170
3rd Battalion Auckland Infantry Regiment, 6th Company
Died of sickness on 22nd September 1917, aged 35

Wilfred Cecil Bedford was born on 6th March 1882 at Ohaupu, Waikate. His parents, Bernard Samuel (1840-1915) and Fanny Eliza (1848-1939), lived at 35 Hepburn Street, Ponsonby, Auckland. Bernard was a schoolteacher and his roots were in England; Fanny (née Scrutton) was born in Sydney. They were married in 1867 in New South Wales, Australia, which suggests that Bernard first emigrated to Australia before settling in New Zealand. Bernard died in June 1915, and later the family moved to 23 Epsom Avenue, Auckland.

Prior to enlisting in the New Zealand Army Wilfred was employed as an Accountant with the firm Sargood Son & Ewen in Dunedin. He signed his Attestation Sheet on 1st June 1916 at Trentham and during his initial training he was promoted to Sergeant. On 15th November he departed from New Zealand with the Otago Infantry Battalion, "J" Company, 19th Reinforcements, and reached Devonport, England on 29th January 1917. The troops then marched into Sling Camp. Wilfred qualified as Corporal on 1st March, and at the end of the month he transferred to the 4th New Zealand Infantry Brigade at Codford Camp, between Salisbury and Warminster. Then on 15th April he joined the 3rd Battalion Auckland Regiment and was posted to 6th Company. After further training at Codford the Company left for France on 28th May.

Wilfred soon became ill and was admitted on 17th June to an isolation hospital suffering from mumps. By mid July he had developed gallstones and was evacuated to England, and admitted to No. 1 NZGH, Brockenhurst. He only survived a further two and a half months, dying on 22nd September 1917 as a result of an abscess on the liver. He was buried on 25th September. Plot A, Row 4, Grave 4.

Wilfred's next-of-kin was listed as his brother Hubert Henry (1880-1942), a Minister of Religion. Other siblings were Frances Edith (1873-1948), Charles Vivian (1875-1930), Gertrude Isabella (1876-1939), Bernard Eustace Aubrey (1878-1904) and probably Marion Lucy Calder Bramshaw (1890-1948). These persons originally were commemorated on the family grave at Purewa Cemetery, Auckland (E/48/51-52-53). Regrettably, the cemetery has been vandalised and there is no headstone evident.

Acknowledgement: Geoff Hall, Auckland

ERNEST NICHOLSON PLAYER

Sergeant, 27185
3rd Battalion, Wellington Regiment, 7th Company
Died of wounds on 16th October 1917, aged 29

Ernest Nicholson Player was the son of David Preston Player (1848-1915) and Ellen Eliza, née Stratford (1853-1934). He was the husband of Elizabeth Eileen, née Lennon (1887-1955), and father of Patricia (b. 1917).

David Preston Player was born in Greenwich, London, the son of Edward and Margaret Ann Ralston (née Preston). Edward in 1859 was a widower, so he decided that year to make a new life for himself in New Zealand. He sailed with his family on board the ship *Alfred The Great* and wrote an account of his journey (which is now kept at Alexander Turnbull Library in Wellington). He was also co-editor of the onboard magazine produced for passengers.

The Player family settled in the Wellington area, and in 1865-6 Edward was listed on the Electoral Roll for Hutt constituency. He worked as a hatter first, and then later a clerk, and was a member of the "Eight-hour day working committee" which played its part in legislation leading to the control of working hours.

Edward's son, David married Ellen Eliza on 10th February 1873 at Wellington, her birthplace. Her parents, George Alder Stratford (1807-1863) and Mary Ann, née Hollingshead (1820-1895) also came from London and they were married in 1841 at St. James's Church, Clerkenwell.

David and Ellen Player raised a large family of ten children:

Ellen Margaret	*b. 20 November 1873*	*Wellington*	*d. 12 April 1903*
Kate Edith	*b. 29 December 1874*	*Wellington*	*d. 19 November 1941*
David Edward	*b. 25 April 1876*	*Wellington*	*d. 11 February 1877*
Maude Preston	*b. 24 August 1877*	*Wellington*	*d. 26 April 1930*
George Preston	*b. 4 August 1879*	*Wellington*	*d. 18 June 1922*
Olive Stratford	*b. 27 March 1884*	*Greytown*	*d. ?*
Ernest Nicholson	*b. 25 March 1888*	*Napier*	*d. 16 October 1917*
Frederick William	*b. 25 March 1888*	*Napier*	*d. 5 April 1966*
Ivy Hollingshead	*b. 18 October 1892*	*Napier*	*d. ?*
Elsie Louisa	*b. 30 January 1895*	*Wellington*	*d. ?*

Ernest Player (from Kevin Bourke, Wellington)

Ernest lived with his parents at 65 Aro Street, Wellington prior to his marriage to Elizabeth Eileen. The wedding took place at Wellington on 15th February 1915 and the service was officiated by Father Peoples. The newly wed couple went to live at 22 Lochiel Street, Khandallah and a year later they moved to 37 Lawrence Street, Wellington. Prior to joining the army Ernest was employed by the Wellington Tram Corporation as a Pay Clerk.

He enlisted with the NZEF on 2nd June at Trentham, was posted to the 19th Non Commissioned Officers and promoted to Sergeant on 31st July. He departed from New Zealand with the 13th Reinforcements to 1st Battalion, "E" Company, New Zealand Rifle Brigade on 15th November 1916 on board HMNZT No. 69 *Tahiti*. The troopship arrived at Devonport, England on 29th January 1917 and Ernest marched into Sling Camp with the 1st Auckland Regiment, where he reverted to the rank of Temporary Sergeant for two months.

Ernest's daughter Patricia was born on 2nd March 1917, and although he knew she had been born he never saw her, and she never knew her father. He wrote to her telling her to be obedient and loving to her mother until he got back from the War - such a tragic tale.

Ernest spent April and most of May at Codford Camp with the No. 3 Reserve Battalion, 4th Brigade prior to leaving for France on the 27th. It was only then that he joined the 3rd Battalion, Wellington Regiment. His movements are not recorded until 4th October 1917, when he was fighting in the 3rd Battle of Ypres (Passchendaele) and received gunshot wounds to his left knee, which necessitated amputation of his leg. He immediately transferred to No. 1 NZGH, Brockenhurst and arrived there on 12th October. He did not survive long, however, owing to the severity of his injuries. He died of his wounds on 16th October and was buried two days later. Plot A, Row 3, Grave 3.

Kevin Bourke, Ernest's grandson, relates that in a very strange twist of fate, some years after the war, his wife, Elizabeth was talking to a new neighbour and discovered that this woman had been a nurse at No. 1 NZGH, Brockenhurst during the time that her husband was there.

Elizabeth had received a letter written by a nurse because Ernest had been too ill to write. It turned out that this neighbour had written the letter herself and remembered the circumstances.

Because of a failure of communication, Elizabeth had received notification of Ernest's death before she was aware of his wounding. This was because death telegrams had a higher priority. Not knowing he was wounded, she had not written nor telegraphed him in hospital. Apparently, he had been desperately waiting to hear from her.

Elizabeth is buried in the Lennon family grave (left) at Karori Cemetery - Area 3, Block C, Row 7, Plot 32.

Acknowledgements:
    Kevin Bourke, Khandallah, Wellington (grandson)
    Richard Anderson, New Plymouth, Taranaki (cousin)

GEORGE ECKFORD LAW

Sergeant, 28160
3rd Battalion, Wellington Regiment, "B" Company
Died of wounds on 4th January 1918, aged 29

George Eckford Law, born on 20th October 1888 was the son of George and Ellen who lived at 22 Nikau Street, Muritai, Wellington.

The original house is still standing although much modernisation has taken place. In the 1940s the land was divided into six building sites for the development of houses.

This settlement, now known as Eastbourne is situated on the eastern side of Wellington Harbour, and Nikau Street has the bush encroaching upon the houses (right).

The Law family owned about an acre of land on which they produced choice cut flowers, which were sent to a florist in Woodward Street in Wellington City several times a week.

Mrs. Law's sister was married to a Mr. Child, a florist (possibly the purchaser of the cut flowers), and they also lived in the same street.

George (junior) attended the local school at Muritai, and his name is mentioned on the Eastbourne War Memorial at the school gates.

By 1916 he was a self-employed farmer at Opatu, Taumarunui. He enlisted with the NZEF at Trentham on 27th June 1916 as a Private in "B" Company, Unit 28. A month later he was suffering from influenza and spent a few days in Wairarapa Hospital.

Then on August 21st he was admitted to the camp hospital at Featherston suffering from measles. Hence his initial military life was dogged with sickness.

George left New Zealand on 16th October 1916 with the Wellington Infantry Battalion, "B" Company, 18th Reinforcements on board HMNZT *Willochra*.

The ship docked at Devonport, Plymouth, on 29th December. George trained at Sling Camp before transferring to 4th Brigade at Codford on 30th March 1917. He was attached to the strength of the 3rd Battalion Wellington Infantry Regiment and arrived in France at the end of May.

Eastbourne War Memorial

On 1st July he was promoted to Lance Corporal, and at the end of the month was detached to the School of Instruction for one week. Further promotion followed: on 5th October he was appointed Temporary Corporal, followed by Temporary Sergeant on 25th October.

George's days at the Front came to an abrupt halt on 20th December 1917 near Ypres, when he was wounded in action with gunshot wounds to his chest and shoulder. He arrived at No. 1 NZGH on 3rd January 1918 and was immediately placed on the Dangerously Ill List. He died the next day, and was buried on 7th January.

Plot A, Row 2, Grave 13.

```
TO
COMMEMORATE
THE UNVEILING OF THE
EASTBOURNE WAR MEMORIAL
ON THE FIRST DAY OF JULY, 1928
BY
HIS EXCELLENCY THE GOVERNOR-GENERAL
SIR CHARLES FERGUSSON BART.
LL.D., G.C.M.G., K.C.B., D.S.O., M.V.O.

PRO ARIS ET FOCIS
```

Copy of leaflet distributed at the unveiling of the Eastbourne War Memorial

George is one of 168 Eastbourne residents who served their country and the Empire during the Great War 1914-1918. 25 men (15%) who went to War made the Supreme Sacrifice and did not return to their loved ones. The foundation stone was laid by the Hon. R. A. Wright, Minister of Education, on Anzac Day, 1927, and the Memorial Gates were unlocked by Lieut. Colonel J. A. Cowles, V. D. on Anzac Day, 1928.

Acknowledgements: Sue de Lange, York Bay, Eastbourne
                   Thelma Lowndes, Eastbourne
                   Pat Milsom, Eastbourne

WILLIAM MILNE MORRISON

Private, 29836
2nd Battalion, Otago Regiment, 4th Company
Died of wounds on 17th October 1917, aged 43

William Milne Morrison, the son of William and Jane, was born on 16th December 1873 at Rakaia, Canterbury. He worked as a sheep station hand for Roberts & Co. at Gladbrook, Middlemarch, Central Otago.

He enlisted with the NZEF on 28th June 1916 at Trentham, and whilst there he found the circumstances rather hard going, and to liven up his disciplined life he decided to smuggle liquor into the camp. However, he was discovered by the authorities and received 168 hours (7 days) detention for his misdeeds! William was posted overseas on 16th October and embarked on the *Willochra* with the Otago Infantry Battalion, "D" Company, 18th Reinforcements. The ship docked at Devonport, England on 29th December and he went straight to Sling Camp for further military training.

He left for France on 1st February 1917, but did not join the 2nd Battalion, Otago Regiment until 25th May near Messines. The next news of him is on 7th June when he was wounded in action on the first day of the Battle of Messines, when 19 large mines were detonated under the German lines. There were many casualties, William being one of them, with gunshot wounds to his spine, resulting in paraplegia.

He immediately transferred to No. 1 NZGH, Brockenhurst, and he died on 17th October. His burial took place two days later in :
Plot A, Row 3, Grave 2.

Next of kin was his sister Mrs. James Leahy, c/o Post Office, Leeston, Canterbury. In his will she was the sole executor and also inherited all William's possessions.

William is commemorated on Middlemarch War Memorial (right).

This was the second loss for the Morrison family. A younger brother James Henry Morrison, Gunner, 13/527 No. 2 Battery, New Zealand Field Artillery, died on 21st October 1916, aged 40. James is buried at A.I.F. Burial Ground, Flers, Somme, France. Grave Ref. I.E.29.

WILLIAM JOHN SMAIL

Private, 32240
1st Battalion, Canterbury Regiment, 2nd Company
Died of wounds on 3rd April 1918, aged 35

A few of the NZEF soldiers who are buried at Brockenhurst were born outside New Zealand. William John Smail is one of these men. He was the son of Thomas and Mary Ann and his birthplace was London, England on 12th May 1882. In 1916 William's next-of-kin was named as his brother Thomas, who at that time lived at 4 Garlies Road, Forest Hill, London.

Prior to William's enlistment with the NZEF, he was employed as a carpenter for J. Stains of Waipukurau, Central Hawkes Bay region. He signed on for military service on 25th July 1916 at Wellington, and departed from New Zealand on 15th November with the 19th Reinforcements to 2nd Battalion, "F" Company, New Zealand Rifle Brigade. Following disembarkation at Devonport, England on 29th January 1917 William marched into Sling Camp where he remained for two months before being sent to France at the beginning of March.

On 3rd June, four days before the British attack on Messines the 2nd Brigade was relieved on the line near Ypres and they marched back to Canteen Corner, a short distance east of the intersection of the Bailleul-Armentieres and Neuve Eglise-Steenwerck roads. This location was the bivouac area for the whole of the 2nd Brigade, and on this day William joined the 1st Battalion, Canterbury Regiment, 2nd Company. That night the enemy shelled the bivouac area with long range high-velocity guns. Although the shooting was accurate and destroyed a cookhouse, there were no casualties.

William's active life ended on 12th October during the 3rd Battle of Ypres – (Passchendaele). He had received gunshot wounds to his right foot and spent his final months as follows:

12.10.17	*Admitted to No. 1 N.Z. Field Ambulance*
12.10.17	*Admitted to No. 3 Australian Casualty Clearing Station*
13.10.17	*Admitted to No. 8 Stationary Hospital, Wimereux*
24.10.17	*Embarked for England per hospital ship*
25.10.17	*Admitted to Military Hospital, Tooting, London*
12.2.18	*Transferred to No. 1 NZGH, Brockenhurst*
2.3.18	*Placed on Seriously Ill list*
4.3.18	*Placed on Dangerously Ill list*
3.4.18	*Died of wounds – septic thrombosis*

William was buried on 6th April 1918. Plot A, Row 3, Grave 15.

CLAUDE RAYMOND READ

**Private, 32708
4th Reserve Battalion, Auckland Infantry Regiment
Died of sickness on 26th February 1918, aged 21**

Claude Raymond Read was born on 27th August 1896 (his Army Records say 1895), the son of William and Betsy of Pencarrow Avenue, Mount Eden, Auckland. His parents came from England - William (1840-1920) from Southampton, Hampshire, and Betsy (1855-1920) from Staffordshire. Claude's siblings were George, Lawrence, Millicent (1883-1919) and Mrs. W. S. Downing - who in 1918 lived in England at Sugley House, Burley, Hampshire.

Claude worked as an Insurance Clerk (Surveyor) for the Royal Insurance Company Ltd. He enlisted with the NZEF on 26th July 1916 at Trentham, and left New Zealand on 15th November on HMNZT No. 68 *Maunganui* with the Auckland Infantry Battalion, "A" Company, 19th Reinforcements. The ship docked at Devonport, England on 29th January 1917 and he marched into Sling Camp.

He never saw active service because he contracted bronchitis and was admitted to No. 1 NZGH, Brockenhurst on 11th April. By 1st June he transferred to Hornchurch in Essex for convalescence and on 4th August he was taken on the strength at Codford Camp, Wiltshire.

Claude was readmitted No. 1 NZGH, Brockenhurst in mid December with nasal obstruction, which developed into meningitis. On 16th February 1918 he transferred to Royal Victoria Hospital at Netley, near Southampton and died there on 26th February - cause of death tuberculosis and meningitis.

Netley, Hospital 1908, Hampshire
Courtesy The Francis Frith Collection, www.francisfrith.co.uk

Claude was buried at Brockenhurst on 1st March, officiated by Reverend W. R. Hutchinson.

He is commemorated on the family grave at Purewa Cemetery Auckland, (Ref: FO45106).

> *In loving memory of*
>
> *William Read husband of Betsy Read*
> *died 4 July 1920 age 80 years*
>
> *Also his wife Betsy died 6 July 1920 age 65 years*
>
> *Also Lieut. L. W. Read 1st Essex Regt.*
> *killed in action France 9 Dec 1916*
>
> *Also Private C. R. Read "A.I.R."*
> *died England 26 Feb 1918*
>
> *Also Millicent Read daughter of William and Betsy Read*
> *died 21 Oct 1919 age 36 years*

Claude's brother, Lawrence William Read, 1st Essex Regiment, has no known grave, and he is commemorated on the Thiepval Memorial, Somme, France. Ref. Pier and Face 10 D.

Acknowledgement: Geoff Hall, Auckland

WALTER WHYTE

Private, 20845
New Zealand Maori (Pioneer) Battalion
Died of sickness on 15th September 1918, aged 24

Walter Whyte, the son of Peter, was born on 31st March 1894 in the Waikato region. Walter worked as a flax cutter for Mr. Dudson at Maketu, near the coast southeast of Tauranga. At that time his father was living at Whangamata, Coromandel region.

Walter enlisted with the NZEF on 27th July 1916 at Narrow Neck Camp, near Auckland. He departed from New Zealand with the Maori Contingent, 10th Reinforcements on 15th November on board HMNZT *Tahiti* (below).

He appears to have contravened orders on several occasions, but at least this proves that he was a lively character. Shortly before his posting overseas he overstayed his final leave and forfeited two days' pay and was confined to barracks for 3 days. Walter's Conduct Sheet implies that parades were held whilst on board ship, because he received the punishment of 3 days confinement to barracks, which seems rather a peculiar penalty considering he couldn't venture far unless he chose to jump overboard!

The ship reached Devonport, England on 29th January 1917 and Walter marched into Sling Camp on Salisbury Plain, where he remained until 1st March.

He then was posted to France and in the first instance was based at the New Zealand training camp at Etaples. He eventually joined the Pioneer Battalion on 25th May in preparation for the successful attack on Messines on 7th June.

Walter then moved with the Pioneer Battalion to wherever their work in building dugouts, gun pits and shelters was required, and eventually settled in the Ypres area prior to the 3rd Battle of Ypres (Passchendaele) in October 1917.

In June 1918, shortly before Walter's active service life was terminated, he again demonstrated that he wanted to lead his life his own way. It appears that he was detected parading with a dirty rifle, and on another occasion he decided to alter his trousers and had to pay half of their cost!

Walter's time spent in France came to an end at the beginning of July 1918 near Hébuterne. He was suffering from inflammation of the peritoneum (peritonitis). Hospitalisation at Rouen preceded his transfer to No. 1 NZGH, Brockenhurst, where he arrived on 19th July.

Walter was placed on the "Dangerously Ill" list on 27th July and died less than two months later on 15th September. He was buried on 18th September, and the ceremony was officiated by the Reverend W. S. Skinner.

Plot A, Row 1, Grave 19.

FARQUHAR McDONALD

Private, 34902
3rd Battalion, Otago Regiment, 8th Company
Died of sickness on 5th January 1918, aged 37

Farquhar McDonald was born on 24th February 1880, at Hokonui, near Winton, Southland, son of Christopher (1838-1917) and Mary (1845-1935).

Christopher McDonald came to New Zealand in 1864 from a tiny hamlet in Ross and Cromarty (now Highland), called Camus-luinie, near Dornie. His father was a crofter and young Christopher was a shepherd who worked for Roderick McKenzie in Applecross. He fell in love with Roderick's daughter, Mary, and was thrown out as she was a class or two above him socially and was also from a "landed" family. Ten years later Mary joined Christopher in New Zealand, by which time he had bought land in Otapiri. The McDonald family has lived in this area ever since.

Christopher and Mary raised five children:

Alexander	born 1875	married and had 2 boys
Roderick	(1877-1940)	never married
Farquhar	(1880-1918)	never married
Mary Ann	born 1882	married – no living children
Christopher	born 1883	married – 2 boys and 1 girl

Farquhar attended Forest Hill East School at Hokonui, after which he took up farming. At the time of joining the NZEF he stated that he was a self-employed farmer at Lora Gorge, Otapiri. He had most probably taken over the running of the farm from his elderly father; the latter was mentioned in Wise's Directory in 1900 as being so employed.

Farquhar's niece, Sheila, cannot imagine why Farquhar (known as Fred) joined up, firstly because he was employed in farming which she thinks would have been a protected job, and secondly because of his age. He would have been 36 when he joined the army.

He enlisted with the NZEF on 25th August 1916 at Featherston. The very next day he was admitted to hospital at the camp suffering from measles. After this initial setback, military training in New Zealand continued before embarkation at Wellington upon the *Athenic* on 30th December, departing with the Otago Infantry Regiment, "D" Company, 20th Reinforcements (2nd draft).

The troops disembarked at Devonport, England on 3rd March 1917 and marched into Sling Camp. After a month Farquhar was taken on strength of the 8th Company and transferred to Codford. He left for France on 28th May 1917.

Nearly five months later he fell seriously ill; on 20th October he was diagnosed as having myalgia and in mid November he was admitted to Southwark Military Hospital, London. He remained there for a month before transfer to No. 1 NZGH, Brockenhurst on 14th December.

He never recovered from his illness and died suddenly of neurasthenia on 5th January 1918. He was buried on 7th January in Plot A, Row 1, Grave 14.

Farquhar is commemorated on his parents' gravestone at Winton Cemetery, Southland (note the spelling of Brockenhurst!).

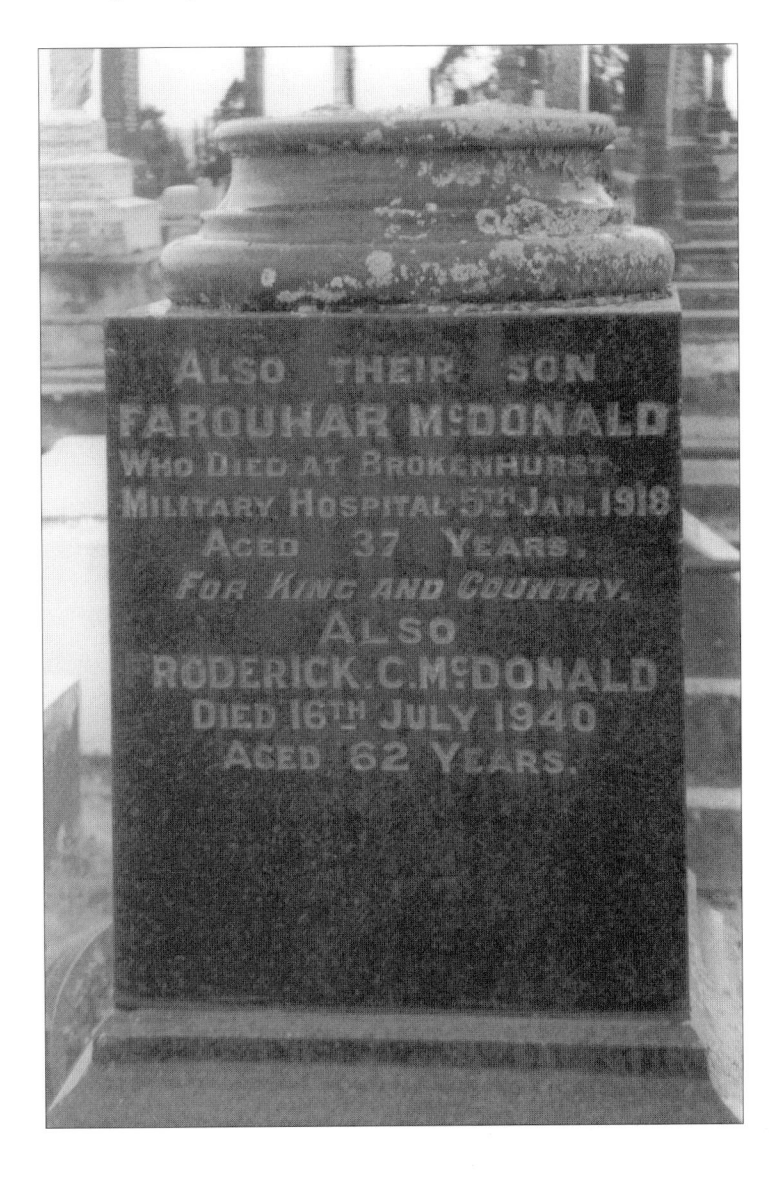

McDonald family grave at Winton, Southland

Acknowledgement:

Sheila Craig (niece, Christopher's daughter)

JERRY RATA

Private, 19411
New Zealand Maori (Pioneer) Battalion
Died of sickness on 20th June 1918, aged 22

Jerry Rata, the son of Herewaka Rata and Te Auraki Hongi Hapeta (her name by her second marriage), was born on 20th December 1895 at Mangamuka, Hokianga, Northland. Jerry was a self-employed farmer prior to enlisting with the NZEF on 4th September 1916 at Narrow Neck Camp, near Auckland.

Jerry departed from New Zealand with the Maori Contingent, 12th Reinforcements on 2nd January 1917 on board the *Opawa* and reached Devonport, England on 27th March. From there he marched into Sling Camp but within two days he was ill with pleurisy and was admitted to Tidworth Military Hospital. He remained there for two months and towards the end of May the medical authorities considered he was fit to return to duty. However, in just over a week he was ill again with pleurisy, and transferred to the New Zealand Convalescent Hospital at Hornchurch in Essex. Towards the end of August he was discharged to the New Zealand (Command) Depot at Codford for fitness training in preparation for posting to the Western Front.

It is evident that Jerry could not endure the rigid discipline enforced because whilst at camp in a spate of drunkenness he broke a carriage window. The punishments awarded amounted to 168 hours detention, a fine of 10 shillings and payment of 10/6d. - the replacement cost of the window.

After another spell at Sling Camp, Jerry eventually left for France on 2nd December. He joined the Pioneer Battalion on 25th December near Ypres, one of 20 reinforcements who arrived on Christmas Day to fill up wastage. No doubt he joined his comrades in the midst of a vague sense of Christmas spirit because on that day every man received parcels from Lady Liverpool's fund, with chocolate and other presents sent from the YMCA. The next day the Pioneers carried on with their task of improving the road system and laying tramlines. In the New Year they worked hard, despite the difficulty of having to cope with frozen ground.

On 21st March 1918, after nearly three months stay in the Ypres area, Jerry was on the move again. The Battalion was required to transfer to the Hébuterne area, north of the Ancre River and the Pioneers spent April at Bertrancourt working on defensive work, digging trenches and wiring. The weather was damp and showery and many men contracted influenza. Jerry fell ill on 12th May with infected lymphatic glands and was admitted to hospital at Rouen. On 25th May he arrived at No. 1 NZGH, Brockenhurst, by which time he was suffering from tuberculosis of the lung.

Jerry survived a few weeks longer and died of phthisis on 20th June 1918. His burial ceremony the next day was officiated by the Reverend A. Mitchell. Plot A, Row 5, Grave 17. By 1922 Jerry's father was deceased and his mother had remarried and she was then living at Cape Runaway, East Coast, North Island.

CHRISTIAN DIEDRICH MARCUSSEN

Corporal, 41218
Otago Regiment, "D" Company, 26th Reinforcements
Died of sickness on 4th December 1918, aged 30

Christian Diedrich Marcussen, the eldest son of Thomas Diedrich and Agnes, was born on 30th March 1888 at Otakou, on the Otago Peninsula. Thomas Diedrich was born in 1852 at Leck, Schleswig-Holstein now in Germany, but at that time in Denmark. Two siblings have been identified, William Martin (1890-1969) and Thomas Diedrich (1896-1918). Christian's schooling commenced at Otakou, then early in 1896 the family moved to Steep Street, Dunedin and Christian and William were admitted to High Street School on 28th January.

A few years later the family uprooted again, this time to Bluff, Southland. The boys' father, Thomas was initially employed as a labourer and he was granted New Zealand citizenship in 1904 at the age of 52. By 1918 he had obtained a position at Bluff Harbour office. It is not known in what capacity he was working, because conflicting reports have come to light. The Southland Times of 18th December 1918 states that he was the harbourmaster, yet John Hall-Jones in his book on Bluff Harbour (1976) does not mention Thomas's name.

In 1915 Christian was employed by the New Zealand Government and working in the Money Order branch of the Greymouth Post Office. It is not known how he met his wife, but he married Sarah Lucilla Tudor Marten, at St. John's Church, Wanganui on 6th September 1915, the marriage ceremony officiated by the Reverend H. Reeve. According to the Wanganui Herald (1915), "Sarah was the daughter of Arthur George and Abigail, a local family. The bridegroom's gift to the bride was a ring set with aquamarines, and her gift to him was a massive gold albert" (a kind of watch chain usually attached to a waistcoat – named after Prince Albert, Consort of Queen Victoria). The honeymoon was spent in Wellington and the couple then went to live in Greymouth, where their daughter, Moya was born on 28th June 1916. An obituary in The Southland Times (1918) reported that Christian was a prominent hockey player, and took a keen interest in football.

Christian enlisted with the NZEF at Greymouth on 30th October 1916 and was promoted to Corporal on 16th November. He joined "D" Company, 26th Reinforcements on 18th January 1917. He left New Zealand on 9th June on board troopship *Willochra* bound for Devonport, England. Upon disembarkation on 16th August the troops marched into Sling Camp. After passing the necessary promotion examination, Christian's rank was confirmed as Corporal on 24th September.

Nothing is mentioned in his army service record until 20th August 1918, when he was relocated to the Durrington Camp, Salisbury Plain. He left for France on 10th September, and marched into camp at Etaples. That very day he fell ill with dysentery, and two weeks later was admitted to No. 2 NZGH, Walton-on-Thames, Surrey. Transfer to the Dysentery depot at Barton-on-Sea, Hampshire took place on 15th November, and he finally arrived at No. 1 NZGH, Brockenhurst on 29th

November, classified as "Dangerously Ill". Christian died of bronco-pneumonia on 4th December 1918 and was buried two days later. The officiating clergyman was the Reverend G. Parr, Church of England Chaplain. Plot A, Row 3, Grave 21.

Christian is commemorated on the War Memorial at Wanganui, his wife's hometown, and also at Bluff, his parents' home.

Wanganui War Memorial

Thomas and Agnes Marcussen suffered a double loss, when their youngest son Thomas Diedrich, Private, 25116, 14th Reinforcements, New Zealand Machine Gun Corps, died on the same day as Christian. This is an unusual coincidence considering that the sons were not together on that day. The Commonwealth War Graves Commission have no details regarding Thomas's death, but it is known that he was buried at Bluff Cemetery, Lagan Street, Bluff, Southland. Ref. Section 66, Block 5. This implies that he was repatriated to New Zealand but died as a result of the War.

Acknowledgements and Sources:

> Bruce Isted, Wanganui
> Robin Purnell, Southampton, England
> Linda Roderique, Bluff
> Hall-Jones, J. (1976) *Bluff Harbour*
> Wanganui Herald, September 1915
> Southland Times, 18 December 1918, p.5

HENRY WI WAKA WI

Private, 19474
New Zealand Maori (Pioneer) Battalion
Died of sickness on 8th February 1918, aged 21

Henry Wi Waka Wi, the son of Wi Kio and Rangiahua Kio was born in 1896 at Whangarei, North Auckland. In 1917 the family was living at Te Kuiti, Waikato region where Henry was working as a farmer for his father.

Henry enlisted with the NZEF on 22nd September 1916 at Narrow Neck Camp, near Auckland. Whilst at this camp he attempted to absent himself without being noticed, to no avail, and had to pay the penalty of forfeiting 12 days pay, plus 21 days confinement to barracks. This was for failing to be present for guard duty.

He departed from New Zealand with the Maori Contingent, 13th Reinforcements on 19th January 1917 on board HMNZT No. 75 *Waitemata*. After the ship docked at Devonport, England on 28th March, the men marched into Sling Camp. On 8th May Henry transferred to the New Zealand Engineers Reserve Depot at Christchurch, near Bournemouth, Hampshire. He was back at Sling in August, and left for France on 1st September.

Henry joined the Maori (Pioneer) Battalion on 14th September, at Bournonville (10 miles east of Boulogne), the day that the Battalion was inspected by the New Zealand Commander-in-Chief, Sir A. J. Godley. On 26th September the Battalion began their transfer to the Ypres area in order to prepare for action in the 3rd Battle of Ypres (Passchendaele).

At the beginning of December Henry fell ill, suffering from debility. His health did not improve so he transferred to England for medical attention, and arrived at No. 1 NZGH, Brockenhurst on 11th December. During the next six weeks his illness developed into pneumonia and he died of this disease on 8th February 1918. His burial three days later was officiated by the Reverend P. J. Minogue, Roman Catholic Chaplain.

Plot A, Row 3, Grave 12.

Henry had a brother who also served in the War, namely Private Thomas Wi, 16/486 who had enlisted before him and departed from New Zealand with the first Maori Contingent on 14th February 1915.

JOSEPH BRIGGS

Private, 38931
1st Battalion, Canterbury Regiment, 2nd Company
Died of wounds on 28th August 1918, aged 23

Joseph Briggs was the son of John and Mary Jane of Waihao Downs, near Waimate, South Canterbury, in the midst of sheep-farming territory. He was born at Woodend, near Rangiora, north of Christchurch, on 23rd September 1896.

Joseph's family came from Cumberland, England. His grandfather Joseph (b.1832/3) was a cordwainer (shoemaker), and grandmother, Isabella (née Lancaster – b.1840/41) originated from Maryport, in the same county. In 1881 six children were living with their parents at Rose Mary Lane, Great Clifton, but their second son, John (b.1864) had left home and was then, aged 16, resident at Holebeck, Arlecdon, Cumberland, employed as an agricultural labourer for Thomas Cook, a farmer with 142 acres.

It has not been ascertained when John emigrated to New Zealand, but he obviously continued working in the agriculture industry on arrival in his new country. His occupation is listed as farmer in Christchurch Parish Records, when he married in 1893 Mary Jane Scoon (1872-1941), from Rangiora, at The Church of St. Barnabas, Woodend, Canterbury. Mary Jane's parents, William and Elizabeth Joyce (née Mawson) were also farmers.

Joseph was born three years later in 1896. At some time between then and 1916 the family uprooted and moved to Waihao Downs, near Waimate, South Canterbury. Prior to enlistment with the NZEF Joseph worked as a labourer for his father, John. He was also a member of 'D' Company, 2nd South Canterbury Regiment.

On 5th October 1916 Joseph signed up for the army at Waimate, and was posted to 'C' Company, 22nd Reinforcements. Basic training took place in New Zealand prior to being posted overseas. He left Wellington on 15th February 1917, on board *Aparima*, arriving at Devonport, England on 26th April. After further training at Sling Camp, on 5th June he joined the 1st Battalion, Canterbury Regiment, 2nd Company, at Basseville, undertaking training for the attack on Passchendaele. He had two spells of training at the School of Instruction.

On 2nd October 1917, exactly a year after Joseph had left his home surroundings, he received gunshot wounds to his face whilst near Passchendaele. He was admitted to the 3rd Australian Field Ambulance, after which he was nursed at No. 12 General Hospital at Rouen. It is assumed that this injury was not serious because he was back at the Etaples army base by 30th November and rejoined the Battalion at New Hutting Camp, half a mile south of Ypres. A fortnight later he was granted 2 ½ weeks leave in England, and he returned to Ypres on 7th February.

Joseph continued to fight for his country for a further six months before being wounded in action for the second time within a year, on 25th August, at the Battle of Bapaume. Prior to this time the landscape in this area had not been ruined because no heavy fighting had taken place there. It had previously been used as a British rest and training area with hutted camps dotted around many miles of open, gently rolling country, interspersed with small woods.

A few days before Joseph's fateful day, there was a limited attack north of the Ancre River in order to gain the general line of the Arras-Albert railway. The 1st Canterbury Battalion were involved in the capture of Bapaume and the high ground to the east of the town. On 25th August the Battalion assembled in front of Grevillers and Biefveillers by 4.30 a.m. The objectives had been met by 7.00 a.m. but at some stage Joseph was severely injured, having received gunshot wounds to his neck and a compact fracture of the spine.

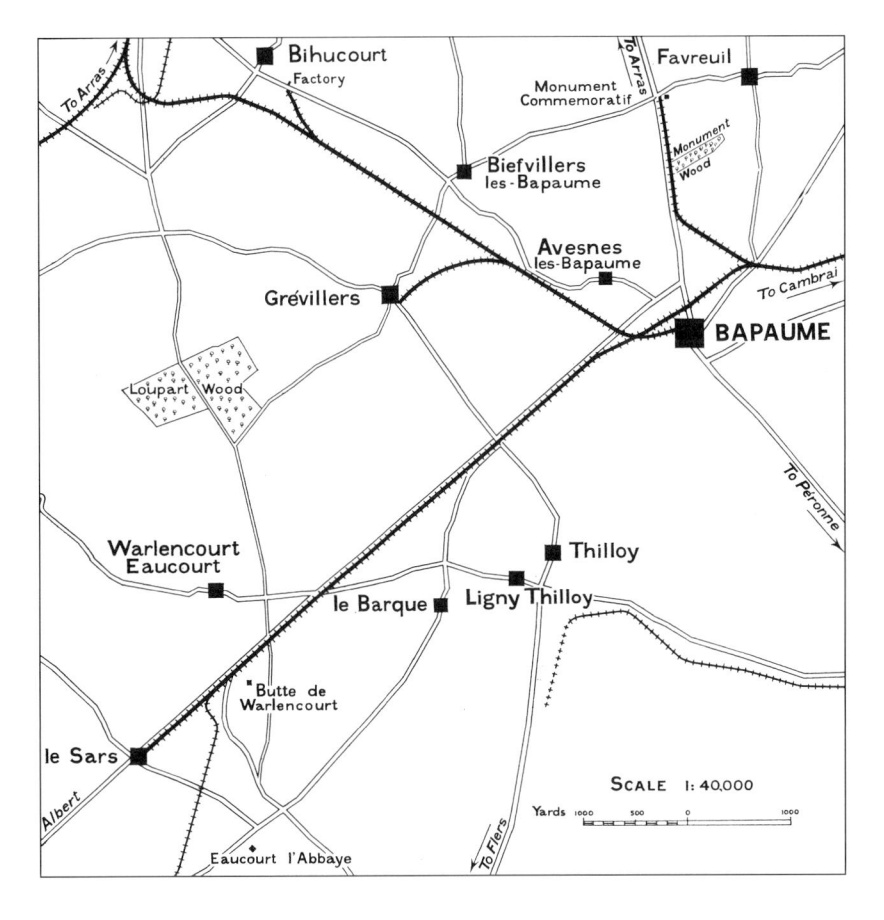

Bapaume

After a brief period at the 1st Australian General Hospital at Rouen, Joseph transferred to England on H.S *Guildford Castle*. He never survived the sea crossing and died on board ship on 28th August 1918. His body was taken to Brockenhurst and buried in St. Nicholas' churchyard on 31st August 1918, alongside fellow New Zealanders.

Joseph is among the few men to be buried at Brockenhurst who never saw No. 1 NZGH Hospital prior to their deaths. He was buried in -

Plot A, Row 4, Grave 19

officiating clergyman the Reverend E. D. Rice, New Zealand Chaplain.

Joseph Briggs is listed on the war memorial at Waimate. Another member of the Briggs family (R.E.) is also included amongst 151 names from the Waimate District, including three nurses. R. E. Briggs must have survived because he is not listed in the Commonwealth War Graves Commission Debt of Honour. The memorial does not differentiate between those who fell in the Great War and those who served their country.

WW1 Memorial Gate at entrance to Victoria Park, Waimate

Sources:

1881 UK Census
FHL Film 1342250, PRO Ref RG11, Piece 5183, Folio 42, Page 31
FHL Film 1342248, PRO Ref RG11, Piece 5175, Folio 109, Page 117
Christchurch Parish Records, Marriage Register SBW3

HARRY PHILLIPS

Private, 39472
2nd Battalion, Canterbury Regiment, 1st Company
Died of wounds on 8th August 1917, aged 28

Harry Phillips was born on 22nd September 1889 at Auckland, the son of Harry and Martha, who both came from Scotland. The family lived at 48 Wynyard Street, Auckland.

In 1916 Harry (junior) was employed as a labourer for the Public Works Department at Otira, north of Arthurs Pass, between Christchurch and Greymouth. The New Zealand Government had a contract with J. McLean and Sons for the construction of the Otira railway tunnel, to be 5 ¾ miles in length (considered to be the longest tunnel in the British Empire) under the Southern Alps, and to complete the rail link between the west coast and Canterbury. Construction was started in May 1908 but by February 1912 (when the work should have been completed) there were still 5 ½ miles to build. J. McLean and Sons were asked to relinquish the contract and the Public Works Department took over. However only another half mile was added before the War began in 1914. The two ends of the tunnel eventually met in 1918 but it was not until the 4th August 1923 that the first train went through. Unfortunately Harry never survived to see the completion of his work.

The Otira railway tunnel under construction, with workers outside.
S C Matthew Collection. F-51297-1/2 (PAColl-0678-01). ATL

Harry enlisted with the NZEF on 14th October 1916 at Greymouth. His next-of-kin was stated as Mr. A. Beban (a friend) of Club Hotel, Greymouth. Harry departed from New Zealand with the Canterbury Infantry Regiment "C" Company, 22nd Reinforcements on 16th February 1917 on board the *Navua*. No doubt he was glad to have a change of scenery, because whilst at Trentham during November he broke out of camp and went absent without leave on two occasions, and when at Featherston camp in December he was Confined to Barracks for seven days for improper conduct.

The troops disembarked at Devonport, England on 26th April 1917 and marched into Sling Camp. A month later on 26th May, Harry left for France and he eventually joined the 2nd Battalion, Canterbury Regiment on 19th June at Basseville. The 2nd Battalion Canterbury Regiment had suffered badly during the Battle of Messines earlier in June so Harry was one of the much-needed reinforcements.

Lieutenant General Sir A. J. Godley, General Officer Commanding II Anzac Army Corps inspected the Brigade on 21st June, and the next day Major-General Sir A. H. Russell, General Officer Commanding the New Zealand Division also inspected the troops. King George V visited the Messines battle area in early July and it was reported that on 4th July the soldiers cheered the King as he drove past.

Harry's period on the Western Front was short-lived as he was wounded in action on 8th July. Ironically, he was awarded a punishment of 14 days Field Punishment No. 2 (which meant extra parades and duties) the day beforehand. Apparently he had been absent from Roll Call and a working party on 6th July. This punishment obviously did not take place because Harry had been taken under the wing of the medical authorities for attention to the gunshot wounds to his head and face.

He transferred to England and arrived at No. 1 NZGH, Brockenhurst on 26th July. By 4th August the hospital staff judged that he would never survive and he was classified as unfit and placed on the New Zealand Roll. He died of his wounds to his face and secondary haemorrhage on 8th August 1917 and was buried two days later.

Plot A, Row 2, Grave 3.

After the War Harry (senior) and Martha moved house and went to live at 12 Paget Street, Ponsonby, Auckland.

GEORGE WILLIAM HESLOP

Private, 44582
2nd Battalion, Canterbury Regiment, 2nd Company
Died of wounds on 24th October 1917, aged 40

George William Heslop (from Gwen Heslop, Stoke, Nelson)

George William Heslop was born on 29th September 1877 at Aorere, near Collingwood, Nelson, the son of George and Emma. George (senior) was a gold miner who later took up land and became a farmer. The Aorere Goldfield was the first gold rush area in New Zealand and both alluvial and quartz reef gold were mined, mainly between 1857 and the early 1900s. George (junior) would have spent his childhood and schooling in the various mining settlements in the Collingwood Goldfields which were established by the early settlers. He had one older brother, Henry Richard and a younger brother, James. There were five sisters. Interestingly, George's grandfather was the first cousin of Llewellyn Grooby's father (see p. 227).

George was a farmer employed by Mr. L. Grant at Rockville, near Collingwood prior to enlisting with the NZEF on 19th October 1916 at Nelson. He was a member of the 25th Reinforcements and was placed in the Canterbury Infantry Regiment, "C" Company. It is interesting to note that he was unable to sign his name and just put an X mark on his Attestation sheet, so his schooling must have been minimal!

Whilst undertaking military training in New Zealand he transferred to 24th Reinforcements and was posted overseas on 14th April 1917, embarking on *Pakeha*. Some problem must have occurred because the ship returned to Wellington on 17th April. The troops eventually re-embarked on 26th April, but they only got as far as Sydney before disembarking again. After a week they were finally on their way towards Devonport, England, where they arrived on 28th July.

George spent time at Sling Camp before leaving for France on 5th September. He joined the 2nd Battalion, Canterbury Regiment on 16th September for further training at Bayinghem, near Lumbres, southwest of St. Omer. On 24th September orders were given to move the next day to the front line near Passchendaele. After days of marching and travel by motorbus the Battalion arrived at the old German Front line at Wieltje, two miles northeast of Ypres. George was involved in the attempt to capture the Gravenstafel and Abraham Heights spur on 12th October. The condition of the ground was very muddy due to recent rains. The men attempted to get round the flanks of the German pillboxes at Bellevue, northeast of Gravenstafel, and despite getting very close their objective was not achieved. During the attack George was injured, with gunshot wounds to his left arm and shoulder.

Immediate evacuation to England was arranged for George and he arrived at No. 1 NZGH, Brockenhurst on 16th October. His wounds were so severe that he survived just a week and died on 24th October 1917. He was buried the next day in Plot A, Row 4, Grave 3.

1917 was a sad year for the Heslop family. George's eldest nephew (son of brother Henry) Bernard Alfred Heslop, Private, 29617, No. 4 Machine Gun Company, N.Z. Machine Gun Corps, was killed at Messines on 10th June, and his mother, Emma, died on 16th October a few days before George.

George's death is recorded on his mother's tombstone (left) at Collingwood cemetery. Both he and Bernard are commemorated on the Collingwood War Memorial.

Acknowledgement: Gwen Heslop, Stoke, Nelson

ANDREW HAMILTON STOBO

Private, 45141
2nd Battalion, Otago Regiment, 8th Company
Died of sickness on 16th July 1918, aged 24

Andrew Hamilton Stobo was born on 7th March 1894 at Invercargill, Southland. He was the middle of three sons in the second family of a Presbyterian minister of the same name, and his mother's name was Jane.

Andrew's father, the Reverend Andrew Hamilton Stobo (1832-1898) was born in Strutherhead, Lanarkshire, Scotland, the son of farmers James and Janet (née Hamilton). Andrew (senior) began studying for the ministry in Glasgow in 1847, but he did not complete his studies for several years because of ill health. He worked in parishes in Scotland, and in 1860 he applied to serve the Free Church in the British colonies. He sailed from the Clyde on *Storm Cloud* and arrived at Port Chalmers on 27th April.

He had been appointed as minister for the parishioners of Invercargill and was ordained at the courthouse on 29th June 1860. At this time no church had been built, so for the first three years Andrew held his weekly service in a schoolhouse.

The Reverend Stobo

Eventually, the original First Church was opened on 15th March 1863. Andrew's parish extended many miles and he often made four-day journeys on horseback inland to the Otago gold mining areas to minister to the miners. His weak health could not cope with this style of living and in 1866 he spent three months in Victoria, Australia recuperating. This setback must have prompted Andrew to find a wife to care for him, because on 21st January 1867, at the age of 34 he married Jane Alexander Reid (aged 36) at the First Church, Invercargill. Jane had journeyed from Scotland to join her intended husband. In due course, she gave birth to a son.

Despite his ill health, Andrew continued his work and in 1875 he travelled to London to attend a Presbyterian Conference. However his eyesight was suffering and in 1879 he had a complete breakdown in health and retired from the First Church. He did later take up a home mission in South Invercargill.

Jane died on 11th March 1884, aged 54 years, and Andrew sought another wife to care for him and found a young widow Jane Rankin Mann, née Stirling (1868-1928). They subsequently had three sons, James, Andrew (junior) and Douglas. The boys' father died on 24th December 1898, aged 66, and consequently Jane (no. 2) had to look after the young family on her own. Andrew attended Invercargill Middle School between August 1899 and December 1905 when the family was living at Richmond Grove. He then transferred to Invercargill South School until December 1906, and left at the age of 12. By this time the Stobos had moved to 143 Earn Street, Invercargill. His education continued at Southland Boys' High School in 1907 for an unknown number of years.

In 1915 Andrew was employed as a bank clerk at Invercargill, his home town. He enlisted initially with the New Zealand Expeditionary Force at Trentham on 12th June 1915 at the age of 21, and joined the Otago Infantry, "D" Company, 7th Reinforcements. However, his time in the army did not last long because he was discharged at Tauherenikau, near Featherston, after 191 days' service, as being medically unfit.

Presumably, to toughen up, Andrew decided to take up an open-air life. He found employment with H. McKenzie & Sons as a sheep station hand at Walter Peak Station, beside Lake Wakatipu, opposite Queenstown. Even today, almost a century later, tourists visit the Station to watch the sheep shearing.

Andrew enlisted for the second time on 2nd December 1916 at Lumsden, and volunteered for the 25th Reinforcements "D" Company as a Private. He left New Zealand for overseas on 26th April 1917, departing from Wellington and disembarking at Devonport, England on 20th July. The troops marched into Sling Camp and Andrew was promoted to Lance Corporal.

After further training he left for France on 5th September and upon arriving in camp at Etaples he reverted to the rank of Private at his own request. On 3rd October he marched out to join the Division and on 2nd November he joined the 2nd Battalion, Otago Infantry Regiment, 8th Company near Selles, a training camp midway between Boulogne and St. Omer. The Battalion transferred to the Ypres area on November 13th, and Andrew was involved in the attempt to take Polderhoek Chateau on 3rd December.

Just under a year after leaving Wellington, on 22nd April 1918, Andrew fell ill with diarrhoea. This occurred whilst at the reserve camp on the Somme, near Colincamps, southwest of Hébuterne.

After receiving medical attention in France for six weeks, his case was considered to be serious enough for transfer to England. On 2nd June he arrived at No. 1 New Zealand General Hospital, Brockenhurst, by now suffering from pleurisy with severe effusion. Two days later his name was added to the Dangerously Ill list, due to the diagnosis of tuberculosis of the lung.

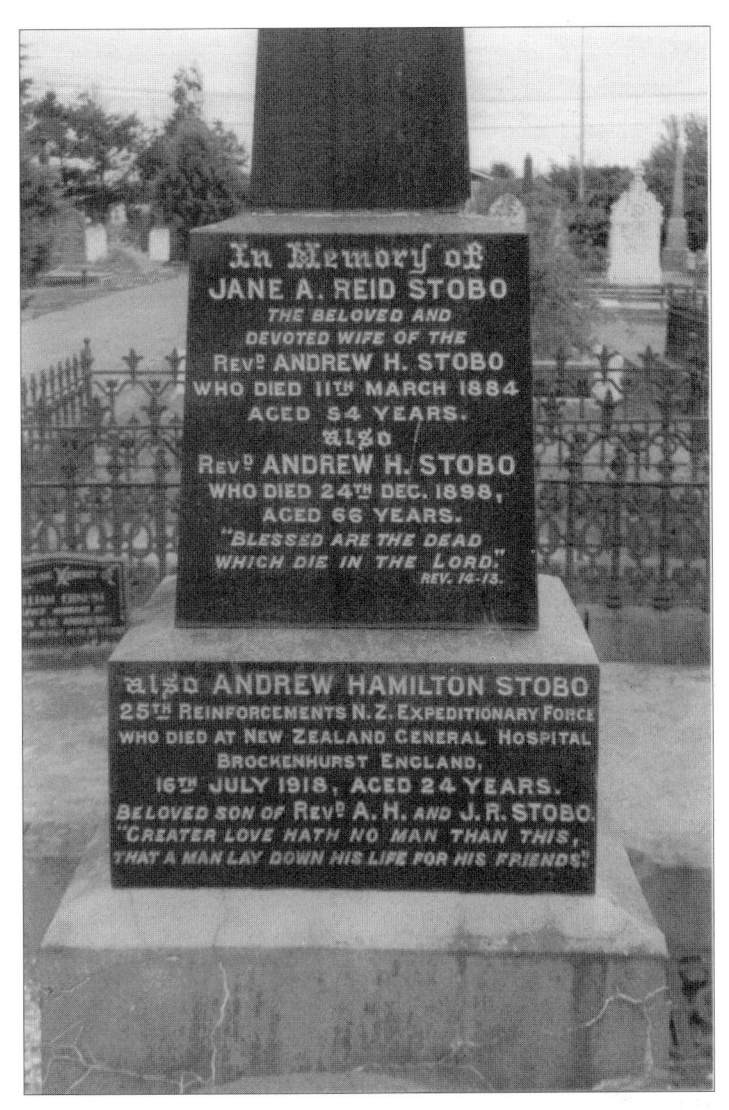

Andrew died on 16th July and was buried three days later. Plot A, Row 1, Grave 18. The Reverend W. R. Hutchinson, Presbyterian minister, officiated at the service.

Andrew is commemorated on Invercargill War Memorial, and on the Stobo family grave at Invercargill Eastern Cemetery (left).

His elder brother James was an outstanding student at Southland Boys' High School between 1905 and 1908, and he later graduated with M.A. with honours at Otago University in 1915. He was well known as a teacher at the Southland Technical School and for other educational work. He named a son Andrew Hamilton Stobo in memory of his brother, the third generation to bear this name.

Acknowledgements and Sources:

    Elizabeth Beer, Invercargill
    Barbara James, Ohope
    John Collie, *The Story of the Otago Free Church Settlement 1848 to 1940*
    Register of Presbyterian Ministers, Deaconesses and Missionaries
    Cyclopedia of New Zealand, Otago/Southland edition
        (photo of Reverend Stobo)

HAROLD LEVI EION HAMBLING

Private, 44481
3rd Battalion, Wellington Regiment, 7th Company
Died of wounds on 28th February 1918, aged 33

Harold Levi Eion Hambling, son of Levi (1860-1935) and Sarah Rebecca, née Hawkin (died 1942), was born on 3rd April 1884 at Woodville, approximately 16 miles east of Palmerston North in the Manawatu region of North Island, a sheep and dairy-farming district.

Harold was the third generation of Hamblings in New Zealand. His grandfather, Charles (1836-1904), and his grandmother Ann, née Prattley (1839-1884) originated in Oxfordshire. Charles and Ann were married on 31st May 1858 at the Parish Church, Fifield, Oxfordshire, and raised a family of six children, Levi being the eldest boy and second child. The family sailed to New Zealand on board the *Winchester* in 1874, arriving at Napier on 26th July. They settled in Woodville and were some of the town's earliest pioneers.

Levi married Sarah Rebecca in 1883 at Woodville. After his mother's death in 1884, his father, Charles, returned to Oxfordshire and married Ann's half sister, Sarah Prattley at Southam, Warwickshire in October of that year. Charles and his second wife very soon returned to Woodville and within a few years Sarah gave birth to seven children, but only three of them survived to adulthood.

Meanwhile Levi and his Sarah had started to produce a family or their own, all born at Woodville. The eldest child was Harold Levi Eion, whose siblings were:

Winnie May	*(b.1887)*	*(Mrs. Grinlinton)*
Clarice Elsie	*(1888-1891)*	
Ruby Ivy	*(1892-1894)*	
Beatrice Clarrissa	*(1897-1907)*	
Lillian Melva	*(b.1900)*	*(Mrs. Taplin)*

Woodville first Methodist Church (from Helen Roy, Feilding)

Charles and Levi were committed to the Methodist Church and they built the first church in Woodville, which was opened in January 1883. Levi was a circuit steward between 1885 and 1905 and he was also choirmaster, with his wife assisting as organist. Later, Levi and Harold built many houses in the area, some of which are still in existence in 2001.

Harold enlisted with the NZEF on 5th December 1916 at Woodville. He left New Zealand on 5th April 1917 with the Wellington Infantry Regiment, "B" Company, 24th Reinforcements on board the *Devon*. The ship reached Devonport, England on 11th June and training at Sling Camp occupied him until posting to the Western Front. He joined the 3rd Battalion, Wellington Regiment, 7th Company on 24th July 1917 in preparation for the attack on Basseville.

Harold survived the Front for two months. He was slightly wounded on 10th August but remained with his unit. He was wounded in action for the second time on 3rd October during the 3rd Battle of Ypres (Passchendaele), the day before the New Zealand Division attacked at Gravenstafel. He received gunshot wounds to his left leg and thigh and it was necessary for his left leg to be amputated at a base hospital in Rouen.

Many New Zealand soldiers were admitted to hospitals in England within days of being wounded, but Harold's situation necessitated him remaining in France to recover from his operation. He eventually arrived at No. 1 NZGH, Brockenhurst on 5th December 1917 but his health never improved, and he died of empyema as a result of his wounds on 28th February 1918. He was buried on 2nd March.

Plot A, Row 1, Grave 15.

Harold is commemorated on the War Memorial at Fountaine Square, Woodville (below), situated in parkland surrounded with trees. The square was named after Thomas Francis Fountaine (1842-1934) whose roots were in Buckinghamshire, England. Along with Harold's grandfather, Charles, he was a pioneer of Woodville and District.

1914-1918

AMBROSE, A.T.	CRUMP, E.F.	HERRICK, N.C.
AMMUNDSEN, R.T.	CURRY, A.B.	HIATT, S.J.R.
ARROW, A.	DAVIE, H.P.C.	HOARE, J.A.
BEAN, W.E.C.	DIXON, C.	HOOPER, C.
BONDI, L.	EBBETT, A.W.J.	HORNE, C.W.
BRAITHWAITE, H.W.	ELWOOD, A.T.	HUGHES, F.
BREARTON, T.H.	GARDNER, T.C.	JENSEN, C.
BURBUSH, D.C.	GREAVES, W.	JENSEN, E.M.
BURBUSH, C.E.	GREENAWAY, F.	JENSEN, W.F.
CAIRNS, R.J.	HAMBLING, H.L.E.	JONES, W.
CAMMOCK, F.H.	HARES, F.	JUNO, W.H.F.
CHRISTIANSEN, C.W.F.	HARRIS, A.	LAITILA, K.
CLULOW, R.	HATWELL, F.A.L.	LEHNDORF, A.R.
COBB, H.F.	HAUCHIE, J.W.	LOADER, E.L.

After the War Harold's parents, Levi and Sarah were resident at 8 Glover Road, Hawera, Taranaki, but it is not known why they went to live there. They later moved to the Auckland area to be near one of their daughters. They are buried in Waikemete Cemetery, Auckland.

Acknowledgements:

    Helen Roy, Feilding
    Mike Foster, Wellington, indexed names from
        "*The Farthest Promised Land*" by Professor Rollo Arnold,
        Victoria University Press, Wellington, 1981

ARTHUR COLE

Private, 41741
1st Battalion, Wellington Regiment, 7th Company
Died of sickness on 12th June 1918, aged 44

Owing to his age and subsequent state of health, Arthur Cole, in hindsight should probably never have been accepted as a fighting soldier. There is a discrepancy regarding his date of birth. His army record states that he was born on 22nd May 1876, but the CWGC records imply that he was born in 1874. It is suspected that the latter date is more accurate, and that on enlistment Arthur falsified his age in order to gain admission to the NZEF.

Arthur's birthplace was Foxton, Manawatu, and he was the son of Edwin and Harriet (née Durrant). Edwin's roots were in Kent, and Harriet came from Portsmouth. They arrived independently in New Zealand in approximately 1860, and were married at Wellington on 8th May 1870. Besides Arthur, it is known that Harriet gave birth to three other children: Mabel (Mrs. Sherrock), Alice (Mrs. Tunnicliffe) and Florence, b.1878 (Mrs. Anderson). The Cole family would have attended Foxton School and some may well be pictured below.

Wooden School building with group of children outside, Foxton.
W J Harding Collection. G-000344-1/1 (PAColl-3042) ATL

Judging from the number of children in the photograph it is a wonder how they all fitted into the small school building!

Prior to joining the New Zealand army, Arthur was employed as a labourer for Mr. Maden, a Contractor of Foxton. Arthur lived at Robinson Street in the same township. He enlisted with the NZEF at Palmerston North on 12th December 1916 and departed from New Zealand on 14th March 1917 on the *Ruapehu*, with the Wellington Infantry Regiment, "B" Company, 23rd Reinforcements.

The ship docked at Devonport, England on 21st May, and Arthur marched into Sling Camp on Salisbury Plain for the standard one-month's training. He left for France on 21st June and joined the 1st Battalion, Wellington Regiment, 7th Company on 9th July in preparation for the attack on Basseville. In the event, he was never involved in this attack because he was in hospital between 18th July and 2nd August, suffering from influenza.

In mid December Arthur transferred temporarily to the 3rd Canadian Tunnelling Company for one month. Then in mid January 1918 he was detached to a Sanitation School for two weeks to be taught how to keep his fellow comrades in a healthy state, i.e. ensuring that the Field latrines and ablutions were satisfactorily maintained. However, despite this tuition, Arthur himself suffered from unsanitary conditions because on 16th May he was sent to hospital with diarrhoea, which developed into enteritis.

The medical authorities decided it was necessary to transfer him to England, and Arthur arrived at No. 1 NZGH, Brockenhurst on 22nd May 1918. He was immediately placed on the Dangerously Ill List because his condition had deteriorated rapidly, and he was diagnosed as having tuberculosis of the lung. Arthur died of this disease on 12th June 1918 and was buried two days later.

Plot A, Row 5, Grave 13.

The officiating clergyman was the Reverend A. J. Jacob.

Arthur's next of kin was named as his sister Alice (Mrs. Tunnicliffe) of Manunui, Main Trunk Line. Another sister Mabel (Mrs. Sherrock) lived at Tiakitahuna, Palmerston North.

HENRY CHARLES SIDFORD

Rifleman, 41638
4th Battalion, 3rd New Zealand Rifle Brigade, "A" Company
Died of wounds on 21st January 1919, aged 37

Henry Charles Sidford was born on 8th May 1881 at Dunedin. His parents Arthur Beggs (1851-1916) and Deborah, née Pettigrew (1855-1916) came from Dublin, Ireland, and they both emigrated to New Zealand in the 1870s. They were married on 27th February 1877 at Knox Church, Dunedin, and their first son, Arthur Hulton was born on 12th May the following year. The family first lived at Royal Arcade, Dunedin, but by 1900 they had moved house and settled at 6 Kent Terrace, Wellington.

Henry worked as a Clerk for the Wellington Harbour Board. He named his eldest brother, Arthur, as next-of-kin when he enlisted with the NZEF. At that time the brothers were living at 7 Caroline Street, Wellington.

Wellington Harbour Board Offices. PA1-o-100-18

Henry signed his Attestation Sheet on 13th December 1916 (possibly influenced to do so by the death of both his parents earlier that same year) and departed from New Zealand with the NZRB Reinforcements, "G" Company on 5th April 1917 on board the *Devon*. The troops disembarked at Devonport, England on 11th June and went straightaway to Sling Camp.

On 6th July Henry was posted to France and joined the 4th Battalion, 3rd NZRB, "A" Company on 9th August 1917 at Basseville, southeast of Messines. His period at the Front lasted for two months before he was admitted to hospital suffering from scabies. He was not pronounced fit enough to return to Etaples until the beginning of February 1918, and he finally rejoined his unit in the Field near Hébuterne in the Upper Ancre on 26th April. After four months in action, he was wounded on 29th August 1918 whilst fighting east of Favreuil in the Battle of Bapaume (see map p. 179). The 4th Rifles were positioned in the railway siding and were unable to make any advance owing to the determined resistance of the enemy. Henry received gunshot wounds to his back and chest, the seriousness of which resulted in paraplegia.

Henry was classified as Dangerously Ill, and immediately evacuated to England, arriving at No. 1 NZGH, Brockenhurst on 8th September. He must have temporarily recovered from his injuries because he survived a further three and a half months. However, his death on 21st January 1919 was perhaps a blessing in disguise in view of his paralysis. He was buried on 23rd January. Plot A, Row 2, Grave 22.

Henry is commemorated on the family grave at Karori Cemetery, Wellington (below), Area 8, Block G, Row 14, Plot 12. His mother, Deborah, died on 13th February 1916 (aged 60), and his father, Arthur died on 12th August the same year (aged 65).

Acknowledgement and Source:

    Estelle Longstaffe, Dunedin
    1900 Wise's NZPO Directory

EDWARD WILLIAM HENRY LAWRENCE

Private, 45872
3rd Battalion, Wellington Regiment, 7th Company
Died of wounds on 6th November 1917, aged 23

Edward William Henry Lawrence was born on 3rd April 1894, the only son of William Henry (1865-1949) and Rose Young, née Lett (1871-1945).

Rose Young was the second daughter of a large family of sixteen children (12 boys and 4 girls) of Charles (1837-1918) and Sarah Lett, née Watson (1848-1917). At the age of seventeen Rose married William Henry Lawrence at the Registrar's Office, Wellington, on 20th September 1887.

William Henry and Rose Lawrence (from Lesley Keil, Masterton)

William Henry Lawrence was born in Upper Hutt, near Wellington. At the time of his marriage to Rose he was working as a railway engineer at Kaitoke, and he later became a carpenter. They appear to have lived in several locations - their two girls Rose Isabella (1887-1957) and Daisy (1892-1972) were born at Pakuratahi, Kaitoke in the Wellington area, and Edward William Henry (1894-1917) was born at Manakau, south of Levin. The family then moved to Newman in the Wairarapa region, prior to settling in First Street, Lansdowne, Masterton in 1902. Edward was admitted to Masterton District High School (No. 1114) on 19th June 1905, after which he attended Lansdowne School, Masterton (No. 85) in 1909.

Edward worked as a carpenter for his father prior to enlisting with the NZEF. He signed on to join the army on 20th December 1916 at Masterton and departed from New Zealand with the Wellington Infantry Regiment, "B" Company, 24th Reinforcements, (1st Draft), on 5th April 1917 on board HMT *Devon*. The ship docked at Devonport, England on 11th June and Edward marched into Sling Camp, where he remained for a few weeks before proceeding overseas to France on 6th July.

On 24th July he joined the 3rd Battalion, Wellington Regiment, 7th Company, in preparation for the attack on Basseville. A few days later, on 3rd August Edward was admitted to No. 4 New Zealand Field Ambulance with conjunctivitis. This was soon cured and he shortly afterwards rejoined his unit.

On 4th October he was wounded in action at Passchendaele, with gunshot wounds to his right buttock. He transferred to England straightaway and was admitted to No. 1 NZGH, Brockenhurst (Balmer Lawn section) on 12th October. He was classified as Dangerously Ill on 4th November and died of his wounds two days later. His burial took place on 8th November. Plot A, Grave Row 1, Grave 13.

Original grave marker, Brockenhurst
(from Lesley Keil, Masterton)

Headstone provided by
Edward's parents

Rose and Bill never got over the loss of their only son, and made a pilgrimage to England in 1921 to visit his grave. Also in his memory every year, on the anniversary of his death, they put "In Memoriam" notices in the local newspaper:

ROLL OF HONOUR

IN MEMORIAM

LAWRENCE – In loving memory of E. W. H. (Ted) Lawrence (Twenty-fourth Reinforcements), who was wounded at Passchendaele, France, on October 4, 1917, and died at Brockenhurst, November 6, 1917.

> Our thoughts they ever wander
> To a soldier's honoured grave,
> For we see you in the photo
> In the home you died to save.
> To live in the hearts of those we love is not to die.

(Inserted by his loving father, mother and sisters)

"LAWRENCE E," is listed on the Cenotaph (left) at Queen Elizabeth Park, Masterton, just a few names above his uncle's, (his mother's brother), "JOHN McCLAREN LETT", (Australian Imperial Forces), who was killed in action at Passchendaele on 27th September 1917, seven days before Edward was wounded.

In later life Rose and Bill Lawrence moved to Marine Parade, Napier, where they had a guesthouse, "Lansdowne House", named after their previous residence. They are both buried at Park Island Cemetery, Tamatea, Napier.

Acknowledgement: Lesley Keil, Masterton

THOMAS CAMPBELL

Private, 46288
2nd Battalion, Auckland Regiment
Died of wounds on 13th October 1918, aged 34

Thomas Campbell was born on 14th August 1884 at Mercury Bay, Coromandel. He was the son of Thomas Duncan (1856-1948) and Anne, née Hall (1857-1925). Thomas (senior) was born in Stirling, Scotland and Anne came from County Cavan, Ireland. She arrived in New Zealand in 1875, and in January 1882 she married Thomas Duncan at Papakura. Their first child Mary (Mrs. C. J. Moody) was soon born followed by Thomas in 1884. By this time the family were living at Mercury Bay where Thomas (senior) was employed as a mill hand. Other children were Ann (Mrs. T. Dunkley, b.1888) and William (b.1893).

In 1890 the family had settled at Wairoa Road, Papakura where father was a farmer. Thomas (junior) was admitted to Papakura Public School on 27th January that year (Register No. 246). Interestingly, his mother Anne is listed on the 1893 Waipa Electoral Roll (No. 343), which indicates that she would be one of the first women in the world to exercise her vote! At that time her occupation was Domestic Duties (i.e. housewife)!

Before Thomas enlisted with the NZEF on 1st January 1917 he was employed as a platelayer for the New Zealand Government Railway. After basic military training in New Zealand, he left Wellington on board *Tofua* on 26th April 1917 with the Auckland Infantry Regiment "A" Company, 25th Reinforcements bound for Devonport, England, where he disembarked on 20th July. Further training at Sling Camp followed, prior to posting to France on 5th September. He joined 1st Battalion, Auckland Regiment at the training camp near Lumbres on 27th October. Then in December he found himself attached to the Australian Tunnelling Company for a month before rejoining 1st Battalion, Auckland Regiment on 19th January 1918.

At the beginning of May 1918 Thomas was ill suffering from mumps, which was followed by a brief stay in hospital with scabies. He did not join the 2nd Battalion, Auckland Regiment until 27th August, and just three days later on 30th August he received gunshot wounds to both his knees, which promptly ended his active military life. This happened towards the end of the Battle of Bapaume (21st August-1st September). It was necessary for both his legs to be amputated as a consequence of his wounds and this trauma proved fatal for him. Thomas was admitted to No. 1 NZGH on 1st October, but only lived a further fortnight and died on 13th October 1918. The burial ceremony was officiated by Rev. W. R. Hutchinson on 16th October. Plot A, Row 5, Grave 18.

After Anne's death in 1925, Thomas Duncan continued to live at Wairoa Road, Papakura. By now he was a stable keeper for a large racing establishment in the area. In 1941 he moved to live with his married daughter Ann (Dunkley) at 12 Union Street, Papakura, where he died in 1948 in his 92nd year.

The parents' grave headstone at Papakura Cemetery, Great South Road reads:

In loving Memory
of
ANNE
BELOVED WIFE OF
THOMAS DUNCAN CAMPBELL
DIED MARCH 30TH 1925
AGED 68 YEARS

ALSO HER BELOVED HUSBAND
THOMAS DUNCAN CAMPBELL
DIED MARCH 10TH 1948
AGED 91 YEARS, 11 M^{THS}

ALSO THEIR BELOVED SON
46288. PVTE. THOMAS CAMPBELL
DIED OF WOUNDS OCT. 13TH 1918
AGED 34 YEARS

Thomas is also commemorated on the memorial on the Soldiers' Statue, Papakura.

Acknowledgements: Geoff Hall, Auckland (information and photographs)
1900 Wise's NZPO Directory

WILLIAM DOUGLAS MAYALL

Private, 35474
New Zealand Machine Gun Battalion, "B" Company
Died of wounds on 28th April 1918, aged 25

William Douglas Mayall, born on 28th March 1893 at Footscray, Melbourne Australia was the sixth child of eight of James William and Elizabeth.

William's family originated from the Lancashire/Yorkshire borders of England. His grandparents were Giles and Sarah Elizabeth (née Platt). After Giles's death in 1865, Sarah married James Bottomley a year later. The 1881 Census lists the following members of this family living at Diggle, on the outskirts of Oldham, and on the edge of Saddleworth Moor.

James Bottomley	60	born Saddleworth, Yorkshire	Farmer of 7 acres
Sarah Bottomley	43	" Oldham, Lancashire	Wife
James William Mayall	21	" Oldham, Lancashire	Butcher
George Mayall	19	" Oldham, Lancashire	Loom Tuner
Albert Bottomley	18	" Saddleworth, Yorkshire	Iron Driller
Frank Bottomley	14	" Saddleworth, Yorkshire	Errand boy
Ester Bottomley	12	" Saddleworth, Yorkshire	Scholar

James William Mayall (1860-1928) married Sarah Elizabeth Alice Holden (1861-1920) on 7th September 1881 at St. Chad's Church, Saddleworth. Their first child, Harold was born on 15th December 1881 prior to their emigration to Ballarat, Victoria, Australia. They left England in February 1883, accompanied by James's brother, George Edward Mayall and his wife Millicent (née Sollis) who had married shortly beforehand.

James and Elizabeth went directly to Ballarat, and their second child, Robert was born on 22nd June 1883. Two further children were born in Ballarat, Maud Elsie (b.1886) and Ida Vivian (b.1888). The brothers and their families then moved to Footscray, Melbourne where four more children were born: Ethel Annie (b.1890), William Douglas (b.1893), Hedley Hadfield (b.1895) and Vera Alice (b.1896).

James and his brother George set up a butchery business in Footscray and in 1890 G & W Butchers were established in Barkley Street (this could be 86 Buckley Street, which was a business address until 1900). The next year the brothers expanded their partnership and ran a second shop at 1 Hopkins Street. In 1896 they split up, with George at Buckley Street and James at Hopkins Street, and in 1898 Elizabeth ran a shop at 27 Manson Street, Newport, probably for one year only.

James migrated to Dunedin, New Zealand as a steerage passenger aboard the S.S. *Talune*, which departed from Melbourne on 14th June 1900 and arrived in Dunedin via Hobart and Bluff on 23rd June. His wife and children followed on the next voyage of the same ship, leaving Melbourne on 26th July 1900, arriving Dunedin on 4th August.

The family established themselves in South Dunedin at Bradshaw Street. In 1903 James is recorded as working as a butcher at 113 Rattray Street. In 1904 he was a butcher at 75 Great King Street, and the next year he was the manager of Thos. Smith & Co., Butchers at 131 George Street. He remained in this position until 1916 when he returned to managing his own butchery business.

William Douglas was educated at Macandrew Road and Arthur Street Normal Schools and George Street Primary School. He left school in June 1907 aged 14. He soon went to work in the furniture making industry, and on the 1914 General Electoral Roll for Dunedin North Electorate he is recorded as being a chair maker. Sometime after this he left Dunedin, and in 1917 when he enlisted with the NZEF he was working as a cabinetmaker for Doyle Bros., Wellington. When he signed on he nominated his mother as next-of-kin, her address given as 38 Forth Place, Dunedin.

William signed his Attestation Sheet on 8th January 1917 at Dunedin and departed from New Zealand with the Army Service Corps, 26th Reinforcements on 12th June on the *Maunganui*. The ship docked at Devonport, England on 16th August and William went to Sling Camp. A month later he transferred to the Machine Gun Corps in the capacity of Driver and was posted to the New Zealand Machine Gun Depot at Grantham, Lincolnshire. He must have found the temptation of celebrating too great over the New Year period 1917-18 as he went absent without leave between 28th December and 3rd January. He served 7 days detention and forfeited 7 days pay.

He left for France on 18th January 1918 and marched into camp at Camiers. He remained there until 5th March when he joined the New Zealand Machine Gun Battalion, "B" Company at Polygon Wood, east of Ypres. On 25th March the New Zealand Division proceeded south to the Upper Ancre valley to repel the German offensive. His stay at the Front was brief, for he was wounded in action on 1st April with gunshot wounds to his head whilst at la Signy Farm, south of Hébuterne

William straightaway left France, and arrived at No. 1 NZGH, Brockenhurst on 13th April. He died from his wounds on 28th April and was buried two days later. The officiating clergyman was the Reverend W. R. Hutchinson.

William's mother, Elizabeth died in 1920, and in 1922 his father James re-married to Olive McPherson; she died two years later in August 1924. James again re-married to Jessie Paterson Beer (née Wilkinson) in 1925. In later life he was a taxi proprietor, living at 48 Howe Street, Dunedin and he died in 1928. The family grave at Northern Cemetery, Dunedin, Block 152, Lot 11C could not be found by the author. Many of the headstones are damaged and demolished.

Acknowledgements and Source:

Allan Pope, Motueka, Nelson
Estelle Longstaffe, Dunedin
UK 1881 Census, FHL Film 1342042, PRO Ref. RG11, Piece 4364, Folio 80, page 9
Sands and McDougall Directory, Melbourne, 1890-1900
Stone's Directory, Dunedin, 1914

CYRIL ERNEST ROGERS

Rifleman, 48570
2nd Battalion, 3rd New Zealand Rifle Brigade
Died of sickness 19th April 1918, aged 30

Cyril Ernest Rogers was born on 1st February 1888 at Tuakau, south of Auckland. He was the youngest son of Samuel Smith and Martha Elizabeth (née Fry). He had ten siblings (possibly 11):

Elizabeth Mary	b. 1870	m William Anderson Savage in 1896
Stanley Edward	b. 1880,	m Beatrice Stoneham
	(drowned Leigh, 24 August 1936)	
Ethel C		m Dave Blackburn
Margaret I		m Ron W Blackburn (brother to Dave)
Arthur (Bill)		m Millicent Mace (WW1 veteran)
Ellen		m Patrick Walsh
Annie E		m ? Penk
Florence		m Jack Peers
Ernest		died as a toddler after eating unripe tawa berries
George Henry		killed in action 3rd October 1917

Samuel and Martha (below) came from the west country of England. Samuel was born on 22nd November 1839 in St. Augustine's Parish, Bristol, whilst Martha, who was 14 years younger (b.1853), came from Weston-Super-Mare, Somerset.

During Cyril's early years the family moved from Tuakau to Little Omaha, near Leigh, where his father Samuel was a farmer.

Cyril (aged 10)   and shortly after enlisting, January 1917

Cyril worked as a contractor at Port Waikato prior to enlisting with the NZEF. He signed on at Auckland on 18th January 1917 as a Private, and at the end of his preliminary military training on 25th July, he was promoted to Corporal. The next day he departed from New Zealand with "G" Company, NZRB Reinforcements (2nd Draft) on troopship *Ulimaroa* bound for Devonport, Plymouth, England.

He disembarked on 24th September and went straight to Sling Camp. Three days later he transferred to the New Zealand Rifle Brigade base at Brocton, Staffordshire. Here he joined "A" Company, 5th Reserve Battalion with the rank of Rifleman. The 23rd October saw Cyril proceeding overseas to France, and he joined the 2nd Battalion, 3rd New Zealand Rifle Brigade, "D" Company on 2nd November 1917.

His health was beginning to fail, however, because the next day, on 3rd November he was admitted to No. 3 Field Ambulance, followed by New Zealand Stationary Hospital, suffering from measles. By 7th November his condition had deteriorated and he was placed on the "Seriously Ill" list with bronchial pneumonia, which necessitated him being transferred to No. 1 NZGH, Brockenhurst, Balmer Lawn section. He had recovered sufficiently by 19th December to be removed from the "Seriously Ill" list.

Cyril was discharged from No. 1 NZGH on 26th March 1918, and went once more to the New Zealand Rifle Brigade base at Brocton. This transfer proved to be fruitless because he was back at Brockenhurst by 3rd April, suffering from lobar pneumonia, and placed on the "Dangerously Ill" list. Cyril died of the disease on 19th April and was buried the next day.

Plot A, Row 5, Grave 11.

His unfortunate history is a classic case of being sent back to his unit before he was physically fit.

Cyril's siblings all signed a "Consent" document in 1919 stating that the payment of any balance that may be due to his estate by the Defence Department was to be made to his sister, Mrs. Florence Erin Peers, of 24 Millais Street, Grey Lynn, Auckland.

One of Cyril's brothers, Private George Henry Rogers, 38750, 1st Battalion, Wellington Regiment (right) also lost his life in the War. He was killed in action on 3rd October 1917 during the Third Battle of Ypres (Passchendaele).

His body has never been found, and he is commemorated on the Tyne Cot Memorial to the Missing at Zonnebeke, West-Vlaanderen, Belgium.

Both Cyril and George are remembered on the War memorial at Leigh.

Three members of this large family are buried in Leigh cemetery - Samuel, Martha and brother Stanley.

Samuel died on 14th February 1914, aged 74 and his wife Martha, who died on 26th April 1919, aged 66 is buried alongside him.

Stanley drowned in Leigh harbour on 24th August 1936, aged 56 when his dinghy capsized while he was lifting crayfish pots.

Wooden crosses placed on the graves of Samuel and Martha Rogers
by Cliff and Phyl Blackburn (photographed by Jim Lee, Leigh)

Acknowledgements:

    Velma Savage, Dargaville (great nephew's wife)
    Phyl Blackburn, Warkworth (nephew's wife) – information and photos
    Jim Lee, Leigh
    Lynne and Kevynne Hyde, Stanmore Bay

JOSEPH WILLIAM BOWER

Gunner, 52940
New Zealand Field Artillery, 13th Battery, 3rd Brigade
Died of wounds on 2nd September 1918, aged 21

Joseph William Bower, the son of Donald Calder and Flora (née Stevenson) was born on 8th November 1896 in Blueskin, Otago. He was the fourth generation of Bowers in New Zealand. His great grandparents, David (1797-1837) and Isabella (née McDonald) were Scottish. David died aged 40 leaving Isabella destitute with 10 children. One son David and his wife sailed to New Zealand on the *Philip Laing* in 1848 with the Free Church Migrants as early Otago settlers and he encouraged and arranged assistance for his mother and her four youngest children to follow, which included a son Joseph (b.1837). They arrived in Port Chalmers on the *Larkins* in September 1849, when Joseph was 12.

Joseph (son of Isabella) first worked in the Clutha area of Otago sawing timber. In 1860 he married Johanna Calder, after which he was a farmer until his retirement. Their sixth child of ten was Donald Calder (1869-1919). Donald married Flora Stevenson (1870-1949) in 1893 and they had two children, Jean Campbell (1894-1960) and Joseph William (1896-1918). The family moved to the Wairarapa region and the children attended Parkvale School at Carterton. As a young man, Joseph William worked as a cheese maker at Greytown (the family home township) with his father, most probably at the Dairy Factory (below).

Dairy products ready for transport from the Co-op Dairy Factory in Greytown
G 48475-1/2. S. C. Smith Collection (PAColl-3082) ATL

Joseph enlisted with the NZEF on 25th January 1917 at Greytown. He departed from New Zealand on 14th July with the New Zealand Field Artillery (NZFA), 28th Reinforcements (1st Draft) on board the *Waitemata* and disembarked at Devonport, Plymouth on 24th September. He marched into camp at Aldershot the next day and stayed there for one month before being sent to France. He joined the 13th Battery on 12th November and within two days he was posted to the Ypres area. During the first week in December the NZFA moved into the Front line.

In February 1918 Joseph spent a few days at No. 1 New Zealand Field Ambulance suffering from scabies, but he soon rejoined his unit. However, during the Battle of Bapaume (see map p. 179) he received gunshot wounds to his left hip and left buttock on 26th August. His injuries were serious enough for immediate transfer to England and he was admitted to No. 1 NZGH, Brockenhurst on the 30th. Joseph died on 2nd September 1918, with his burial two days later. The officiating clergyman was the Reverend W. R. Hutchinson (Presbyterian Chaplain). Plot A, Row 5, Grave 17.

Joseph is commemorated on his school Roll of Honour board at Carterton, on his parents' grave at Greytown (now a very worn and indistinguishable headstone) and also on the memorial gates at the park entrance, Greytown. These gates were dedicated on ANZAC Day, 1923 and an avenue of lime trees was planted in commemoration of the servicemen lost in the Great War.

Entrance to Greytown Park with WW1 soldiers' names beside the gates

Jean, Joseph's sister, did not marry so there do not appear to be any descendants from this side of the family.

Acknowledgement: Shirley Scadden, Masterton (cousin)

WILLIAM JAMES RAINEY

Rifleman
47076
3rd Battalion, 3rd New Zealand Rifle Brigade, "C" Company
Died of sickness on 21st august 1918, aged 37

William James Rainey was born on 31st March 1881 at Winchester, near Temuka, Canterbury. His parents William and Agnes, from Belfast, Ireland emigrated to New Zealand circa 1877. William (junior) was employed as farm labourer for Mr. Richard Austin at Danebury, Mayfield prior to going to War. His sister Margaret was named as next-of-kin, of Clandeboye, Temuka, and with legatee as Mr. G. Rainey (elder brother) of Glenavy, on the Waitaki River.

William enlisted on 26th January 1917 at Ashburton and departed from Wellington on 26th April with "J" Company, New Zealand Rifle Brigade (NZRB) Reinforcements. After arrival at Devonport, England on 20th July 1917 he marched into Sling Camp and a week later was taken on strength of No. 3 NZGH at Codford. Then on 27th October William was sent to the NZRB base at Brocton, Staffordshire for further training. He left for France on 7th December and joined the 3rd Battalion, 3rd NZRB, "C" Company. He suffered with feet problems and spent the next few months in and out of hospital in France. He eventually transferred to England and was admitted to No. 1 NZGH, Brockenhurst on 27th July 1918 suffering from a totally different problem - valvular disease of the heart. On 10th August he was placed on the Seriously Ill List suffering from ulcerative endocarditis. William died on 21st August 1918, and was buried two days later. Plot A, Row 3, Grave 18.

His name is listed on Temuka War Memorial and Mayfield Memorial Hall (below).

HORACE DAVID MATUSCHKA

Private, 52449
2nd Battalion, Auckland Regiment
Died of sickness on 25th January 1918, aged 28

Horace David Matuschka was born on 3rd January 1890 at Auckland. He was the son of Lewis (1864-1937) and Elizabeth Anne (1869-1913) who lived at Carruth Road, Papatoetoe, Auckland. Lewis was born in Australia and moved to New Zealand in the 1870s. School records indicate that Horace had three sisters - Magdalene (b.1900), Ethel May (b.1902) and Amy Elizabeth (b.1906).

Horace enlisted with the NZEF on 28th January 1917 at Ashburton, Canterbury, near to where he had been working as a teamster (a driver of a team of horses) for Mr. T. Baxter of Seafield.

He departed from New Zealand with "C" Company, Otago Infantry Regiment, 26th Reinforcements on 12th June 1917 on board HMNZT *Maunganui*, arriving at Devonport, England on 16th August. Training at Sling Camp took place before posting overseas to France for action on the Western Front. Horace undertook further training at the base camp at Etaples before joining the 2nd Battalion, Auckland Regiment on 11th October to play his part in the 3rd Battle of Ypres (Passchendaele).

Horace's period at the Front was short-lived, because he fell sick on 21st November, suffering from influenza. He then spent the next two months in France under the care of the medical authorities before transfer to England and admission to No. 1 NZGH, Brockenhurst on 11th December.

By this time his illness had developed into pneumonia and on 16th December Horace was placed on the Seriously Ill list. He never recovered and died on 25th January 1918 of lobar pneumonia. His burial was officiated by the Reverend W. R. Hutchinson on 31st January.

Plot A, Row 3, Grave 13.

Louis and Elizabeth Anne are buried in the Flat Bush Wesleyan Cemetery, Chapel Road, Flat Bush, Manukau City, Auckland.

Acknowledgement:

Les Woolnough, Manurewa, Auckland

JOHN TANA WARENA

Private, 19661
New Zealand Maori (Pioneer) Battalion
Died of sickness on 1st November 1917, aged 23

John Tana Warena, the son of William and Ari was born on 10th May 1894 in the Waikato region; the exact location is not known. The Maori population farmed this region before the Europeans settled in New Zealand, and archaeological evidence shows that thousands of hectares were under cultivation with kumara (sweet potatoes) and other crops.

John probably came from an area of land where the Maoris had retreated after the Waikato Land War of 1864. Relations between the two cultures during the 1850s had been soured owing to the Europeans' seizure of Maori land for settlement. The Maoris retreated to what is known as "King Country", which extended roughly from the towns of Otorohanga in the north to Taumarunui in the south, and from Lake Taupo to the western coast.

John's job prior to joining the army was as a carpenter for Mr. J. Johnson at Morrinsville, northeast of Hamilton. He enlisted with the NZEF at Morrinsville on 30th January 1917. At that time his father was deceased and his mother was living at Wanganui.

He departed from New Zealand with the Maori Contingent, 17th Reinforcements on 26th April on the *Turakina*. The ship docked at Devonport, England on 20th July and John marched into Sling Camp. He left for France on 5th September in the Reserve Group and was attached to strength at Etaples on 8th September.

John never reached the Front line because he fell ill on 2nd October with influenza and tuberculosis of the lung. Within three weeks he was a patient at No. 1 NZGH, Brockenhurst. He survived less than a fortnight longer and died on 1st November 1917. He was buried on 3rd November in Plot A, Row 2, Grave 12.

John's brother also died in the Great War only days before him on 20th October 1917. He was Private Kitohi Warena, 16/1354 New Zealand Maori (Pioneer) Battalion who is buried at Kaikohe Maori Cemetery near Kaikohe, on SH 12, approximately 200 miles north of Auckland.

JOHN THOMPSON CONNELLY

Rifleman, 49874
2nd Battalion, 3rd New Zealand Rifle Brigade, "D" Company
Died of wounds on 26th April 1918, aged 34

John Thompson Connelly worked as a mill hand for Ross Glendinning and Company at Peel Forest, north of Geraldine, South Canterbury. This forest is one of New Zealand's most important areas of indigenous podocarp (conifer) forest, which consists of totara, kahikatea and matai.

He was born on 25th July 1883, the son of Henry and Susan, whose roots were in Ireland. They had settled in New Zealand in the 1870s.

John's parents were both deceased when he enlisted with the NZEF on 3rd February 1917 at Timaru, South Canterbury, so he nominated his sister Mrs. Mary Stewart of 40a Bayview Road, Dunedin as next-of-kin. He departed from New Zealand with "J" Company, New Zealand Rifle Brigade Reinforcements on 12th June 1917 on the *Maunganui*. The ship arrived at Devonport, England on 16th August and he marched into Tidworth Camp on Salisbury Plain the same day. Shortly afterwards, he transferred to Brocton, Staffordshire for further training.

His departure for France took place on 23rd October, and he joined the 2nd Battalion, 3rd New Zealand Rifle Brigade on 2nd November. On 16th November the New Zealanders took over Divisional command and Headquarters were set up in a hutted Anzac Camp, to the south of Ypres at Chateau Segard. John was detached to No. 2 Field Company, New Zealand Engineers from 25th November until the last week in February 1918. During this period the engineers constructed additional huts, repaired roads, built stables for horses, built protective walls against aeroplane bombs, and carried out many other tasks in preparation for enemy action the following spring.

John's efforts during the winter proved fruitless for himself, because on 19th April 1918 he was wounded in action in the Hébuterne area, receiving gunshot wounds to his neck and left arm, resulting in paralysis. His injuries were so serious that he immediately transferred to England and arrived at No. 1 NZGH, Brockenhurst on 24th April. He died two days later, on 26th April and was buried on 29th April, the same day as Private William Henry Steele, 6/4148, 2nd Battalion, Auckland Regiment (p. 119) and Corporal James Lilley, 43623, New Zealand Field Artillery (p. 212).

After the War John's legal next-of-kin was his brother William Connelly (b. 25.7.1883), of 21 Elizabeth Street, Timaru, because his sister Mary, had died in the meantime.

JAMES LILLEY

**Corporal, 43623
New Zealand Field Artillery
Staff of Transport "Leitrim"
Died of sickness on 24th April 1918, aged 35**

James Lilley was born on 13th April 1883 at Sefton, Canterbury, the son of Reuben and Margaret. James was one of eight children, with four brothers and three sisters. Reuben (1848-1899) was born at Woodbridge, Suffolk, England. His wife, Margaret (1846-1906) came from Belfast, Ireland. They emigrated to New Zealand in about 1870 (according to James's Attestation Sheet). Reuben died on 18th October 1899, aged 51. He was listed as a Carrier at Sefton in the 1900 Wise's NZPO Directory, so probably died suddenly after a short illness.

James was a farmer at Cust, but joined the New Zealand Permanent Force as a soldier on 1st August 1902, aged 19. His mother Margaret died in October 1906, and is buried at Balcairn Cemetery, near Sefton alongside her husband Reuben. James served mostly at Alexandra Military Depot at Wellington, as a Gunner, followed by Bombardier. He continued to be based at Wellington until 6th February 1917 when he transferred to the NZEF. He departed from New Zealand on 16th April with the Royal New Zealand Artillery for duty as a gunner on board S.S. *Leitrim*.

A year later on 18th April 1918 James was admitted to University War Hospital, Southampton, England ex staff of Transport *Leitrim*. He was placed on the Seriously Ill list suffering from cellulitis on the face, and died on 24th April. His body was taken to St. Nicholas Church, Brockenhurst for burial; the service was officiated by Reverend A. J. Jacob on 29th April. Plot A, Row 2, Grave 16.

James's next of kin was Mrs. Mary May Hayes of Southbrook, Canterbury. His name is commemorated on his parents' headstone (below) at Balcairn Cemetery, along with his brothers and sisters.

PERCY EMANUEL HOLST

Rifleman, 49959
1st Battalion, 3rd New Zealand Rifle Brigade, "A" Company
Died of wounds on 12th May 1918, aged 35

Percy Emanuel Holst was born on 3rd February 1884 at Lyttelton, near Christchurch, Canterbury. His father, Emanuel Octavus originated from Halse, Denmark whilst his mother Elizabeth was an English girl from Cosham, near Portsmouth.

Percy was employed as an Architect for Edmund R. Wilson of Invercargill, Southland. He married Florence Priscilla Stone on 10th August 1915 at Invercargill, the ceremony being conducted by the Reverend E. Streete. A daughter Helga Morey was born on 13th June the following year, 1916. Emanuel was deceased when his son enlisted with the NZEF in 1917. Percy's army History Sheet implies that his mother was still alive then, and she had been living in New Zealand since the 1850s.

Percy enlisted with the NZEF and joined with 30th Reinforcements on 21st February 1917 at Invercargill, leaving behind his wife and daughter at 199 Ythan Street, Invercargill. Within weeks he was promoted to Corporal. He remained in New Zealand for a longer period than most men, possibly owing to his marital situation, and eventually departed overseas on 16th November 1917. HMNZT No. 97 *Tahiti* sailed from Wellington with Percy amongst members of "G" Company, New Zealand Rifle Brigade Reinforcements. The ship arrived at Liverpool on 7th January 1918 and the troops marched into camp at Brocton, Staffordshire. Here Percy was demoted to the rank of Rifleman because he failed to pass an army examination.

He left for France on 20th March and marched into camp at Abeele for a brief period before joining the 1st Battalion, 3rd New Zealand Rifle Brigade, "A" Company near Hébuterne on 27th March. His days at the Front were extremely short-lived because he received gunshot wounds to his left leg on 6th April. At the end of the month he was invalided to the United Kingdom and admitted to No. 1 NZGH, Brockenhurst.

Percy lived just six weeks longer, and died on 12th May with his burial the next day. The Reverend E. E. Walden conducted the service.

Plot A, Row 4, Grave 15.

After the War Florence was resident in Christchurch. She lived to an old age, and died in the same city in 1962.

CLETUS PATRICK O'BRIEN

**Sapper, 37651
New Zealand Engineers, Tunnelling Company
Died of sickness on 17th July 1918, aged 32**

Cletus Patrick O'Brien's parents, Michael and Norah left Ireland for New Zealand in the 1860s. Cletus was born on 29th January 1886 at Brighton, Westport, Westland.

He was a miner for the Westport Coal Company at the Denniston Mine. Westport is situated on the mouth of the Buller River, and a spur of the main railway line ran up the Denniston Incline to the Mount Rochfort Plateau 1,960 ft. above sea level.

The Denniston Incline showing the Brake head works. West Coast Historical and Mechanical Society Collection. F-091658-1/2. ATL

The coal was considered the best quality in the world and, amongst other things, was supplied for ships of the Royal Navy. It was transported in railway wagons down a self-acting incline, such that descending full wagons drew the empty ones up. At Conn's Creek below, steam locomotives of the New Zealand Railways took the coal 11 ½ miles to Westport. The area was nicknamed Coalbrookdale after the mining district in Shropshire, England.

Initially, the only access to the mine was by riding in or on the wagons on the incline. However, numerous accidents occurred due to wagons breaking away and hurtling off the line. The practice of wagon riding was eventually banned after a serpentine foot-track had been dug for the miners to reach their work.

In 1917, Norah was a widow, living at Cape Foulwind, near Westport. Cletus enlisted with the NZEF on 10th March 1917 and on 26th April he embarked at Wellington on the *Turakina* with the 5th Tunnelling Company Reinforcements. He was admitted to the ship's hospital on two occasions before arriving at Devonport, England on 20th July. A few weeks were spent at the Royal Engineers Camp at Christchurch, near Bournemouth before transfer to France.

By January 1918 Cletus was no longer capable of undertaking an active life owing to a cerebral tumour. He spent several weeks in stationary hospitals in France before admission to No. 1 NZGH, Brockhurst on 4th March. He survived a further four months and died on 17th July 1918. Cletus was buried two days later, with the Reverend P. J. Minogue officiating.

Plot A, Row 5, Grave 15.

Source:

> Meyer, R. J (1989)
> *Coaling from the Clouds – The Mount Rochfort Railway*
> N.Z. Railway & Locomotive Society, Wellington

ROBERT WILLIAM MARSHALL

Rifleman, 51658
1st Battalion, 3rd New Zealand Rifle Brigade
Died of wounds on 26th October 1918, aged 22

Robert William Marshall's grandfather, also named Robert, came from Stirling, Scotland. Robert (senior) had a son, David who was Robert's father. David married Jemima (née Sutherland) at Port Chalmers, Otago on 13th March 1895. Robert, born at Glenomaru, near Balclutha, Otago on 23rd January 1896 was the eldest of five children, two boys and three girls. His siblings were

> Irene (Ian Shackleton's mother)
> Mason Mary
> David Gordon (Margery Byrne's father) and
> Margaret Grace

David, Jemima and their family settled in Westport, Westland in the early 1900s.

Prior to enlisting with the NZEF, Robert was a sawmill hand working with his father for the Marlborough Timber Company in the Nydia Bay area, Pelorus Sound, Marlborough.

Timber milling began in this area in 1876 with William Brownlee, and later a rival firm (which became the Marlborough Timber Company) set up in the upper Opouri valley in 1907. John Craig, the manager, and his partners the Reese brothers gained the milling rights. They needed to get the timber out of the forest and down to Nydia Bay for transportation by ship so they built a steep incline from the bay, right over the 1500 feet high saddle and into the Opouri valley where they established their mill.

Robert Marshall (from Margery Byrne, Westport)

The timber was then hauled over the saddle by a steam winch and drawn by a pair of horses on rail trolleys down to the 900-foot long wharf at Nydia Bay, which could accommodate five steamers at once. Most of the timber was shipped to Lyttelton to help build the city of Christchurch. The Company operated in the Opouri Valley for about 20 years, but everything was cut out by the early 1920s.

Although it has been established that wives often accompanied their husbands and lived in the timber milling area, it is most probable that Jemima remained at the family home at 100 Peel Street, Westport looking after her other four children, whilst Robert and his father lived in a settlement in the Opouri Valley, a very isolated location. Despite the rustic living, facilities for the workmen were provided. In Nydia Bay, William Gould, a local farmer, built a store and after a while he put down a grass tennis court and turned his woolshed into a dance hall. His brother John owned a launch and made a small fortune charging people £1 for a one-way trip between Havelock, the nearest village and Nydia Bay.

Robert enlisted on 10th March 1917 at Havelock, and departed from New Zealand with "G" Company, New Zealand Rifle Brigade on the *Maunganui* on 12th June. On 18th August he was posted to Tidworth Camp on Salisbury Plain, and during the next two months he transferred to Brocton Camp, Staffordshire. He left for France on the 18th October and joined his Battalion, "A" Company on 24th October at Colembert, situated between St. Omer and Boulogne. The Battalion remained in this area until 8th November, undertaking training and reorganisation.

In May 1918, Robert was sick with mumps and spent time in hospital recovering. His days as an active serviceman ended on 29th July when he was wounded in action near Hébuterne with gunshot wounds to his back.

Robert was immediately evacuated to England, and arrived at No. 1 NZGH, Brockenhurst on 2nd August. He never recovered from his injuries and died on 26th October. He was buried two days later in Plot A, Row 2, Grave 20.

Acknowledgements and Sources:

> Margery Byrne, Westport (niece)
> Ian Shackleton, Nelson (nephew)
> Leaflet on The Nydia Track, Department of Conservation
> Marlborough Sounds Maritime Park, NZ Lands and Survey leaflet

JAMES WILLIAMS

Private, 19779
New Zealand Maori (Pioneer) Battalion
Died of sickness on 30th September 1918, aged 21

James Williams, the son of William Moka and Ellen, was born on 27th April 1897. The family came from Mangamuka, Hokianga. James worked as a barman for Mr. J. Nicholson at Kohukohu, adjacent to the harbour.

View of Kohukohu Harbour, looking towards the hotel and general store on the waterfront. F-29831-1/2. Northwood Collection. ATL

James enlisted with the NZEF on 22nd March 1917 at Kohukohu. His initial military training took place at Narrow Neck Camp, near Auckland. In the middle of June he was granted a final leave before proceeding overseas, but he decided to extend his freedom and return a day late. However, the authorities were wise to his ploy and docked him one day's pay as a result!

James departed from New Zealand with the Maori Contingent, 21st Reinforcements on 15th August 1917 on board HMNZT No. 92 *Ruahine*. The ship reached Glasgow, Scotland on 2nd October and straightaway he transferred to the south of England and was attached to the New Zealand Engineers Reserve Depot at Christchurch, near Bournemouth, Hampshire.

Whilst at Christchurch, James fractured his clavicle and was admitted to No. 1 NZGH, Brockenhurst nearby for treatment. His stay in hospital was followed by a spell at the New Zealand Convalescent Hospital at Hornchurch, Essex. On 15th November he moved to Codford Camp for light training to bring his fitness up to the satisfactory standard for life on the Western Front. He arrived in France on 4th April 1918 and marched into camp at Abeele.

James joined the Maori (Pioneer) Battalion on 10th April at Bertrancourt, southwest of Hébuterne. The next day the Battalion had eleven men wounded in their billets from German shelling, so they moved out into bivouacs in the paddocks where there was less danger from enemy fire.

On 21st July, when the Pioneer Battalion were in the Front line, between Rossignol Wood and Hébuterne, James fell ill suffering from debility and anaemia. His condition deteriorated rapidly, so he transferred to England and arrived at No. 1 NZGH, Brockenhurst on 6th August. A week later it was established that he had tuberculosis of the lung and his name was added to the "Dangerously Ill" list. James died of this disease on 30th September 1918. The Reverend Jacob officiated at his burial, which took place on 2nd October.

Plot A, Row 3, Grave 19.

The Williams family had suffered another loss. James's brother, Corporal Willie Williams, 20624, New Zealand Maori (Pioneer) Battalion, died that same month on 4th September 1918, aged 26. He is buried in Bagneux British Cemetery, Gezaincourt, Somme, France. Grave Ref. VI.F.16. Gezaincourt is located just outside Doullens, to the southwest of the town.

WILLIAM JOHN SHOTTER

Private, 59467
1st Battalion, Wellington Regiment, 11th Company
Died of wounds and sickness on 9th March 1919, aged 27

William John Shotter was the last NZEF soldier who died at Brockenhurst.

He was born on 23rd December 1891 at Masterton, the son of David (b.1868) and Mary (b.1869). David's family originated in Funtington, near Chichester, Sussex. A George James Shotter (b.abt.1801) married Elizabeth, née Maidment (b. abt.1805). They raised a family of five children: Richard (b.1825), Charles (b.1827), George Henry (1831-1920), John (b. 1832) and Fanny (1833-1934).

George (senior) died in England, and Elizabeth married again, to Thomas Cole. Thomas, an agricultural labourer, Elizabeth and all the children emigrated to New Zealand on board the 560 ton vessel *Gertrude*, departing from Gravesend on 19th June 1841 and arriving at Port Nicholson on 30th October. Many years later, in 1868, David Shotter was born into this family, which had settled at Makara, near Wellington and were working in the timber industry.

William's mother, Mary came from Masterton and she gave birth to him in her home-town. The family moved to Wallace Street, Karori, near Wellington during William's early childhood and he attended Karori School between 1898 and 1900.

View of Karori, from above the Karori tunnel. F-55362-1/2. ATL

William worked as a labourer for W. Bruce of Wellington prior to enlisting with the NZEF on 17th May 1917 at Wellington. He embarked upon transport No. 92 *Ruahine* on 15th August 1917 with the Wellington Infantry Regiment, "B" Company, 29th Reinforcements (2nd Draft). The ship docked at Glasgow on 2nd October and William would have endured the long train journey from Scotland to Sling Camp on Salisbury Plain.

He left for France on 19th November and joined the 1st Battalion, Wellington Regiment, 9th Company, and on 8th February 1918 he was taken on strength at Abeele.

William's army records reveal that he was transferred temporarily to different battalions during his remaining time in France. On 26th March he joined No. 1 New Zealand Entrenching Battalion which had been sent to the Somme. A month later he was posted to the 2nd Battalion, Wellington Infantry Regiment. At the beginning of July he fell ill with influenza and was admitted to hospital at Rouen. He was fit enough to return to duty at the end of August and rejoined the 1st Battalion, Wellington Regiment.

His active military life ended on 4th November 1918, just one week before the Armistice, when he was wounded in action at the Battle of Le Quesnoy, receiving gunshot wounds to his right thigh. He was admitted to No. 1 South African Hospital on 6th November and embarked on a hospital ship bound for England on Armistice Day, 11th November.

William received medical attention at the Military Hospital, Endell Street, London for six weeks prior to transfer to No. 1 NZGH, Brockenhurst on 24th December. He died on 9th March 1919 as a result of his gunshot wounds and purulent bronchitis. His burial on 11th March was officiated by the Reverend G. C. Williams.

Plot A, Row 4, Grave 23.

Sources: Bull's Wellington Almanack, Street & Trade Directory 1865
Electoral Roll 1865-6 for Porirua

MATTHEW JAMES WATSON

Sapper, 59173
New Zealand Engineers, Tunnelling Company
Died of sickness on 4th April 1918, aged 29

Matthew James Watson was one of the few men buried at Brockenhurst who, perhaps, should never have been assessed fit enough for the army owing to lack of fitness and sickness.

Named after his father, he was born on 9th June 1888 at Waitara, near New Plymouth. Matthew (senior) was born in England, and he met and married Malinda, a New Zealand girl after his emigration.

Matthew (junior) was employed as a bushman near Taumarunui when he initially enlisted with the NZEF on 15th January 1915. However, he was discharged three weeks later whilst at training camp with the 4th Reinforcements by reason of a weak back. He then went to work in a different industry, and in 1917 he was a labourer for the Vacuum Oil Company, and lived at 6 Liverpool Street Auckland. His mother by this time was a widow living in New Plymouth.

Matthew rejoined the Army in 1917 and signed his attestation sheet for the second time on 21st May at Auckland. He departed overseas from Wellington with the New Zealand Engineers, Tunnelling Company (7th Draft), sailing with the 32nd Reinforcements on 21st November on HMNZT No. 96 *Maunganui*. The ship docked at Liverpool, England on 8th January 1918 and Matthew marched into Sling Camp. His stay there was brief, however, because four days later he transferred to the New Zealand Engineers Reserves Depot at Boscombe, near Bournemouth.

The next month, in February 1918, Matthew was admitted to No. 1 NZGH, Brockenhurst with tuberculosis of the lung. He survived less than two months longer, and died on 4th April. Archdeacon A. J. Jacob officiated at his burial on 6th April.

Plot A, Row 1, Grave 16.

DAVID IVON PORTEOUS

Sapper, 62881
New Zealand Engineers, Divisional Signal Company
Died of sickness on 14th November 1918, aged 33

David <u>Ivon</u> Porteous was born to a farming family who lived at "Seaview", Beaconsfield, Otago (15 miles north of Dunedin). The farm was so named because it was on the top of Porteous Hill, 400 metres above sea level at its summit, with views down to the township of Warrington and out to the Pacific Ocean. Beaconsfield no longer exists in name because it is now absorbed into the Kilmog Hill area where State Highway One travels north and south.

Ivon's grandparents, Archibald (a farmer) and Agnes (née Brown) were Scottish and remained in Scotland all their life. It was Ivon's father, John who emigrated to New Zealand. John was born in Midlothian County, Scotland, probably in 1832. However his two marriage certificates and his death certificate do not concur regarding his exact date of birth. John sailed to New Zealand on board the *Pladda* from Glasgow, arriving at Dunedin in about August 1860. He married Isabella Phillips on 8th October 1863. She was apparently 23 at the time of her marriage, but again dates and ages conflict. She was born in Scotland in 1840 or 1844 and it is believed her father was a shipmaster. Isabella died from pneumonia on 22nd July 1883 listed as aged 39. From John's first marriage there were two boys and five girls.

John Porteous working his team of horses on Porteous Hill,
above the township of Warrington, with the Pacific Ocean to the left
and the tidal estuary of Blueskin Bay on the right (from Ruth Porteous)

Beatrice Oliver Brunton (1854-1943) was Ivon's mother. She was born in Bonnyrigg, Midlothian, Scotland to David Brunton (a farmer) and Elizabeth (née Oliver). Beatrice came to New Zealand when she was aged 5 ½ with her parents and three sisters, Janet, Mary Ann and Charlotte. They sailed from London as steerage passengers on board the *Mariner* arriving in Otago in June 1859.

John remarried on 27th November 1884 to 30 year old Beatrice at Waitati, near Evansdale, Otago. Ivon was born on 23rd July 1885 at the farm at Beaconsfield, and Ruth Porteous has ascertained that he was an only child for his mother. Ivon probably attended school at Seacliff, a coastal community about two miles north of Warrington.

Ivon was employed by the New Zealand Public Works Department as an Electric Lineman. He had left the family home and was living at 326 Tuam Street, Christchurch prior to enlisting with the NZEF on 16th July 1917. He departed from Wellington with the Specialist Company, 34th Reinforcements on 8th February 1918 on board HMNZT No. 100 *Ulimaroa*. The ship docked at Liverpool, England on 29th March and Ivon marched into the Signals School at Brocton, Staffordshire. He then joined the Signals Unit at Stevenage, Hertfordshire before leaving for France on 30th April, where he was attached to the Sixth Signals Depot. He obviously had a cheeky character, for whilst in France he forfeited one day's pay and was confined to barracks for seven days for failing to salute an officer!

Ivon fell ill in October 1918 with influenza. Then a fortnight later, on 1st November he was poisoned by gas near Le Quesnoy on the first day of the Battle of the Sambre (1st-11th November), the final conflict in the Great War. His situation was critical so he immediately transferred to No. 1 NZGH, Brockenhurst, arriving there on 7th November. He died from bronchial pneumonia on 14th November 1918, three days after the Armistice was signed. The Reverend Hutchinson conducted the burial ceremony, which took place on 16th November. Plot A, Row 5, Grave 19.

Ivon is commemorated on a memorial at Merton Cemetery, Otago, along with other local lads who lost their lives in the War. His father, John died from heart disease at Port Chalmers on 18th October 1919, stated as aged 87, and his grave is at St. Barnabas Church cemetery, Warrington. His eldest son John, from his first marriage inherited the farm. In 1922, Beatrice was living at 48 Fitzroy Street, Caversham, Dunedin. For the last thirteen years of her life she was cared for at Ross Home, Dunedin, after suffering a stroke, and she died from pneumonia on 26th November 1943. Beatrice is buried at Merton, Otago near the memorial to her son Ivon.

Members of the Porteous family are still farming land near Warrington. John (junior) passed the farm on to his second son Graham, and Cliff Porteous took it over from Graham (his father) in 1967. Over the years the farm had increased in size, totalling about 300 acres. In 1995, the majority of the land was sold, with 40 acres remaining on which to run 30-35 beef steers, and a new house was built for Cliff and his family.

Acknowledgements: Ruth Porteous, Warrington, Otago (wife of great nephew)
John Scragg, Waikouaiti, Otago

TEMETE SMITH

Private, 20015
New Zealand Maori (Pioneer) Battalion
Died of sickness on 27th December 1918, aged 21

Temete Smith, the son of Kere and Tira Herehere of Bethlehem, Tauranga, was born on 5th May 1897. Prior to enlisting with the NZEF he worked as a labourer at an orchard at Whakatane, Bay of Plenty.

Temete signed his Attestation Sheet on 26th July 1917 at Rotorua and departed from New Zealand with the Maori Contingent, 23rd Reinforcements on 22nd November on HMNZT No. 95 *Willochra*. The ship reached Liverpool, England on 7th January 1918 and three days later Temete was in the south of England at Boscombe, near Bournemouth, attached to the New Zealand Engineers Reserve Depot. He remained there until 27th March when he left for France, and in the first instance he was based at Etaples. A few days later he transferred to the camp at Abeele and then joined the Pioneer Battalion on 10th April at Bertrancourt, near Hébuterne in the Upper Ancre Valley. He would have been in the company of Private Jerry Rata, 19411, Maori (Pioneer) Battalion (p. 174).

Temete spent just two days at the Front because he fell ill on 12th April suffering from trench fever. This developed into tuberculosis of the lung and after hospitalisation in France he was evacuated to England and arrived at No. 1 NZGH, Brockenhurst on 28th April. His health never improved and in September it was written on his army medical record "he was still a cot case".

Temete died on 27th December 1918 and was buried three days later. The Reverend W. Skinner, Roman Catholic Chaplain conducted the service.

He was buried in Plot A, Row 4, Grave 22.

MEIHANA HUTA

Private, 20026
New Zealand Maori (Pioneer) Battalion
Died of sickness on 24th March 1918, aged 21

Meihana Huta, son of Mrs. Hoepo Huta, was born on 1st January 1897 at Poroporo, near Whakatane, Bay of Plenty. Before joining the army he worked as a labourer for Mr. J. Shaw.

Meihana enlisted with the NZEF on 26th July 1917 at Rotorua, and a remark on his medical report was "seems a good recruit". Like many others, he disobeyed the rules, and whilst at Narrow Neck Camp, near Auckland he committed the offence of staying out beyond the allotted time, for which he received the punishment of three days confinement to barracks. On 22nd November he embarked upon HMNZT No. 95 *Willochra* at Wellington, with the 23rd Maori Reinforcements (see also Private Temete Smith, p. 225). On 10th January 1918, three days after disembarkation at Liverpool, England Meihana marched into the New Zealand Engineers Reserve Depot at Boscombe, near Bournemouth. He was, by then, ill with pleurisy.

On 19th February Meihana was admitted to No. 1 NZGH with tuberculosis of the lung. Within a fortnight he was placed on the "Dangerously Ill" list and he died on 24th March. His burial two days later was officiated by the Reverend P. J. Minogue (Roman Catholic Chaplain). Plot A, Row 2, Grave 15.

Meihana is commemorated at Whakatane Memorial Rest Room (below). His Royal Highness the Duke of Gloucester unveiled the Roll of Honour on 21st December 1934. 46 men from the region served their country, and 10 died as a result of the War.

Acknowledgement: Joe Longson, Kawerau

LLEWELLYN GILBERT GROOBY

Private, 68405
1st Battalion Canterbury Regiment, 12th Company
Died of wounds on 9th January 1919, aged 20

Llewellyn Gilbert Grooby (known as Lyn) was born on 16th October 1898, at Motueka, Nelson, the youngest child of Edward and Elizabeth.

Llewellyn's grandparents, Edward (1815-1880) and Sarah (née Hudson, c.1818-1907) came from Greasely, Nottinghamshire, England. On 1st May 1842 they set sail from Gravesend with their eldest children Harriett (3) and John (1), bound for New Zealand aboard the 363 ton barque *Sir Charles Forbes*, the first ship to sail from London to Nelson direct. Edward's brother Francis (1818-1899) and his family accompanied them. The ship arrived at Nelson on 22nd August. Edward and Francis's parents, Francis (senior, 1787-1858) and Sarah (née Morley, 1788-1876) soon followed suit, and sailed to Nelson on *Phoebe* in 1843 with six children. The Groobys were among the first Europeans to settle in the Nelson area.

The Grooby extended family initially lived on land owned by a Mr. Jenkins at Brook Street, Nelson. They leased 300 acres, clearing the fern-covered land, and by 1845 had built three cob cottages, fenced and cultivated eight acres, and obtained a variety of animals, including thirty goats. In 1849 the family moved to Motueka north west of Nelson. Their combined skills were listed as carter, sawyer and gardener. They eventually bought land in Pangatotara nearby.

Llewellyn's father, also named Edward (1851-1931), was the third son and seventh child (of 10) of Edward and Sarah. He married Elizabeth (née Wratten) and they had five children (one daughter and four sons), Llewellyn being the youngest. His siblings were Inez Mabel (b.1889), Charles Edward (1890-1968), Leslie Harold (1891-1956) and Laurence Robert (1894-1918).

The children went to Brooklyn Nelson School with Llewellyn in attendance between 5th July 1909 and 12th December 1913 (Register No. 322).

Russell Marshall confirms that his grandmother was a first cousin of Llewellyn, and that Llewellyn's father, Edward, and a grandfather of George Heslop (p. 183) were first cousins. It is an interesting coincidence that members of the same family are buried in the same cemetery so far from the land of their birth.

Llewellyn was working for a local fruit farmer, Mr. J. Jones, prior to joining the NZEF. Of the 93 New Zealanders who are buried at Brockenhurst, he was the last man to enlist, which he did at the age of 19 at Motueka on 17th October 1917. He was initially posted to "A" Company, Canterbury Infantry. After basic military training in his home country he embarked aboard HMNZT No. 103 *Maunganui* at Wellington on 9th May 1918, with "C" Company, 37th Reinforcements. The ship arrived at Liverpool, England on 24th June and Llewellyn marched into Sling Camp. Shortly afterwards he transferred to Larkhill nearby. During this time his youthful energy was spent in a bout of gambling for which he was awarded 72 hours detention, this activity being expressly forbidden by Camp Standing Orders!

On 10th September Llewellyn left for France, and three days later he joined the 1st Battalion, Canterbury Regiment, 12th Company at Haplincourt Wood, southeast of Bapaume. The next day, 14th September, the Battalion moved to huts to the west of Biefvillers, a peaceful area out of the range of the enemy's bombing planes. Llewellyn's days at the Front were brief because he was wounded in action on 5th November 1918 (six days before the Armistice was signed) when he was involved in action in Mormal Forest, near Herbignies, east of Le Quesnoy. This is one of the last photographs taken, showing New Zealand troops on the Western Front.

Men on the last New Zealand front line before Le Quesnoy, France, shortly before the Armistice. Making New Zealand Collection. F-1996-1/2 MNZ. ATL

Llewellyn received gunshot wounds to his head and a fractured skull. He was admitted to No. 1 NZGH, Brockenhurst on 22nd November and placed on the "Dangerously Ill" list. He died on 9th January 1919 and was buried two days later in Plot A, Row 5, Grave 20.

Edward and Sarah suffered another loss because their third son, Laurence Robert Grooby, Trooper, 58408, Canterbury Mounted Rifles, was killed in action on 27th October 1918, aged 24. He is buried in Ramleh War Cemetery, Israel. Ref. BB. 42.

Acknowledgements and Source:
  Allan Pope, Motueka
  Marshall R. *Notes on the life and times of the Grooby Family of Nottinghamshire, England and Motueka, New Zealand*

Appendix A1   NEW ZEALAND IMMIGRANTS 1840-1849

Family name	Origins	Ship	From	Departure	To	Arrival	Settled
Prebble (married Harris)	Kent	Aurora	London	18.09.1839	Port Nicholson	22.01.1840	Prebbleton Nr. Christchurch
Shotter	Funtington Sussex	Gertrude	Gravesend	19.06.1841	Port Nicholson	30.10.1841	Makara Wellington
George (married Newell)	Cornwall	Oriental	Plymouth	22.06.1841	New Plymouth	07.11.1841	New Plymouth
Grooby	Greasley Nottinghamshire	Sir Charles Forbes	Gravesend	01.05.1842	Nelson	22.08.1842	Nelson, then Motueka
Rusden (married Newell)	Helston Cornwall	Blenheim	Plymouth	01.07.1842	New Plymouth	19.11.1842	New Plymouth
Grooby	Greasley	Phoebe	England	16.11.1842	Nelson	29.03.1843	Nelson, then Motueka
Bower	Scotland	Philip Laing	Greenock	23.11.1847	Port Chalmers	15.04.1848	Blueskin, Otago
McAnulty	Drummally Co. Fermanagh	Ann	Belfast		Auckland	16.05.1848	Otahuhu, Auckland
Bower	Scotland	Larkins	London	06.06.1849	Port Chalmers	11.09.1849	Blueskin, Otago

Appendix A2   NEW ZEALAND IMMIGRANTS 1850-1859

Family Name	Origins	Ship	Departure	To	Arrival	Settled
Giblin	Cambridge	Mariner	London	07.04.1850	Port Chalmers	06.08.1850	Stoke, Nelson
Fendall	Crambe, Yorks	Sir George Seymour	Gravesend	04.09.1850	Lyttelton	17.12.1850	Fendalton, Christchurch
Newell	Cornwall	St. Michael	Plymouth		New Plymouth	02.12.1852	
Fraser	Carlrossie, Rosshire, Scotland	Strathfieldsaye	Greenock	22.01.1858	Port Chalmers	8.4.1858	Dunedin, then Invercargill
Haxton	Fireshire, then Kent				Wellington	1858	Wellington
Player	London	Alfred the Great	London	07.12.1858	Port Nicholson	17.4.1859	Wellington
Brunton (married Porteous)	Bonnyrigg, Midlothian	Mariner	London	02.01.1859	Port Chalmers		
Anderson (married Haxton)	London	Montmorency	London		Wellington	1859	Wellington

231

Appendix A3   NEW ZEALAND IMMIGRANTS 1860-1870

Family Name	Origins	Ship	From	Departure	To	Arrival	Settled
Stobo	Strutherhead Lanarkshire	Storm Cloud	Greenock	27.01.1860	Port Chalmers	27.04.1860	Invercargill
Porteous	Midlothian	Pladda	Greenock		Port Chalmers	16.08.1860	Blueskin, Otago
Kennedy	Kirkolm Wigtownshire	Aboukir	Greenock	26.09.1864	Port Chalmers	05.01.1865	Dunback, Otago
Cole	Kent				Port Nicholson		Wellington, then Foxton
Durrant (married Cole)	Portsmouth			1860s	Port Nicholson		Foxton
O'Brien	Ireland			1860s			Westport, Westland
Lilley	Woodbridge Suffolk			circa 1870			Sefton, Canterbury

Appendix A4

NEW ZEALAND IMMIGRANTS 1871-1880

Family Name	Origins	Ship	From	Departure	To	Arrival	Settled
Johnstone				1873	Oamaru		Isla Bank, near Invercargill
Allington	Stretton-on-Dunsmore	Crusader	Plymouth	03.11.1873	Lyttelton	01.02.1874	Rangiora, then Papanui
Woodley	West Hagbourne Berkshire	Crusader	Plymouth	03.11.1873	Lyttelton	01.02.1874	Wairarapa
Raper (married Holt)	Doncaster Yorkshire	Atrato	London	10.02.1874	Port Chalmers	08.06.1874	Dunstan, near Clyde, Otago
Hambling	Fifield, Oxfordshire	Winchester		03.05.1874	Napier	26.07.1874	Woodville
Poole (married Johnstone)	Sandwich, Kent	Gareloch	Gravesend	23.11.1874	Port Chalmers	13.02.1875	Isla Bank, near Invercargill
Morice	Elgin, Inverness			mid 1870s			Gisborne
Harris	Oxford			1870s			Paenga, near Murchison
Hanrahan (married Geoffrey)	County Cork Ireland			1870s			Wedderburn
Sidford	Dublin			1870s			Dunedin, then Wellington
Campbell	Stirling, Scotland			1870s			Papakura, Auckland
Rainey	Belfast, Ireland			circa 1877			Winchester, near Temuka

Appendix B   NZEF DEPARTURE FROM NEW ZEALAND

Year	Rfts.	Dep.	Name	No.	Troopship	Arr.
			Sailed to Egypt			
1914	Main Body	16 Oct	Adams, C. G	2/180		3 Dec
			Fraser, N. D	9/407	No. 5 Ruapehu	3 Dec
	2nd	14 Dec	McAnulty, J	17/126	No. 14 Willochra	29 Jan
			Fendall, F. S	11/764	No. 14 Willochra	29 Jan
			Kennedy, A	8/1272	No. 14 Willochra	29 Jan
1915	3rd	14 Feb	Rapona, K	16/525	No. 20	25 Mar
	ex Samoa	17 April	Clark, F	12/2183		25 May
	5th	13 June	Allington, S,	6/2052		30 July
		13 June	Davies, S. A	4/895		
		13 June	Duncan, W. M	3/667		
		13 June	Johnstone, W. E	8/2020		
	6th	14 Aug	Baird, H. J	7/1440		
		14 Aug	Gilbert, A	2/1975	No. 27 Willochra	
		14 Aug	Newell, D. R	8/2687	No. 27 Willochra	
	2nd Maori	18 Sep	Akena, R	16/598	Waitemata	26 Oct
	2nd Maori	18 Sep	Tuhoro, P	16/769	Waitemata	26 Oct
	2nd Maori	18 Sep	Matenga	16/810	Waitemata	26 Oct
	1st NZRB	18 Sep	Booker, A. B	23/77	Waitemata	26 Oct
	7th	9 Oct	Morice, W. L	23/831	Tahiti	18 Nov
		9 Oct	Kirk, W. B	24/484	Tahiti	18 Nov
		9 Oct	Broadbridge, T.	24/693	Tahiti	18 Nov
		9 Oct	Barter, J. H	10/2852		18 Nov
		9 Oct	Edman, H. L	6/3007		18 Nov
		9 Oct	Game, C. F	2/2127		18 Nov
		9 Oct	Monahan, J.J	10/3035		18 Nov
		9 Oct	Page, W. C	5/563		18 Nov
		9 Oct	Stirrat, A. M	8/3081		18 Nov

Year	Rfts.	Dep.	Name	No.	Troopship	Arr.
1915			**Sailed to Egypt**			
	8th	13 Nov	Dunbar, W. D	8/3434		20 Dec
		13 Nov	Tait, C. R	2/2557		20 Dec
	Tunnelling	18 Dec	Ainslie, W	4/1323	Ruapehu	18 Feb
	Company		**Sailed to Devonport, Plymouth, England**			
			Sailed to Egypt			
1916	9th	8 Jan	Arrowsmith, A	6/3609		8 Feb
			Cooper, W. C	15/149		12 Feb
			Harris, A. L	6/3729		12 Feb
			Haxton, G. W	10/3592	Maunganui	12 Feb
			Bennett, S	2/2575		14 Feb
			Rhoades, H	8/3745		14 Feb
	3rd Bn. NZRB	5 Feb	Blackham, J	25/948		13 Mar
	4th Bn. NZRB	5 Feb	Lynch	26/965	Mokoia	15 Mar
	10th	4 Mar	Lankey, C. J	24/2019		10 April
	11th	1 April	Campbell, E. D	4/2060		2 May
		1 April	Steele, W. H	6/4148		3 May
		1 April	Woodley, A	10/4218	Maunganui	3 May
	12th (1st Draft)	1 May	Holt, W	11167	Ulimaroa	9 June
		1 May	Healey, W	11279	Ulimaroa	9 June
		1 May	Adams, T. C	11589	Ulimaroa	9 June
		1 May	Meek, E. P	11896	Ulimaroa	9 June
		1 May	Giblin, E. G	12032	Ulimaroa	9 June
	4th Maori	6 May	Hura, R	16/1339		23 June
	12th (2nd Draft)	6 May	Hurrell, G	10603		23 June
	4th Bn. NZRB	6 May	Geoffrey, J	13000	Navua	22 June

Year	Rfts.	Dep.	Name	No.	Troopship	Arr.
1916			**Sailed to Plymouth, England**			
	13th	27 May	Brown, F. H	13406	No. 55 Tofua	27 July
	13th	27 May	O'Connor, H	24215		26 July
	2nd Bn. NZRB	19 Aug	Williams, P. L	20271	Aparima	25 Oct
	2nd Bn. NZRB	25 Sep	Mogg, W. J	26129	Devon	21 Nov
	18th	11 Oct	Cliff, J. E	17697	Tofua	29 Dec
		16 Oct	Law, G. E	28160	Willochra	29 Dec
		16 Oct	Morrison, W. M	29836	Willochra	29 Dec
	19th	15 Nov	Bedford, W. C	27170		29 Jan
		15 Nov	Player, E. N	27185	No. 69 Tahiti	29 Jan
		15 Nov	Read, C. R	31708	No. 58 Maunganui	
		15 Nov	Smail, W. J	32240		29 Jan
	10th Maori	15 Nov	Whyte, W	20845	Tahiti	29 Jan
	20th (2nd Draft)	30 Dec	McDonald, F	34902	Athenic	3 Mar
1917	12th Maori	2 Jan	Rata, J	19411	Opawa	27 Mar
	13th Maori	19 Jan	Wi, H. W. W	19474	No. 75 Waitemata	28 Mar
	22nd	15 Feb	Briggs, J	38931	Aparima	26 April
		16 Feb	Phillips, H	39472	Navua	26 April
	23rd	14 Mar	Cole, A	41741	Ruapehu	21 May
	24th (1st Draft)	5 April	Hambling, H. L. E	44481	Devon	11 June
		5 April	Sidford, H. C	41638	Devon	11 June
		5 April	Lawrence, E. W	45872	Devon	11 June
		12 April	Lilley, J	43623	Leitrim (Gunner on board)	
	24th (2nd Draft)	14 April	Heslop, G. W	44582	Pakeha	28 July

Year	Rfts.	Dep.	Name	No.	Troopship	Arr.

Year	Rfts.	Dep.	Name	No.	Troopship	Arr.
1917						
	5th Tunnelling	26 April	O'Brien	37651	Turakina	20 July
	17th Maori	26 April	Warena, J. T	19661	Turakina	20 July
	25th	26 April	Campbell, T	46288	Tofua	20 July
		26 April	Rainey, W. J	47076		20 July
		26 April	Stobo, A. M	45141		20 July
	26th	9 June	Marcussen, C. D	41218	Willochra	16 Aug
	26th	12 June	Mayall, W. D	35474	Maunganui	16 Aug
		12 June	Connelly, J. T	49874	Maunganui	16 Aug
		12 June	Marshall, R.W	51658	Maunganui	16 Aug
	26th	12 June	Matuschka, H. D	52449	Maunganui	16 Aug
			Sailed to Plymouth, England			
1917	28th (1st Draft)	14 July	Bower, J. W	52940	Waitemata	24 Sep
	28th (2nd Draft)	26 July	Rogers, C. E	48570	Ulimaroa	24 Sep
	29th (2nd Draft)	15 Aug	Shotter, W. J	59467	No. 92 Ruahine	2 Oct
	21st Maori	15 Aug	Williams, J	19779	No. 92 Ruahine	2 Oct
	31st	16 Nov	Holst, P. E	49959	No. 97 Tahiti	7 Jan
			Sailed to Liverpool, England			
	23rd Maori	22 Nov	Smith, T	20015	No. 95 Willochra	7 Jan
		22 Nov	Huta, M	20026	No. 95 Willochra	7 Jan
	32nd	21 Nov	Watson, M. J	59173	No. 96 Maunganui	8 Jan
1918	34th	8 Feb	Porteous, D. I	62881	No. 100 Ulimaroa	
	37th	9 May	Grooby, L. G	68405	No. 103 Maunganui	24 June

Appendix C1   EVACUATION FROM THE SOMME SEPTEMBER/OCTOBER 1916

Name	Field Amb.	Date	CCS	Date	Stationary Hospital	Date	Hospital Ship	Date
BENNETT, S				5.9.16	No. 11 Rouen	6.9.16	Maheno	10.9.16
RAPONA, K	No. 2	9.9.16		9.9.16	No. 5 GH, Rouen	11.9.16	Asturias	13.9.16
LYNCH, R.W					No. 11, Rouen	13.9.16	Asturias	15.9.16
WOODLEY, A	XV Corps	14.9.16			No. 8 GH, Rouen	18.9.16	Panama	19.9.16
DUNBAR, W. D			No. 36	17.9.16	No. 3, Rouen	18.19.16	Panama	19.9.16
KENNEDY, A	No. 1 NZ	18.9.16	No. 36	18.9.16	No. 8 GH, Rouen	19.9.16	Asturias	20.9.16
COOPER, W. C	No. 45	18.9.16			No. 1 Can. GH, Etaples	19.9.16	Asturias	22.9.16
CLARK, F	(3rd occasion)				No. 5 GH, Rouen	22.9.16	Maheno	23.9.16
EDMAN, H. L					No. 11, Rouen	23.9.16	Maheno	23.9.16
BLACKHAM, J	XV Corps	15.9.16			No. 9 GH, Rouen	21.9.16		23.9.16
BROADBRIDGE, T	XV Corps	17.9.16			No. 3, Rouen	19.9.16	Aberdonian	25.9.16
TAIT, C. R	No. 2	21.9.16	S.M.D.	22.9.16	No. 3, Rouen	24.9.16	Aberdonian	25.9.16
BAIRD, H. J					No. 9 GH, Rouen	25.9.16	Aberdonian	25.9.16
ADAMS, C. G	XV Corps	16.9.16			No. 2 GH, Etretat	18.9.16	Llanfranc	26.9.16
ARROWSMITH, A					No. 3, Etaples	18.9.16	Asturias	27.9.16
LANKEY, C. J	1/3 North	21.9.16	No. 13	21.9.16	No. 23 GH, Etaples	23.9.16	Asturias	27.9.16
GIBLIN, E. G	XV Corps	19.9.16	No. 38,	20.9.16	No. 9 GH, Rouen	22.9.16	Western Australia	27.9.16
HARRIS, A. L					No. 5 GH, Rouen	23.9.16	Carisbrooke Castle	8.10.16
GAME, C. F			No. 38	25.9.16	No. 11, Rouen	28.9.16	Glengorm Castle	23.10.16
ALLINGTON, S	XV Corps	28.9.16	No. 36	28.9.16	No. 26, Etaples	1.10.16	Panama	10.11.16

Appendix C2 — EVACUATION FROM THE FRANCE OCTOBER 1916-DECEMBER 1917

Name	Field Amb.	Date	CCS	Date	Stationary Hospital	Date	Hospital Ship	Date
FENDALL, F. S	No. 2 Can	28.10.16			No. 11 Rouen	29.10.16	Llanfranc	7.11.16
GILBERT, A					No. 2 Le Havre	24.11.16	Gloucester Castle	27.11.16
HOLT, W	No. 1 NZ	17.11.16	No. 1 Aus	20.11.16	No. 2 Wimereux	21.11.16	St. Andrew	2.12.16
HURA, R	No. 2 NZ	19.11.16	No. 1 Aus	23.11.16	No. 13 Boulogne	26.11.16	St. David	2.12.16
TUHORO, P	No. 1 NZ	30.10.16	No. 1 Aus	31.10.16	No. 7 St. Omer	3.11.16	St. David	2.12.16
O'CONNOR, H			No. 1 Can	4.11.16	No. 13 Boulogne	29.11.16	St. Andrew	11.12.16
DAVIES, S. A	No. 1 NZ	14.12.16			No. 13 Boulogne	16.12.16	St. Andrew	18.12.16
MORICE, W. L	No. 1 NZ	27.12.16	No. 1 Aus	27.12.16	No. 8 Wimereux	3.1.17	Glenart Castle	10.1.17
FRASER, N. D	(never left Etaples)				No. 24 Etaples	18.10.16	Glenart Castle	13.1.17
ADAMS, T.C.	No. 3 NZ	2.1.17	No. 1 Aus	2.1.17	No. 8 Clemenceux	29.1.17	Princess Elizabeth	31.1.17
MORRISON, W. M					No. 13 GH Rouen	7.6.17	?	9.6.17
JOHNSTONE, W. E	No. 77	7.6.17	No. 53	7.6.17	No. 13 Boulogne	8.6.16	St. David	12.6.17
GEOFFREY, J	No. 10 Aus	4.6.17	No. 2 Aus	8.6.17	No. 9 GH Rouen	9.6.17	Western Australia	13.6.17
BEDFORD, W. C	No. 4 NZ	15.6.17	No. 53	17.6.17	No. 7 St. Omer	18.6.17	St. David	11.7.17
PHILLIPS, H	No. 4 NZ	8.7.17	No. 2 Aus	8.7.17	No. 83 GH Boulogne	13.7.17	St. Denis	22.7.17
MONAHAN, J. J	No 3 NZ	31.7.17	No. 2 Aus	31.7.17	No. 10 GH Rouen	2.8.17	Warilda	23.8.17
AINSLIE, W		15.8.17	No. 19	15.8.17	No. 11 Rouen	19.8.17	St. George	24.8.17
LAWRENCE, E. W	1/2 S. Mid	5.10.17	No. 4	5.10.17	No. 53 GH Boulogne	5.10.17	Jan Breydel	12.10.17
PLAYER, E. N			No. 3 Aus	4.10.17	No. 7 Can GH Etaples	5.10.17	Stad Antwerpen	12.10.17
WARENA, J. T					No. 24 GH Etaples	2.10.17	Stad Antwerpen	12.10.17
BROWN, F. H	No. 1 NZ	13.10.17	No. 3 Can	13.10.17	No. 3 Can Boulogne	14.10.17	?	15.10.17

239

Name	Field Amb.	Date	CCS	Date	Stationary Hospital	Date	Hospital Ship	Date
HESLOP, G. W	No. 1 NZ	13.10.17	No. 3 Aus	13.10.17	No. 2 Can Outreau	16.10.17	St. Denis	17.10.17
SMAIL, W. J	No. 1 NZ	12.10.17	No. 3 Aus	12.10.17	No. 8 Wimereux	13.10.17	France	24.10.17
BOOKER, A. J	No. 1 NZ	13.10.17	No. 10 Aus	13.10.17	No. 2		?	25.10.17
McDONALD, F			No. 15	20.10.17	No. 15 African GH Abbeville	22.10.17	Jan Breydel	13.11.17
HAMBLING, H. L. E	No. 11 Aus	3.10.17	No. 3 Can	3.10.17	No. 10 GH Rouen	4.10.17	Western Australia	3.12.17
MATUSCHKA, H. D	No. 1 NZ	21.11.17	No. 17	21.11.17	No. 57 GH	23.11.17	?	10.12.17
WI, H. W. W			No. 10 Aus	2.12.17	No. 54 Boulogne	3.12.17	St. David	10.12.17
NEWELL, D. R	No. 3 NZ	3.12.17	No. 20	3.12.17	No. 10 GH Rouen	4.12.17	?	11.12.17
ROGERS, C. E	No. 3 NZ	2.11.17			No. 7 GH	4.12.17	?	11.12.17

Appendix C3 EVACUATION FROM THE FRANCE 1918

Name	Field Amb.	Date	CCS	Date	Stationary Hospital	Date	Hospital Ship	Date
LAW, G. E	No. 3 NZ	20.12.17	No. 2 Can	20.12.17	No. 2 Aus Wimereux	29.12.17	St. Denis	2.1.18
HEALEY, W	No. 2 NZ	11.1.18	No. 3 Can	18.1.18	No. 7 Boulogne	20.1.18	Jan Breydel	24.1.18
CAMPBELL, E. D	No. 3 NZ	27.2.18	No. 2 Can	28.2.18	No. 5 GH	1.3.18	?	6.3.18
AKENA, R					No. 8	9.3.18	?	14.3.18
STEELE, W. H	No. 3 NZ	5.2.18	No. 2 Can	8.2.18	No. 53 GH Boulogne	9.2.18	?	2.4.18
MAYALL, W. D	No. 2 NZ	1.4.18			No. 11 Rouen	10.4.18	Panama	12.4.18
CONNELLY, J. T	No. 1 NZ	19.4.18	No. 3	19.4.18	No. 9 GH Rouen	21.4.18	?	23.4.18
SMITH, T	No. 3 NZ	12.4.18	No. 29	13.4.18	No. 1 Aus GH Rouen	15.4.18	Carisbrooke Castle	27.4.18
HOLST, P. E	No. 1 NZ	6.4.18			No. 3 GH	9.4.18	?	29.4.18
RHOADES, H	No. 3 NZ	25.4.18	No. 3	28.4.18	No. 16 GH	30.4.18	?	10.5.18

Name	Field Amb.	Date	CCS	Date	Stationary Hospital	Date	Hospital Ship	Date
PAGE, W. C						1.4.18	Western Australia	19.5.18
COLE, A	No. 50	16.5.18	No. 29	18.5.18	No. 3 GH Rouen	19.5.18	?	21.5.18
RATA, J	No. 3 NZ	12.5.18	No. 56	16.5.18	No. 9 GH Rouen	19.5.18	Guildford Castle	23.5.18
STOBO, A. M	No. 3 NZ	22.4.18	No. 56	27.4.18	No. 10 GH Rouen	29.4.18	Warilda	1.6.18
CLIFF, J. E	No. 1 NZ	29.6.18	No. 56	2.7.18	No. 9 USA GH	3.7.18	Grantully Castle	6.7.18
WHYTE, W	No. 1 NZ	15.7.18	No. 29	15.7.18	No. 1 Aus GH Rouen	17.7.18	Western Australia	18.7.18
RAINEY, W. J	No. 3 NZ	29.6.18			No. 10 GH Rouen	6.7.18	Western Australia	26.7.18
MARSHALL, R. W	No. 1 NZ	29.7.18	No. 29	30.7.18	No. 11 Rouen	31.7.18	Esseonibo	1.8.18
WILLIAMS, J	No. 2 NZ	21.7.18			No. 2 Can. Outreau	25.7.18	Carisbrooke Castle	4.8.18
WILLIAMS, P.L	No. 1 NZ	26.7.18			No. 8 GH Rouen	28.7.18	Grantully Castle	7.8.18
BRIGGS, J	No. 1 NZ	25.8.28	No. 56	25.8.18	No. 1 Aus GH Rouen	27.8.18	Guildford Castle	28.8.18
BOWER, J. W	No. 1 NZ	26.8.18	No. 3	27.8.18	No. 12 GH Rouen	28.8.18	Grantully Castle	29.8.18
MOGG, W. J	No. 1 NZ	22.8.18	No. 56	22.8.18	No. 9 USA GH Rouen	23.8.18	Grantully Castle	29.8.18

Name	Field Amb.	Date	CCS	Date	Stationary Hospital	Date	Hospital Ship	Date
SIDFORD, H. C			No. 3	30.8.18	No. 2 GH Le Havre	3.9.18	Grantully Castle	7.9.18
STIRRAT, A. M	No. 1 NZ	5.9.18	No. 59	7.9.18	No. 3 Rouen	8.9.18	Grantully Castle	18.9.18
MARCUSSEN, C. D					No. 46 Etaples	13.9.18	Brighton	24.9.18
CAMPBELL, T	No. 1 NZ	30.8.18	No. 29	31.8.18	No. 12 GH Rouen	1.9.18	?	1.10.18
MEEK, E. P	No. 3 NZ	5.10.18	No. 21	5.10.18	No. 3 Aus GH	7.10.18	St. Denis	11.10.18
HAXTON, G. W	No. 3 NZ	1.11.18	No. 19	1.11.18	No. 9 USA GH	3.11.18	?	4.11.18
PORTEOUS, D. I	No. 5	1.11.18	No. 38	2.11.18	No. 3	3.11.18	?	6.11.18
McANULTY, J			No. 38	29.10.18	No. 6 GH Rouen	30.10.18	?	9.11.18
SHOTTER, W. J		4.11.18			No. 1 S.African GH	6.11.18	?	11.11.18
GROOBY, L. G	No. 2 NZ	6.11.18	No. 19	6.11.18	No. 2 GH Le Havre	19.11.18	?	21.11.18

BIBLIOGRAPHY

Allen, Lt. Col. S. S. (1920) *2/Auckland 1918* Whitcombe & Tombs, Auckland

Annabell, Major N. (1927) *The Official history of the New Zealand Engineers during the Great War 1914-1918* Evans, Cobb & Sharp

Austin, Lt. Col. W. S. (1924) *The Official history of the New Zealand Rifle Brigade* L. T. Watkins, Wellington

Burton, O. E. (1922) *The Auckland Regiment* Whitcombe & Tombs, Auckland

Byrne, Lieut. A. E. (1921) *Official History of the Otago Regiment* J. Wilkie & Co., Dunedin

Byrne, J. R. (1922) *New Zealand artillery in the field, 1914-1918* Whitcombe & Tombs, Auckland

Cowan, James (1926) *The Maoris in the Great War* Whitcombe & Tombs, Auckland

Crawford, T. S. (1999) *Wiltshire and the Great War – Training the Empire's Soldiers* DPF Publishing, Reading

Cunningham, T & H. (1927) *The Wellington Regiment 1914-1919* Ferguson & Osborn

Drew, H. T. B. (ed) (1923) *The war effort of New Zealand* Whitcombe & Tombs

Ferguson, Capt. D. (1921) *The history of the Canterbury Regiment NZEF, 1914-1919* Whitcombe & Tombs

Flude, A. G. (2001) *The First Immigrant Ships*

Foljambe, Arthur William de Brito Savile. Earl of Liverpool (1916) *The New Zealand hospital ship "Maheno": the first voyage July 1915 to January 1916* Whitcombe & Tombs

Foljambe, Arthur William de Brito Savile. Earl of Liverpool (1917) *The voyages of His Majesty's New Zealand hospital ships "Marama" and "Maheno"* Whitcombe & Tombs

Harper, G. (2000) *Massacre at Passchendaele* Harper Collins, Auckland

Laffin, J. (1965) *Anzacs at War. The story of Australian and New Zealand battles* Abelard-Schuman, London

Laffin, J. (1994) *A Western Front Companion 1914-1918* Alan Sutton, Stroud, Gloucestershire

Leary, L. P. (1918) *New Zealanders in Samoa* Heinemann

Luxford, J. H. (1923) *With the Machine Gunners in France and Palestine: the official history of the New Zealand Machine (Gun) Corps in the Great War* Whitcombe & Tombs

McCarthy, C. (1995) *The Somme – the day-by-day account* Cassell

McCluskey, Major A. J. (2001) *Medical Bursary 1999* in The Gallipolian, Spring 2001

Neill, J. C. (ed.) (1922) *The New Zealand Tunnelling Company 1915-1919* Whitcombe & Tombs, Auckland

New Zealand Departments of State & Public Institutions (1917) *Featherston Military Training Camp* Brett Printing

New Zealand Departments of State and Public Institutions (1918) *The Codford Wheeze* Codford

New Zealand Departments of State and Public Institutions (1918) *Historic Trentham, 1914-1917. The story of a New Zealand Military Training Camp* Wellington

Nicol, C. G. (1921) *The story of two campaigns: official war history of the Auckland Mounted Rifles Regiment 1914-1919* Wilson & Houghton

Paterson, S. (2001) *Conditions: Evacuation of the sick and wounded from Gallipoli* - paper written after The Joint Imperial War Museum/Australian War Memorial Battlefield Study Tour to Gallipoli, September 2000

Perfect, C. T. (1920) *Hornchurch during the Great War* Benham & Co., Colchester

Phillips, J., Boyack, N., and Malone, E. P (eds.) (1988) *The Great adventure. New Zealand soldiers describe the first World War* Allen & Unwin, Wellington

Powles, Lt. Col. C. G. (ed.) (1928) *The history of the Canterbury Mounted Rifles 1914-1919* Whitcombe & Tombs

Pugsley, C. (1991) *On the fringe of hell – New Zealanders and military discipline in the First World War* Hodder & Stoughton, Auckland & London

Pugsley, C. (1995) *Te Hokowhitu a Tu: the Maori Pioneer Battalion in the First World War* Reed

Robinson, I. G. H. G. (ed Ward, C.) (2000) *Dear Lizzie – a Kiwi soldier writes from the battlefields of World War One* Harper Collins, Auckland

Sinclair, K. (1991) *A History of New Zealand* Penguin Books (NZ) Ltd. Auckland

Stewart, H. (1921) *The New Zealand Division 1916-1918 Official History of New Zealand's effort in the Great War, Vol. 2 – France* Whitcombe & Tombs

Studholme, J. (1928) *New Zealand Expeditionary Force* W. A. G. Skinner, Wellington

Vicar and PCC of Brockenhurst (1996) *New Zealanders in Brockenhurst – The No. 1 New Zealand General Hospital 1916-1919*

Waite, Maj. F. (1919) *The New Zealanders at Gallipoli* Whitcombe & Tombs

Wellcome Institute Library, London *Report of New Zealand General Hospital, Brockenhurst, Hampshire for 1918.* on Microfilm. Ref: FOOOO956B00

Weston, Lt. Col. C. H. *Three Years with the New Zealanders.* Skeffington & Son, London

Whitehead, I. R. (1999) *Doctors in the Great War.* Leo Cooper

Wicksteed, M. R. (1981) *A Short history of the New Zealand Army.* Wellington

Wilkie, Maj. A. H. (1924) *Official history of the Wellington Mounted Rifles Regiment in the GeatWar 1914-1919.* Whitcombe & Tombs

INDEX

Names indexed in **bold** are those men who are buried at Brockenhurst

A
Adams C G 46
Adams T C 140-141
Ainslie W 104-105
Akena R 92
Allington S 66-67
Ancre, Upper 30
Anzac Day Service 37-38
Armentières 24
Arrowsmith A 114

B
Baird H J 95-96
Basseville 28
Barter J H 90
Bedford W C 159
Belton Park 16
Bennett S 113
Blackham J 106-107
Bollom E W 38
Booker A B 78-79
Bower J W 206-207
Briggs J 178-180
Broadbridge T C 86-87
Brocton 14
Brown F H 151

C
Campbell E D 126-130
Campbell T 198-199
Casualty Clearing Station 34
Christchurch, Hampshire 15
Clark F 42
Cliff J E 149
Codford 17
Cole A 191-192
Connelly J T 211
Cooper W C 112

D
Denniston Mine 214-215
Davies S A 68-69
Dunbar W D 101
Duncan W M 76-77

E
Edman H L 88
Egypt 8-10
Etaples 13, 34-35
Ewshott 15

F
Field Ambulance 33
Featherston 7-8
Fencibles, Royal New Zealand 4-5, 50
Fendall F S 53-55
Flers-Courcelette 25-26
Fraser N D 47-49

G
Gallipoli 21-22
Game C F 102
Geoffrey J 143-144
Giblin E G 137-139
Gilbert A 74-75
Grantham 16
Gravenstafel 29
Grooby L G 227-228

H
Hambling H L E 188-190
Harris A L 109-111
Haxton G W 43-45
Hazebrouck 10-11
Healey W 147-148
Heslop G W 183-184
Hobson, Captain William 3
Holst P E 213
Holt W 145-146
Hornchurch 16-17
Hospital Ship 35
Hospitals –
  Stationary & General 34-35
  No. 1, Brockenhurst 36
Hura R 125
Hurrell G 142
Huta M 226

J
Johnstone W E 62-65

K
Kennedy A 56-60
Kirk W B 83-85

L
Lankey C J 118
Law G E 163-165
Lawrence E W H 195-197
Lemnos 21
Lilley J 212
Lynch R W 108
Lys River 24

M
McAnulty J 50-52
McDonald F 172-173
Machine Gunners 16
Main Dressing Station 33
Marcussen C D 175-176
Marshall R W 216-217
Matenga T 93-94
Matuschka H D 209
Mayall W D 200-201
Meek E P 131-136
Mersa Matruh 21, 81
Messines 27
Mogg W J 155-158
Monahan J J 91
Morbecque 10-11
Morice W L 80-82
Morrison W M 166

N
Narrow Neck Camp 8
New Zealand Company 3
New Zealand Medical Corps 15, 77
New Zealand Field Artillery 9, 15
New Zealand Maori (Pioneer) Bn. 8
New Zealand Rifle Brigade 14
Newell D R 70-73

O
O'Brien C P 214-215
O'Connor H 150
Otira Tunnel 181

P
Page W C 98-100
Passchendaele 29
Phillips H 181-182

Player E N 160-162
Porteous D I 223-224

Q
Quesnoy, Le 31

R
Rainey W J 208
Rapona K 61
Rata J 174
Read C R 168-169
Regimental Aid Post 32
Rhoades H 115-117
Roquetoire 10-11
Rogers C E 202-205

S
Samoa 20
Senussi 21
Shotter W J 220-221
Sidford H C 193-194
Sling Camp 11-12
Smail W J 167
Smith T 225
Somme 25
Steele W H 119
Steenbecque 10-11
Stirrat A M 89
Stobo A H 185-187

T
Tait C R 103
Tophouse Hotel 86
Trentham 7-8
Tuhoro P 97

W
Wakefield, Edward Gibbon 3
Warena J T 210
Watson M J 222
Whyte W 170-171
Wi H W W 177
Williams J 218-219
Williams P L 152-154
Woodley A 120-124

Y
Ypres 27, 29